# CLIMBS AND PUNISHMENT

**Felix Lowe** is best known by his alter ego *Blazin' Saddles*, whose incredibly popular Eurosport blog has become the go-to place for an irreverent and authoritative take on the world of cycling. Over the past decade Felix has covered the major cycling races in the pro calendar, writing for Eurosport, *Cycle Sport* and the *Telegraph*. He also writes a monthly column for *Cyclist* magazine.

www.transworldbooks.co.uk

# CLIMBS AND PUNISHMENT

Riding to Rome in the Footsteps of Hannibal

Felix Lowe

BANTAM PRESS

LONDON · TORONTO · SYDNEY · AUCKLAND · JOHANNESBURG

TRANSWORLD PUBLISHERS
61–63 Uxbridge Road, London W5 5SA
A Random House Group Company
www.transworldbooks.co.uk

First published in Great Britain
in 2014 by Bantam Press
an imprint of Transworld Publishers

A CIP catalogue record for this book
is available from the British Library.

ISBN 9780593073346

Addresses for Random House Group Ltd companies outside the UK
can be found at: www.randomhouse.co.uk
The Random House Group Ltd Reg. No. 954009

The Random House Group Limited supports the Forest Stewardship Council®
(FSC®), the leading international forest-certification organisation. Our books
carrying the FSC label are printed on FSC®-certified paper. FSC is the only
forest-certification scheme supported by the leading environmental organisations,
including Greenpeace. Our paper procurement policy can be found at
www.randomhouse.co.uk/environment

Typeset in 11/16.25 pt Berkeley Book by Falcon Oast Graphic Art Ltd.
Printed and bound in Great Britain by
Clays Ltd, Bungay, Suffolk

2 4 6 8 10 9 7 5 3 1

'We will either find a way, or make one.'

HANNIBAL (218 BC)

FRANCE

Rhône

ALPE D'HUEZ

Lautar
Galibic
Izoar

BOURG D'OISANS

LA
CHAL

MONT VENTOUX

MENS

Col
Agnel

AVIGNON

Mazan

COSTIGLIOL
SALUZZ

OLARGUES

SOMMIÈRES

CARCASSONNE

DUILHAC-SOUS
-PEYREPERTUSE

CÉRET

MONTSENY
Turó de l'Home

Empúries

BARCELONA

N

Blain Saddles

W

E

HANNIBAL

S

**ITALY**

*Battle of Trebbia*

**ALBA**

**GAVI**

**CAVAZZONE**

**CASTELNUOVO DI GARFAGNANA**

**SAN GIMIGNANO**

**SANT'ANNA**

**PERUGIA**

*Lago Trasimeno*

**NARNI**

*Lago di Bracciano*

**ROME**

# TRAINING:

# GRAN CANARIA

VALLEY OF THE TEARS.

I'D BEEN WARNED THAT I'D LEAVE a little bit of myself on the climb – I just hadn't expected to see so much of it splattered across the tarmac.

I really couldn't help it. There was no warning, just a sudden urge to retch. Luckily none of the others were watching. Ray is ahead on his swanky £5,000 racing machine, which probably weighs less than what I had for lunch, now reduced to road carrion for the vultures that must be gathering overhead. They can spot a dead man riding a mile off.

Our support car slows until I edge a bit closer. Ray's girlfriend Maria drives while her friend, also called Maria, sits in the back with the boot open. Camera in hand, Maria 2 records my every pained pedal stroke for posterity. I try to smile but the thought of cheese makes me queasy. I shake my head instead. Such intrusion really isn't on. Being videoed taking a dump would feel less of a violation.

I'm overcome with a sudden surge of sympathy for the countless riders I've witnessed hitting the wall on sharp Tour de France ascents and imploding dramatically – just as prying TV cameras are thrust up close. Angered by the idea of my own suffering being broadcast to millions worldwide, I desperately wave the lens away.

Cut to commercial – there's nothing to see here. Just one man's inner struggle to keep his solids down and his frown stolid.

But still Maria films my plight. This is a cycle-suffer scene bordering on the pornographic – something that'd even be illegal in Amsterdam. It's all I can do to whisper a feeble 'stop' and gesticulate forlornly one last time, almost losing my balance on the coarse double-digit gradient.

There's nothing caring, compassionate or Christian about either Maria. The least they could do is give me a tug with a 'sticky bidon'. If I go any slower I'll just stop and roll over, unable and unwilling to unclip. It's now a tussle between body and mind. My knees throb, my lower back tightens and my lungs gasp. But something inside drives me on.

For large stretches of this ascent I've resisted the temptation to do a Wayne Rooney and flirt with the 'granny'. But now, amid the crowning hairpins of this punishing climb, I cave in and pop on to the smallest ring of my triple chainset. I glance down at the big sprocket in a drooling daze. It has thirty-two teeth. The same amount that I feel like dislodging from Ray's gaping jaw every time he turns round to gee me up.

'Come on, *Blazin' Saddles*! Don't be such a weakling. We're almost there now.' His words tumble down the mountain like falling rocks for me to dodge. Weakling? I've only just taken up this sport and I'm clearly out of my depth. Some 1,300 metres out of my depth, to be precise. So give me some slack. I should be sitting in the car, not wedged on this saddle.

The momentary respite that follows my granny gear ignominy is an opportunity to reach round and procure a gel from my back pocket. This should rid me of the taste of bile in my mouth and provide the final juice boost I need to reach the summit.

What in God's name am I doing here, you ask. I've fled the chills and ills of England to do a spot of winter riding in the Canary Islands – seeking sunnier climes for some challenging climbs. In the name of a good story, I asked my host Ray – an evergreen Irish ex-pat with Celtic freckles and an age deficit on Chris Horner – to take me on the hardest route Gran Canaria has to offer.

'That'll be the VOTT,' he said. 'It's dangerous, dark and evil – the most villainous piece of road-building contrived by man.'

'Sounds promising. What does VOTT stand for?'

'The Valley of the Tears – and it usually does what it says on the tin.'

So you can understand my trepidation as I clawed my way through an undulating 60-kilometre ride along the coast this morning – up and over one peak, and along to a rather run-down town called San Nicolás: the gateway to the hurt locker I'm currently enduring.

'I'm bricking myself,' I half joked in a piece to camera as we edged our way out of civilization after a lunch somewhat overshadowed by the bleak task in hand. An overcooked tuna steak with chips is hardly what I'd ask for as my last meal – but it had to do. The waiter didn't bring any salt to the table. Perhaps he thought there was enough encrusted on the back of my bib shorts.

'There's going to be no flat or downhill at all for the next 25 kilometres.' I continued my groundlessly upbeat monologue as Ray rode slightly further up the road. 'It's steep, peaking over 25 per cent and averaging around 14 per cent. I'm not prepared for this. I'm six foot six. I'm 90 kilograms. That's 21 kilos more than Brad. Even Bradley couldn't do this climb. Not without Froomie to help him – and I haven't got Froome. Although I do have Ray. Ray can be my Froome. Ray's going to be my Froome . . . and then I'll beat him at the end.'

Except there's been no beating apart from the one dealt to me. The terror kicked off with six ramped switchbacks called the Devil's Guts – best described as a mini, steeper Alpe d'Huez condensed into one brutal kilometre. For some inexplicable reason I took it upon myself to attack my mentor on the first bend. Big mistake. He surged ahead. I was as cumbersome as an elephant trying to pursue a panther.

Yesterday I wore my polka-dot jersey but that just made me feel like a charlatan. I'm no King of the Mountains, I'm a Joker with a warped grasp on reality. At best I'm an Ace of Hearts – but judging by the palpitations, that's one organ this climb might well club to death. Especially now that we're on the hardest, longest slog. The Devil's Guts was simply the climb's colon – a mere stinker of a warm-up. We're now on to the interminable uphill ravel of the small intestine – and I'm about to be chewed up, devoured, broken down and spat back out. Much like my lunch which, if not decorating the road – I'm ashamed to say – is now vaporized in my pants. For you can add bowel-stirring to belly-punching and stomach-crunching on the list of verbal understatements that best describe my current pickle. Hardly anyone's idea of fun. But that's the hold El Valle de las Lágrimas has on me. Aptly, grimacing has become my default expression, and I'm now the lead in some warped film where a meek and bashful Brit is reduced to a stuttering heap of flatulence and tortuous lament.

I've only got myself to blame. I'm trying to go from bike virgin to racing snake without doing any of the amateurish stuff in between. I haven't even shed the hairy skin of my former self – my bushy, scrawny legs earn me the nickname of 'El Pelo' from the locals.

In the absence of anything remotely pertaining to base fitness and riding pedigree, I simply take on as much food as possible in the twisted belief that it's the fuel, and not the engine, that counts most. I ordered last night's 400-gram Uruguayan steak actually banking on it containing traces of the kind of steroids that seem all the rage nowadays in the pro peloton. I'm living in some kind of delusional microcosm where extra calories are the answer to everything. Perhaps this is the type of thinking that torments the pros for whom doping is the only way forward?

Finally, after the best part of three hours of largely self-inflicted torture, we reach the top of the VOTT. I'm pounding all over. My entire body is riddled with multiple stabbing sensations as if someone, somewhere, has made a miniature voodoo doll in my form, and takes malicious pleasure in sticking needles into its lower back, neck, knees, thighs and – a low blow indeed – perineum.

And yet it doesn't take long for morale to surge with the excitement of discovering that the island's toughest test has not killed me, nor even rendered me speechless.

'I wanted the valley to live up to its name,' I tell Ray as he films my victory speech with his camera phone. 'But I just sweated out those tears. A lot of them came out in other ways too . . . that tuna and chips at lunch – God, big mistake. But we've done it, we're up in the clouds now. And it's all down to you, Ray. I was cursing you throughout, under my breath. I could see you, up the road, in your BMC Swiss Cycling Technology top. And the only thing that kept me going was the thought that I looked much cooler in my Cinzano kit.'

It's easy to joke now that I'm off the bike and stuffing my trap with a banana and a Mars bar from the support car. The prospect of a 35-kilometre ride back home doesn't even faze me, although I'm aware of the two remaining short climbs on the agenda. They'll be a pleasure after what we've just done. In fact, looking upwards I can see the top of the island's tallest point – the Pico de las Nieves, so called because of the snow that often clads the summit. From a previous ride I remember the Pico as an easier conquest than the catalogue of pain I've just experienced. In fact, from this intersection we could feasibly tackle the final 6 kilometres and there's something stirring inside me that could probably be described as temptation.

'Don't even think about it,' says Ray, reading my mind. 'Look at you. You're dead. There's no way you're ready for a VOTT-Pico double. I'm surprised you've even made it this far.'

# PROLOGUE:

# BARCELONA

THERE'S A CARNIVAL ATMOSPHERE IN THE Catalan seaside town of Castelldefels, 20 kilometres south of Barcelona. It's Friday, 6 September and Stage 13 of the 2013 Vuelta a España is reaching its climax. Unknown French youngster Warren Barguil has rumbled his more experienced rivals with a late surge in the final 2 kilometres and now solos up the ramped finish towards his first major scalp as a professional. Choosing the inside line close to the barriers, the 21-year-old whippet-lean rider is almost entirely obscured by cheering fans as he zips past my vantage point, some hundred metres from the line. Seven seconds later, with Barguil preparing to pump his fists in celebration, veteran Italian Rinaldo Nocentini grimaces as he leads the futile chase. Fifteen years Barguil's senior, Nocentini knows that a gilt-edged chance to nail his own first major win has just gone begging.

Tomorrow the Vuelta – the third and final of cycling's Grand Tours after the Giro d'Italia and Tour de France – heads north towards the Pyrenees. I, too, will leave Barcelona behind and seek out the mountains. For the best part of a decade this has been my job – to cover and follow bike races professionally; to write about the exploits of elite cyclists who now, tragically, are, like Barguil, much younger than me. But this time it's different. This is as far as my journey with the Vuelta goes. I'm only in Castelldefels because, quite coincidentally, today's stage happens to clash with the Grand Départ of my own Grand Tour.

After years of covering the world's biggest bike races, I'm swapping the sofa for the saddle, exchanging my laptop for Lycra and doing my very own Tour d'Europe. Tomorrow I'm riding to Rome the roundabout route: across the Pyrenees, along the south of France, over the Alps and down the spine of Italy.

It might be worth adding, on the eve of this 2,800-kilometre odyssey, that I took up cycling less than a year ago . . .

Being a non-cycling cycling fanatic was always a source of surprise to everyone I met. Carving out a career in something as specific as professional cycling and yet not actually riding a bike was quite an anomaly. Just imagine a chancellor without an economics degree, or the tubby finger-licking presenter from *MasterChef* not actually knowing how to cook. I never intended not to ride a bike. I guess I just never got round to doing it.

At university I nipped to lectures sporadically on a red mountain bike that was clearly designed for someone at least a foot smaller than me. After graduating I moved to Paris, a city hardly conducive to bike riding, except of course on one day of the year when the world's biggest cycling race comes to town and causes the famous Champs Élysées to shut down and play host to a grandstand sprint finale. Subsequent stints in London and Sydney hardly inspired me to swap jeans for bib shorts (my time Down Under coincided with the wettest Australian summer on record). Throughout my twenties I successfully managed to keep my interest in the sport on a purely professional plane – like someone who refuses to take work home with them. It helped that none of my friends initially shared my passion for cycling, nor did they understand just how or why I could sit down and watch an entire race from start to finish on television.

This infatuation with the two-wheeled world started one wet summer back in the 1980s, when the Tour whizzed past the bottom of the garden of the holiday home in Normandy where my family were staying. Every day me and my brothers would buy the latest copy of *L'Équipe* to check the results – and when we returned to Blighty it was with genuine delight that we discovered Channel 4's daily highlights programme with Richard Keys, Phil Liggett, Paul Sherwen and the catchiest theme tune known to man.

By the time I moved to Bordeaux for a year during my studies, the Tour had become the highlight of my summer – more so than World Cups or Olympic Games. It was 2003, the hundredth anniversary of the Tour and the year Europe was engulfed by an almighty heatwave. In the sweltering temperatures old folk were dropping like flies all over the country – while flies had taken over the entire centre of Bordeaux, where a strike by the local refuse collectors meant sacks of rubbish overflowed bins, piling up and festering in the heat. I had a bar job in the evenings and so was free to watch entire stages from the comfort of my cool sitting room with my French flatmate, who had never met an Englishman so engrossed by his country's national sporting event. When the Tour came to town, and Dutchman Servais Knaven won from an opportunistic break, I was there cheering him on in the crowds. It was just days after Joseba Beloki had crashed in the melting tarmac on a fast downhill and the yellow jersey, Lance Armstrong, had avoided the sprawling Spaniard by bunny-hopping over a ditch, dodging a gendarme and riding cross-country through a field before rejoining the road on the descent of the Côte de la Rochette.

That Tour – which saw a resurgent Jan Ullrich (back to his best after a series of setbacks involving drink-driving, disco pills, injury and weight fluctuations stemming from an insatiable appetite for bratwurst) come within one minute and one second of ending Armstrong's then-record-equalling string of victories – remains my favourite. Perhaps because it was the first time I had been able to follow the race in its entirety from start to finish. By being in France, I also felt closer to the action, swept along in the annual all-consuming circus that is 'La Grande Boucle'.

Little did I know back then that two years on, once I'd finished my degree and started my first job, I'd be covering the race professionally. I'd moved to Paris to keep up my French and avoid making any career-defining decisions. Being the shilly-shallier that I was back then, a few months of Parisian loafing seemed like a good idea – especially seeing as I had no desire to follow my friends to London and take up a job in the City: something that appealed about as much as cheesegrating my limbs in a Beloki-style crash. When the chance to join the rapidly expanding internet department at Eurosport's head office in the suburb of Issy-les-Moulineaux came up, it was a no-brainer. After all, it's a dream of most guys to be paid to watch and write about sport. And for me to be able to do this in Paris, alongside other young people from all over Europe, was fist-pumping, back-of-the-net stuff.

In those early days, sorting out who did what in the *Eurosport.com* office was fairly simple: the question 'Who wants to do this?' would be followed by a show of hands and that was that. By the same logic that put me in charge of all Arsenal's live minute-by-minute football commentaries (back in a time when the Gunners were Manchester United's big rivals), I was made the winter sports editor (being the only person in the office who'd ever been on a snowboard). From this lofty perch, I carved out a niche writing ridiculously elaborate articles on obscure (yet criminally underrated) winter sports such as ski jumping and biathlon.

Reporting on the antics of ski-jumping sensations Sven 'Honey Wings' Hannawald and Adam 'The Flying Moustache' Malysz, I built up something of a reputation as Eurosport's 'Balzac of Bischofshofen' – although I always preferred the more understated 'Zakopane Zola' or, high praise indeed, the 'Goethe of Garmisch-Partenkirchen'. In my 2004/05 ski-jumping season review I managed to spend the first seven paragraphs talking about a Finnish proverb and the national characteristic of *sisu* – a dogged and proud refusal to lie down and be beaten – before concluding that one of the Austrian jumpers had 'suffered from a tapering of form indirectly proportional to the lavish generosity of his prodigious proboscis'. Fan mail soon came flooding in, with one Scandinavian chap thanking me for 'bringing the sport alive' and making Eurosport the go-to destination for ski-jumping coverage. Others were less impressed: a disgruntled reader from Poland took issue with me overlooking the lifetime achievements of moustachioed national icon Malysz in favour of cheap shots at his frivolous facial furbelow. If I valued my kneecaps then a visit to Warsaw was not advised, he suggested.

With the winter sports season coming to an end in a sequinned flourish with the ice-dancing world championships, my boss called me into his office and asked if I liked cycling. I told him that, yes, I was a big fan of the Tour de France.

'Great. How about being our cycling editor now all the triple Salchows are done?'

And so started my career as a cycling journalist. Fast forward several years and, my ability to turn the prosaic world of ski jumping into a jamboree of pun-fuelled mirth not forgotten, I was asked by Eurosport to write a lighthearted weekly satirical cycling blog, which was christened *Blazin' Saddles* (my initial suggestion of 'Lanterne Rouge – the last say on cycling' was overruled).

Written in the third person and renowned for its barbed wit and caustic analysis, *Blazin' Saddles* fast built up a small cult following. For many it was entirely apt that the blog was often abbreviated as 'BS', but most people appreciated its intentions. For me it was a complete hoot, and a chance to poke fun at a sport so often mired in controversy. Then along came Twitter and the subsequent inundation of anonymous *nom de plume* bloggers. Social media took the cycling world by storm, opening so many doors as riders, fans and journalists could all of a sudden interact. *Blazin' Saddles* went daily during the Grand Tours and soon my alter ego had truly taken on a life of its own. Twitter wasn't to every cyclist's taste, though. Bradley Wiggins compared its users to the crowd in the Colosseum. And when an irate Wiggo, en route to winning the Tour de France in 2012, had a pop at the 'bone idleness' of those critics who 'sit under a pseudonym on Twitter', I almost took it to heart that he thought I was an utter 'cunt'. What he didn't appreciate was that it took a lot of effort and application to become among those he so liberally labelled 'fucking wankers'.

By the time Britain had been given their first ever Tour de France winner, I was freelancing full time, with about 80 per cent of my work being pedal related. But as the nation took to the saddle following Sir Wiggo's Olympic time trial victory and Team GB's gold rush in the London 2012 velodrome, I had yet to get on a bike . . .

The phone rings. It's my friend Justin, a multimedia programmer for a number of cycling websites. He's up at the Castelldefels finish area with softly spoken Dave, a silver-haired former Irish Olympic cycling coach. They want to know if I'm 'aboot' (Justin is Canadian). I am more than a boot – I'm a shoo-in to meet up.

Having waded through a mass of blue, white, red and yellow (the Catalan 'national' colours), I reach the barriers. Justin tosses over his press accreditation and green bib, and this bearded lanky Brit manages to put in a convincing enough turn as a fresh-faced, compact and bespectacled Nova Scotian to gain entry to the media area, located inside the walls of the old castle to which Castelldefels owes its name.

Inside the press room journalists are frantically beavering away in all-too-familiar scenes. We grab some complimentary sandwiches and head out to the courtyard. Next to a line of small electric cars that are being used to shuttle lazy VIPs up and down the track to and from the castle, we catch up and share stories. Nearing the end of our *bocadillos* we look up and see Warren Barguil, the stage winner from the Argos-Shimano team, standing three paces away. The man of the moment is then ushered into one of the electric cars for what looks to be a painfully staged, sponsor-pleasing photo shoot.

Justin manages to record some footage as I congratulate boyish Barguil, ten years my junior, on his victory. I've always been naturally lean but Barguil really takes the biscuit (yet clearly stops short of actually eating it). Alongside this sinewy beanpole, whose legs still bear the scars of a recent crash earlier in the race, I, sandwich debris lingering in my whiskers, look positively obese. And if my own hairless legs look like they have been dragged through a field of nettles, it's because a couple of hours ago they were not so hairless.

Barguil freewheels down the hill on his pristine Felt bike, leaving Dave and me to jump into the same electric car while Justin films us for a segment on their *Road Reel* website. The seat is still warm from Barguil's bottom. I do my best to absorb some of his powers. I feel as if this was always meant to happen, that it's a sign that I'm in the driving seat of my own cycling destiny. I'm starting my journey in the exact same position as the most recent stage winner of the Vuelta. It can't get much more serendipitous than that. And I also ride a Felt!

'There are very few people that I would attempt to smuggle into the Vuelta press enclave,' tees-up Dave with that languid yet harmonic voice from the relative freshness of the passenger seat. 'None of them were around today so we had to settle for Felix Lowe, aka *Blazin' Saddles* from Eurosport, who was here in no professional capacity. He was actually being a cycling fan. Felix, what was it like for you out there today?'

Well, Dave, I did what cycling fans do best and almost caused a high-speed horror smash by trying to get too close to the action. For years I've poked fun at fans coming a cropper – most recently in the Tour de France, when a fight ensued between spectators on Alpe d'Huez after one of them tripped another who was running in the wake of lone leader Tejay van Garderen. But today it was very nearly me who would have gone to the top of the YouTube 'epic fail' charts. Remember the hapless fan on Alpe d'Huez who felled lone leader Giuseppe Guerini inside the final kilometre of stage 10 of the Tour de France back in 1999? Or the gendarme who caused a gruesome pile-up when he stepped out in front of Wilfried Nelissen and Laurent Jalabert during a fast sprint finish in 1994? The French police force may have been quick to deny it, but both incidents occurred just moments after the squinting perpetrators thought to themselves, 'Woah, this new zoom lens really does take you into the heart of the action.'

Having made the short journey from Barcelona by train, I had managed to catch the publicity *caravane* in time to snare a free red cap and a slice of pizza, but not – much to my chagrin – any cooling lotion for my inflamed, newly hairless legs (yes, yes . . . more on that later). My initial plan to hike out of town to the ominously named Alto del Rat Penat second-category climb was met with mild amusement by the locals – and it soon became clear why. With the thermometer pushing 30 degrees and the peloton less than an hour away from passing through Castelldefels ahead of their undulating loop into the hills, I had to lower my ambitions somewhat and instead settled for a shaded spot on the side of the road beside the intermediate sprint. In a climbing-heavy race where sprinters have about as much chance of winning the points classification as Lance Armstrong has of making a third coming, intermediate sprints are a bit of a formality. But who knows, perhaps today someone will try and impress the sponsors with a mad dash.

Lying on my back on the side of the road just after the end of the barriers, I took a number of practice shots with my zoom lens as amateur cyclists rode under the kite en route to tackling the climb, the start of which was located another six kilometres away. About twenty minutes later, the leading group of riders – including that man Barguil, three from the front – passed through the sprint with about as much fanfare as the opening of a new Lidl in Swindon. The escapees had taken up position on the opposite side of the road, leaving a vast open space which I helped to fill by shuffling up a few centimetres closer to the action in anticipation of the bunch. The sheer size of the 170-strong peloton, however, meant that when it whooshed by minutes later at top speed it occupied the whole road – from barrier to barrier. Through my lens I could see the rainbow stripes of Philippe Gilbert – yesterday's stage win ending an almost year-long victory drought as world champion – coming closer and closer, protected by his BMC team-mates in red and black.

One eye shut and a finger on the button, I held my poise as the peloton passed within a whisker of my left elbow. Not only could I feel the air move, I could hear what sounded very much like numerous riders giving someone a right earful for letting their angular limbs stray too close to the spokes of their €15,000 bikes. To make it even more tragic, I ran out of space on my memory card just as the peloton reached the line so my recklessness was not even rewarded with a blurred photo of a scowling Gilbert. How cringeworthily ironic it would have been had the cycling writer known for lambasting feckless fans for their overzealous actions – not to mention riders themselves for their own roles in on-the-road bungles – himself caused a mass pile-up in the Vuelta while goofing around on his day off.

Of course, I don't tell any of this to Dave as we sit there in the cockpit of a glorified dodgem – primarily because I've already forgotten about that close shave and am talking about another. For just hours ago I had been turned down by two Barcelona beauty salons for a full leg wax before being accepted into a third – the aptly named Ave Fénix, or Phoenix. My legs are still very much in flames as Dave and I compare the smoothness of one another's pins, with his tanned and trained limbs putting my pasty, rashed legs to shame. It's odd, I tell Dave, they never looked that white when covered in hair. Anna, the incongruously friendly Chinese girl who spent the best part of an hour inflicting a hitherto unparalleled pain upon my lower body, must have ripped off strips of summer tan as well as my generous man fur. An afternoon in the sun that has seen my follicles go all red and inflamed merely adds to the litany of punishment. The result is as if Heston Blumenthal has taken a blowtorch to a pair of unskinned chicken thighs. Even more disturbing is the green and rather prominent varicose vein on my left calf which has suddenly become apparent – something you'd expect from a 70-year-old grandpa and not a man of 32 about to embark on a very long bike ride indeed.

Sensing my train of thought, Dave segues seamlessly into the next question. 'I believe you have your own little Tour about to start. Would you like to tell us a little bit about that?'

It was May 2012. I had been living in Sydney for seven months to coincide with the Tour Down Under, and was just about to head back to the UK for the summer cycling season and the London Olympics when an email dropped into my inbox with the subject header 'Column in cycling mag'. It was from the editor of a new road cycling magazine that would hit the shelves later in the year under the ingeniously original title *Cyclist* (apparently 'Cadence', the first choice, was already trade-marked by Disney as a DJ-ing penguin with pink hair).

'Would you be interested in producing a monthly column for the magazine in return for cold, hard cash?' he wrote. 'The magazine is aimed at keen riders rather than fans of the pro sport. Let me know when you've got some free time in London and we can meet for a coffee.'

When we went for that coffee it felt like one of those job interviews when it's pretty clear that both parties want the same outcome: he was doing his best to sell the magazine to me and in turn I was pulling out all the stops to ensure I became the back-page columnist. But then came the stumbling block – the moment that, really, was always going to happen at some point in my career.

'The primary aim of the column will be to entertain the readers so we're very keen for you to maintain the lighthearted style with which you write your weekly Eurosport blogs,' he explained. 'The big difference, of course, is that we don't want you to write about the professional scene as much as we want to hear about your own daily experiences on the bike.'

'Ah,' I said, as my face no doubt changed to the colour of the Giro d'Italia's *maglia rosa*. 'There might be a problem there . . . I don't actually cycle.'

'What? You're not telling me you don't ride a bike?'

'I am telling you exactly that,' I winced. As his face filled with disappointment, I made a last-ditch attempt to salvage the situation.

'But that doesn't necessarily have to be a problem. In fact, we could turn it to our advantage. Perhaps the column could be about me, the cycling journalist, finally taking up the sport in his early thirties? People could definitely relate to that – and there'd be ample scope for humour . . .'

Small silence as the brain cogs ticked over.

'You know what, that could work,' he said. 'Kind of "cycling obsessive gets obsessive about cycling" . . .'

'Exactly. Writer to rider – charting my shift from armchair fan to cycling nut. You know what, I've been meaning to start riding for ages. This could be the kick up the backside I need.'

So we shook on it and a few months later I filed my first column for the inaugural edition of the magazine. It was about my lame effort, while back in Sydney, to get into cycling – when I borrowed a bike from a Twitter follower for a week, but failed to get any enjoyment from it, thanks to the combination of having no cleats and no cycling shorts. With my friend Al, who at the time worked for the website *Cyclingnews*, I took the Trek out for some loops of Centennial Park wearing a pair of trainers and my running kit. It had been a disaster – primarily because of the adverse effect the narrow saddle had on my tender undercarriage. I remembered a recent blog I had written making light of Tom Boonen's scrotum rip and winced as the karma set in. On the second ride I wore Speedos stuffed with socks and still pulverized my perineum over every pothole. Despite these setbacks, I told my readers at *Cyclist* that I intended to take up the sport for good back in London; that I would buy a bike, get the right kit and aim to ride the annual Étape du Tour sportive the following July.

My plan to ride a demanding but relatively simple one-day sportive in the Alps soon changed when Dylan, a reader of my very first *Cyclist* column, got in touch, suggesting I join him and a handful of others on their proposed 'Hannibal Expedition' for a gruelling 26-day journey over three mountain ranges and through three countries – shadowing the famous Carthaginian general who, over two millennia ago, followed the same route with a vast army and a pack of elephants.

As bizarre as this endeavour sounded – swapping pachyderms for pedal-power and conquering the road to Rome – my eyes were suddenly opened to the possibilities. With the right training and preparation I could take part in this much bigger challenge. After years of experiencing cycling vicariously, it made sense that I should finally try my hand (or legs) at a Grand Tour of my own. The route not only took us through the three countries that provide the centre stage and backdrop for cycling's major stage races, it tackled a whole host of fabled climbs that every cycling fan has watched countless times on the small screen.

To combat the inevitable pain and suffering that would come hand in hand with such a foolhardy enterprise, I convinced myself it would be a gastronomic journey *par excellence*, powered by local delicacies, fine wines and decadent degustations. I'd also be able to throw back on the crumpled historian's cap from my time at university and delve into the zany story of those thirty-seven elephants and their unlikely Alpine crossing. Just thinking about the prospect of pulling this off made me feel like a breakaway rider who had managed to extricate himself from the peloton and now rode solo at the front of the race. But could this escapee go the distance?

In Castelldefels, Dave and Justin say their goodbyes and we agree to meet up again in a couple of days when me and my riding companions pass through Justin's home town of Girona. I hop on the train back to Barcelona, conscious that my legs look like the result of a night of passion between Mr Eczema and Miss Alopecia. There was no real reason to pay someone to cover them in strips of piping-hot wax before yanking out everything that was aesthetically pleasing about them in a succession of excruciating, emasculating blows. But I had already written one of my monthly *Cyclist* columns on taking a razor to my legs for the first time and so waxing was the logical next step. Besides, I'll now look the part (once the swelling subsides) and it should help me in my quest to get inside the mindset of a pro rider.

I'm staying in a hotel on the Avinguda de Roma. Seeing that Rome is my destination, I thought it would be fitting to dangle it out there as an incentive right at the outset. The hotel also has the benefit of being a short walk from the station, which means I can soon put on a pair of trousers. Waiting for me in the reception is the parcel I have been expecting.

Somewhat belatedly in my preparations for the Hannibal ride, I decided that I should have an official *Blazin' Saddles* kit created. My Scottish friend Scott, who co-hosts the excellent *Velocast* cycling podcast for Eurosport, designed a quite magnificent get-up after I sent over some very specific specifications. The centrepiece of the jersey was one of Hannibal's elephants and the colours were inspired by the maroon and gold of the 'Tower' district of the Tuscan town of Siena, which also boasts an elephant as its emblem.

Given the quick turnaround, Scott's contact Ken (not from Kent), who runs a kit company, could not make the masterpiece in time for a UK delivery ahead of my departure. Instead, Ken kindly agreed to send the kit from his Belgian factory to my hotel in Barcelona. And here it is, in my hands as I take the lift up to my room on the fourth floor.

Like many unfortunate souls at the wrong end of a postal prank, on opening the package I am instantly struck by the brownness of its contents. Scott's jersey design had clearly been a dark red, borderline-maroon colour, but this is a rusty brown that is about as pleasing on the eye as, well, most rusty brown things. What's more, the bib shorts are of the kind of luminous lime that you could probably use to see in the dark. The intention was for my buttocks to be encased in slick dark green as opposed to something that reminds me of Slimer, the first ghost to be thwarted by the Ghostbusters. I wanted the ensemble to be more Portugal-football-kit and less obscure-African-flag.

If the colours are a bit of a let-down, then trying the thing on gives me more cause for concern. Given my height, I ordered the jersey in

XL but was advised by Ken not to opt for the slim-fit version. The net result is a brown tent that I'm meant to wear for the next month. There's so much extra material hanging off my slender frame that none of the lettering or logos from my 'sponsors' can actually be read. While I'm riding, this will no doubt flap in the wind like Marco Pantani's ears, prior to the operation he had to pin them back. But it's too late to reorder another kit. I guess I'll just have to somehow make baggy, brown and electric green cool again.

Looking the part is one thing but if you can't actually pedal over a hill then waxed legs and a loud customized outfit are only going to get you so far. Back towards the end of 2012, with this ride as my ultimate goal, I encountered my first stumbling block – and quite a large one, admittedly. I didn't have a bike. Being an impoverished journalist there was no way I could fork out a four-figure sum for a pair of wheels to feed a hobby that could well prove as short-lived as that time, aged nine, I decided I wanted piano lessons. For three months I made do with borrowing my brother's Bianchi and an old Harry Hall from my brother-in-law – both, like me, six-foot-plus monsters. Then, in a bid to get some serious saddle miles under my belt, I flew out to Gran Canaria with a friend to see just why professional teams such as Alberto Contador's Saxo Bank headed to what the Lonely Planet ominously describes as 'the gay honeypot of the Canaries' for winter training. We took on that man Ray as our guide, and on a couple of hired Cannondales we managed to conquer the island's loftiest peak, the Pico. A week later, I was brought back down to earth with a freezing December ride through Epping Forest. Back on a borrowed bike of diminutive proportions, my body took a hammering and my ever-suspect right knee started to flare up. So when Specialized agreed to loan me a brand spanking new, bright red, extra-large Roubaix Comp for the six months as I prepared for my Grand Tour, you can imagine my riding rapture.

Everything was going swimmingly. I'd done a bike fitting and bought a load of accessories. I'd even turned heads in Richmond Park with my slick carbon-fibre machine before testing out the Olympic road race route in the Surrey Hills. And then, exactly a month after waxing lyrical about my new steed on the back page of *Cyclist*, I was dedicating a column to the bastards who had nicked my pride and joy from my garden shed.

Downcast, I sought solace once again in the Canaries, heading out to be reunited with Ray for that infamous date with the Valley of the Tears. To celebrate our defiance of the mighty VOTT, Ray talked me into shaving my legs for the first time. Despite his conviction that I'd need both a flame thrower and a garden strimmer, a mere beard trimmer and a rusty Gillette sufficed – although the inadvertent creation of a ghastly pair of hair shorts did raise eyebrows on the beach the next day. The VOTT may have been my biggest achievement on a bike in my fledgling amateur cyclist career, but I certainly washed part of my soul down the plug in Maspalomas. I returned to the UK a changed man.

With the first major race of the season – the Giro – out of the way, everything fell gloriously into place when I was invited out to the Alps to take part in the Time Megève Mont Blanc sportive and interview the event ambassador, Greg LeMond. America's first (and only) legitimate Tour de France winner is responsible for one of my earliest memories in cycling – that eleventh-hour time trial win over Laurent Fignon on the Champs Élysées which saw him edge the 1989 Tour by eight slender seconds.

To be able to chew the fat with a legend like LeMond was a defining moment for me, and was infinitely more successful from a professional point of view than my debut TV interview for Eurosport, a year earlier, when Bjarne Riis, the 1996 Tour winner, seemed on the verge of landing a punch on my own sizeable snout. Admittedly, this may have been after I quizzed him about his old nickname, 'Mr 60 Per Cent', a reference to his blood's dangerously high haematocrit level; or it could just well have been the crass remark I made in response to his assertion that his favourite meal was 'a nice, juicy steak' (such meaty issues were a sore point at the time, with his rider Alberto Contador banned for an illegal steroid that the Spaniard blamed on a contaminated piece of beef).

Riis left me rather nonplussed. He refused to let down his defences or open up; I learned nothing about the man that I hadn't already picked up on in various other interviews; I also felt intimidated to the extent that I seriously considered there might be a Danish bounty on my head. With LeMond, however, things were entirely different. What was meant to be a short chat went on for two hours. He told me all about his ongoing spat with Lance Armstrong and his contrasting relationships with the likes of Fignon and his big rival Bernard Hinault; he gave me a fresh (if that's the word) perspective on his amazing 1986 season, which despite all its success was punctuated with numerous toilet-related mishaps. To have a legend of the sport explain to me how he shat his pants and once – quite literally – shed the contents of his bowels all over the face of a team-mate (more on that later), was not only a high point of my career but of my adult life.

Another major bonus that came from the Megève gig was that Saddleback UK, a Bristol-based bike importer, lent me a brand new 62cm frame Felt Z4 to use for what was my first ever amateur race. It rode like a dream – and the understated black, blue and white colours were far easier on the eye than the Ferrari-red bling of the stolen Specialized. After a bit of grovelling on my part, I managed to turn this into a more permanent loan so I could finally train on the same bike that would spirit me across three mountain ranges in a few months' time.

With our departure date looming, the Tour came calling, beckoning me to Paris for the whole of July to cover the centenary race for

Eurosport, as well as deliver a daily ten-minute Tour round-up for the rolling news channel, France 24. François, my old boss from those halcyon Eurosport days, was now one of the presenters at France 24 and managed to pull some strings. The net result was that this anonymous blogger – having already this year branched out by getting a magazine column complete with a picture byline (admittedly one taken back in 2007) – was suddenly trying his hand at besuited live TV cycling punditry. Saying it went like clockwork would be more of a nod to the Festina scandal-hit Tour of 1988 than anything else. I certainly relied on a whole host of stimulants (coffee, Coke and layers of make-up) to keep me performing at a base level. The cameras also had a tendency to catch me with a scowl, while once I spoke of how riders would shave seconds off their time trial efforts by 'wearing special aerodynamic bikes'. Luckily, it wasn't exactly the BBC World Service and so my frequent gaffes were only seen by my family and close friends, who tuned in daily to see me verbally joust with Dan, the charming autocued sports presenter, who had a tendency to steal all my best titbits and palm them off as his own (I soon learned to either hold back the juicy stuff for myself or feed Dan misinformation, which I could subsequently correct while on air).

Despite some kind, if a little biased feedback, my phone was not exactly humming with requests to become cycling's answer to Ben Fogle. Which was a good thing, because after a month in which, besides the odd run along the Seine, my sporting accomplishments included the lunchtime Brie baguette snatch (lifting an ever-decreasing pungent weight from waist to mouth) and the daily game of pavement hopscotch to avoid the steaming piles of Parisian dog mess, I really needed to get back on the Felt and put in some miles. In a bid to get into trim condition ahead of my mammoth ride, I packed August with hefty training: London to Brighton on a wet Thursday, a roll around the Chilterns ahead of my belated birthday barbecue (I had turned 32 under the radar while out in Paris) and a series of hilly rides around my parents' house in Dorset (including Zig Zag Hill – aka the Dorset d'Huez – and Gold Hill, the cobbled street that the lazy baker's boy pushed his bike up in the old Hovis advert).

The final piece of the jigsaw came with two days in the high mountains on the Haute Route Alpine sportive. I flew out to Geneva and joined the other competitors at the ski resort of Val d'Isère ahead of the queen stage of the week-long event, which included three killer ascents and a foray into Italy. Before flying back from Nice, my second of back-to-back stages included the legendary Col d'Izoard, where I would be returning a month later on our Hannibal-inspired tour, and a summit finish at Pra Loup, where Eddy 'The Cannibal' Merckx's long reign at the top finally came to an end in 1975 when he popped sensationally on the final climb of the Tour's fifteenth stage from Nice. Those two days also supplemented my forthcoming quest somewhat, for the Col de Mont Cenis (which we tackled after a chilly dusk slog up the Col de l'Iseran, the highest paved mountain road in Europe) is one of a number of Alpine passes which historians believe could have been the location of Hannibal's march into Italy.

While ideal preparation for my own tour, the Haute Route did leave me as battered and bruised as one of Hannibal's foot soldiers. Opting out of the logistical nightmare of transporting my Felt, I arranged the loan of a snazzy, brand new Look bike – worth €4,500 and weighing less than Bjarne Riis's conscience. Any advantages of being issued with some great weaponry were outdone by the detrimental effect of riding the best part of three hundred brutal kilometres on yet another piece of borrowed equipment designed for someone half a foot shorter. As a result, my final fortnight in London was spent convalescing and fretting over my glass knee, rather than turning the pedals and honing my preparations. Seeking a silver lining, I told myself there would be ample time to ride into some kind of Hannibalic form during those comparatively gentle opening days through the Pyrenean foothills. Besides, London's as kind to cyclists as Jeremy Clarkson is to, well, cyclists – and I didn't want to get hit by a bus or take a spill so close to my own Grand Départ.

Hungry, I head out for my last supper in Barcelona. There's a free table on the terrace of a small restaurant near the hotel and I settle in for a medley of tapas dishes: jamón ibérico, green padrónes peppers, potatoes with a garlic sauce, and deep-fried cod balls. Washed down with the kind of absurdly large beer only ever served to Brits abroad. If I'm going to be burning off calories by the bucket load, then I'd better start loading up now. While eating I notice a steady stream of busty women walking past, some of them even smiling in the direction of my salty cod balls. It's only on closer inspection that I see there's a strip club next door and all these ladies are presumably turning up to work. When the waiter later asks me if I'd like something sweet for dessert, I'm not sure if it's an invitation to shift venues.

The family on the next table – whose young children are strategically placed to avoid the glamorous procession behind – are talking in Italian, and when I catch the eye of the father it's a good opportunity to tell them about the journey I'm about to embark on towards their homeland.

'That's a long trip,' says Paolo. 'In a few days we return to Rome but by plane – not by bike.'

Ho ho. We all have a laugh. I then ask him whether the country is behind Vincenzo Nibali, the Italian who won the Giro in May and who is currently wearing the red leader's jersey in the Vuelta.

Paolo has no idea who I'm talking about. 'I do not follow cycling much,' he admits. This strikes me as a little odd – a bit like an Englishman not knowing who Bradley Wiggins was. 'But we do live in a suburb of Rome where the great Fausto Coppi used to live,' he adds, perhaps proving his previous assertion (Coppi was from the north and never lived in Rome, as far as I'm aware).

While Paolo's young sons Giovanni and Gabriel take it in turns to have a sip from Papa's bright yellow piña colada, I ask him for some restaurant recommendations for when I arrive in his hometown.

'We don't eat out too much in Rome because the food is rather heavy,' he says, which seems rich coming from a man currently tucking into a humongous rare tuna steak topped with fried onions and what appear to be melted slices of Camembert. But he suggests I give the Trastevere area a go – which is handy, as it happens to be where we're staying.

After downing a shot of Strega liqueur that the Italian owner of the restaurant brings with the bill, I return to the hotel for my final night's sleep free from pain and exhaustion. Running through some of the photos I took that day while doing my best to cause a mass pile-up, I come across something quite splendid.

Well after Warren Barguil had taken the victory in Castelldefels I continued taking photos as the remainder of the field came home in dribs and drabs. I have a series of pictures showing Kristof Vandewalle and Zdeněk Štybar – the Omega Pharma Quick-Step team-mates of 'Manx Missile' Mark Cavendish – riding up the final ramp with a man in a black and purple top in tow. The man in the unfamiliar kit is distinctly chunkier than the professional riders and there is no race number attached to his bright yellow Scott bike. He's still being cheered by the crowd, many of whom are presumably oblivious to the fact that this guy is clearly an amateur who has slipped through the net and is quite literally riding his luck. On closer inspection, that man seems familiar. I head back to my earlier preparatory shots and all is revealed: riding through the intermediate sprint in a small group of amateurs is a slightly blurred, heavy-set chap on the same Scott bike, with the same floral tattoos on his right bicep, the same kit and vintage red Barcelona cap underneath his helmet, and the same ironic (you'd hope) bright yellow Livestrong bracelet. This was 60 kilometres from the finish and ahead of the final climb.

I'll never know how, but at some point between there and the finish, Señor Barcelona managed to join the late stragglers of the peloton and ride along with them all the way to the line – without either being given the cold shoulder by the pros or being nobbled by a race official. He rode up the finishing straight of the thirteenth stage of the third biggest stage race of the season and was cheered on by thousands of fans. God knows what he did once he crossed the line – perhaps he was even arrested – but I'm sure it was all worth it. He did what so many of us amateurs have only dreamed of doing: joining our heroes and becoming, for a fleeting moment, one of them; seeing the race through their eyes.

And as I'm smiling to myself at his audacity, it strikes me that over the next three and a bit weeks I'll have the chance to do something very similar. Sure, I won't be riding alongside the pros in the flesh, but I'll be with them in spirit, taking on the very same challenges, riding the same hard miles, reliving the same emotions, perhaps even pining for the same drugs. I'll take on Mont Ventoux, one of the most feared and revered ascents in Tour de France history, a giant upon which I have never set foot let alone wheel, but one which I know so well through years of voracious viewing on television. Then I'll try to emulate the professionals by taking on the famous twenty-one hairpins of Alpe d'Huez twice in one afternoon – just as the peloton did months earlier in the centenary Tour.

Cycling is unique in this respect. Name me another mainstream sport that opens up its doors to the public in the same way. Golf perhaps – provided you have both a hundred quid in green fees and the requisite tweed to get into St Andrews. The Giro, the Tour and the Vuelta are the largest free sporting events on the globe, taking place on public roads rather than containing themselves in stadia. Football fans can't take a ball to Wembley and have a kick around any more than tennis fans can have a knock-up at Wimbledon. But any of us cycling fanatics can take to the road on a bike. What astonishes me the most is that it has taken me so long to get in on the act. Finally I'm doing something about it. For yonks I have earned my crust without taking part in the sport behind my daily bread and butter. I have been peddling my wares without pedalling squares. Now, after a belated yet hasty start, this writer is about to graduate as a proper rider. That tattooed man in black and purple is me – and I have the professional peloton in my sights.

Lying in bed, I recall those choice words from Bradley Wiggins during the 2012 Tour. 'I cannot be doing with people like that,' harrumphed the yellow jersey when quizzed about the new breed of anonymous armchair journalists casting aspersions on Team Sky's top-secret training techniques. 'It justifies their own bone idleness because they can't ever imagine applying themselves to do anything in their lives. It's easy for them to sit under a pseudonym on Twitter and write that sort of shit, rather than get off their arses in their own lives and apply themselves and work hard at something and achieve something. And that's ultimately it. Cunts.'

Now I've never had a serious pop at Wiggo's moral provenance – some readers even accuse me of being a Sky 'fan boy' (which is also hilariously far from the truth) – but Wiggins certainly has a point. And it's one I've taken on board. A year on and I've shed the anonymity and got off my backside and into the saddle. Tomorrow, the raconteur becomes a rouleur.

# STAGES 1-3

# SPAIN

THE NEXT MORNING, ON ARRIVAL AT the designated rendezvous in central Barcelona, the realization dawned on me that I had booked a place on a Saga cycling holiday. It wasn't so much that I was the youngest, as the glaring fact that my fellow riders were considerably older. I hadn't seen as many white hairs in one place since Sir David Attenborough's last polar bear documentary. If it wasn't for Dylan coordinating matters and making introductions, it would have felt like an elaborate hoax. We're cycling to Rome, right? This lot may struggle with the Pyrenees.

My heart thumped and I started to sweat. Had I misunderstood the brief? Misread the small print? Since my sedate month covering the Tour, I'd done my best to get in shape and eat up the miles on my bike. But to what end? To ride at a leisurely pace with people who may need a Stannah stairlift to shunt them up to their hotel room at the end of the day? Perhaps I had overestimated the competition somewhat. I felt like a pumped-up gladiator entering the arena armed with a gory array of sharp weapons only to find, as allies, a group of puny slaves huddled around a shared shield. Even the most positive spin – that I could be their Russell Crowe – didn't bear thinking about.

Soon I had more pressing concerns than my geriatric pedalling domestiques. While they were discussing knitwear, herbal tea and hip replacements during the transfer to the Montseny National Park some 60 kilometres north of Barcelona, I travelled in the front of a separate luggage van with Javier, an Ecuadorian handyman-come-taxi driver, who insisted on using the GPS on his phone for directions while careering one-handedly up a succession of slippery hairpin bends. The sun that had welcomed our arrival in Spain had by now given way to ominous clouds and rain.

Heavily tattooed and pierced, Javier had carefully sculpted his sideburns into sharp points jutting down his jawline. Think Bradley Wiggins, but for the nu-metal generation. Our conversation was pretty fragmented. The gist of his unexpectedly conservative train of thought seemed to be that 'laziness' was to blame for Spain's chronic unemployment figures. Also a trained plumber and electrician, man-for-all-seasons Javier's ability to multi-task would have been impressive had it not resulted in the van almost leaving the road on at least two occasions. Someone upstairs was clearly punishing me for my childish preconception with the age and condition of my riding companions. Come to think of it, one or two of them may have been as young as 45.

I hadn't been as scared as a passenger since the time I was given a ride in the now-defunct Vacansoleil-DCM team car during the 2012 Tour Down Under. With their man Thomas De Gendt in the day's breakaway, the Dutch team received permission to slip out of the ordered line of official vehicles behind the peloton and drive up to the leading group. Behind the wheel was chummy directeur sportif Michel Cornelisse, a former winner of the Tour of Luxembourg, who put his foot down and covered the four-minute gap between pack and break in around about 60 seconds flat, tooting fans on the side of the road as well as reaching behind for a sandwich in the process.

'Michel, it's too fast,' warned mechanic Klas in the back seat.

'They must give us slower cars then,' he laughed before winding down the window and bellowing out, 'Vacansoleil is on fire! Thomas is on fire!'

That afternoon, Michel received two warnings from the race commissaire for his carefree abandon on the road. One more and he was out, they warned. His speeding was strange given what had happened to the team's star rider six months earlier in the 2011 Tour. When a rampaging press car swerved to avoid a tree on the side of the road and veered into the path of Sky's Juan Antonio Flecha, it was Vacansoleil's Johnny Hoogerland who came off worst. The Dutchman slammed into the sprawling Flecha and was thrown over the handlebars and into a barbed-wire fence. Besides ripping his legs and torso to shreds, the impact tore off Hoogerland's shorts and left little to the imagination.

Thankfully things didn't get so prickly in the van to Montseny. Despite his best efforts to the contrary, Javier managed to deliver me and the luggage to the isolated Hotel Sant Bernat – high in the hills of the national park – in one piece. Before the afternoon's proposed warm-up welcome ride, I had to put back together something that *was* in pieces: my bike. This is where I first met Sam – our tour's resident mechanic, historian and GPS mapping guru.

If it was Dylan who first approached me about our Hannibal-inspired tour, it was flamboyant, loud-suit-wearing, long-haired Australian archaeologist Sam who gave birth to the initial concept. Like Hannibal (and myself), Sam has two brothers. Back in 2009, the Woods brethren made a six-part BBC documentary about Hannibal's famous march on Rome, which saw the endearingly goofy trio ride pannier-laden hybrids from Cartagena in southern Spain, up the Iberian peninsula, over the

Pyrenees and Alps, down the backbone of Italy to Rome, and then further south to the toe before crossing the Mediterranean to Tunisia. Carefully bringing alive the Hannibal legend by exploring all aspects of the Second Punic War between Carthage and Rome, the boys even managed to shoehorn a good wrestle into each episode – although highjinks would often morph into a nervous group hug.

The experience – Hannibal, not hugging – was the inspiration behind the signature event of Sam and Dylan's global bike-touring company, Ride & Seek, which the pair set up following a chance encounter at a Sydney wedding (both their wives were at high school with the bride). Having dabbled as a Milan-based British squash champion with a masters degree in international affairs, Dylan had recently moved Down Under to start a family after various stints as a ski and bike guide in France. Blending Sam's archaeology armoury, Dylan's previous guiding experiences and their shared love of cycling and travel, all the ingredients were there for something special.

While riding and coordinating a European bike tour prised them away from their immediate families in Australia, it was a great chance for Dylan to catch up with his Liverpudlian father, Terry – my designated room-mate for the entire journey to Rome. Father and son could not have been more different. The one: taller, greyer, thicker set and both bumbling and ponderous; the other: lean, lithe, assured and confident. While Dylan could segue seamlessly between multiple European languages and accents, Terry's primary means of articulation were Scouse and snoring – although he had grumbling and groaning down to a tee as well.

But if Dylan owes his luxuriant locks and olive complexion to his Mauritian mother, then the seeds of his cycling passion were clearly sown by his dad. Together they used to ride around the Fens near their home in Cambridge or the French countryside while on summer holidays. As a family, the Reynoldses even defied a fierce headwind to ride from John O'Groats to Land's End. While Terry's interest in – and ability on – bikes somewhat dwindled once his son flew the nest, the previous year's inaugural Barcelona–Rome tour reacquainted him with two wheels. He, too, was now back for what he described as 'more suffering on a daily basis'.

Joining Terry for a second successive stab at riding to Rome was Bob, an American cycling fanatic whose reputation preceded him. In emails leading up to the event, Dylan had spoken in mythical tones about a 70-year-old retired man from Seattle who promised to return and ride the route on a wooden bike. And here he was, chatting away with Sam as he opened his case to reveal his pride and joy – a $7,000 Renovo made to measure out of three different types of African hardwood. It was one of sixteen bikes – including a 1983 fully restored Eddie Merckx in Molteni orange, a 1995 Davidson custom-made tandem which Bob rides with his wife Sandy, and a 1997 Trek in US Postal colours (the outing of Lance Armstrong was a sad day in the Berg household) – that Bob keeps on display either in his garage-cum-museum at Seattle, or at his holiday home in Idaho.

Bob assembled his shiningly varnished wooden bike with all the dexterity of someone who, among other things, I'd soon discover made his money manufacturing what he described as 'electronic butt plugs' for men with dodgy prostates. I, on the other hand, cobbled together my carbon-fibre Felt with all the cack-handedness of someone thinking about combining a bike ride with testing out one of Bob's back-door devices. We were the only two of the group to have brought out our own steeds, the others preferring to ride some hired Specialized bikes sourced by Dylan and Sam. 'I should be putting together three titanium bikes that we've been given by a sponsor,' said Sam as he helped me untangle my chain. 'But the Spanish customs officials have confiscated them at the airport. Looks like Javier will have to drop them off once they're released.'

Over a meet-and-greet lunch I was relieved to see a vanguard of demonstrably young faces who had already arrived at the hotel ahead of the Saga reinforcements. Old school friends of Dylan's, Richard and Suren were in their late thirties and were down to ride with us until Carcassonne, where they would call time on the sporty leg of Suren's prolonged engagement celebrations (previous stag destinations had included weekends in Brighton and Ibiza). His advanced kit and quasi-toned physique suggested that Suren was a potential sparring partner – even if the premise for his inclusion on the tour seemed to come from the Oliver Reed school of cycling. Richard and Suren were busy rolling back the years with Terry, who had earlier, rather humbly, assured the room that 'my only claim to fame is that I'm Dylan's dad' before jokingly asking whether anyone had any amphetamines.

Such self-deprecation blended with caustic wit prompted several nervous laughs from the remainder of the group, who probably should have counted their lucky stars that the convict jokes had yet to be rolled out (there would be many of those – as well as cricket-related wisecracks which would come back to haunt us Brits). This Antipodean contingent featured: semi-retired academic John and air-conditioning-unit importer Kay, a couple (or so I presumed) from Wollongong; Bernadette, a pencil-thin chiropodist from Ballarat, near Melbourne; nurse Michaela and radiographer Sharon, both from Sydney; Ted, one of Sam's old archaeology lecturers at university, and his partner Camilla, a fellow ancient historian who had just completed a doctorate. Ted, Camilla and Michaela were only down to ride the first leg to Avignon – but the others, like me, had signed up for the full monty.

After a light lunch of soup and salad we all went to get ready for the proposed warm-up ride. Not wishing to make any enemies too fast, I decided to keep the garish brown and green kit under wraps until the first full stage. Things, nevertheless, started ominously – and it wasn't just the drizzle falling from the grumbling grey clouds hanging overhead.

On the first bend of the entire tour, the rider in front of me came a cropper and crashed. It was Michaela, the only one of our group opting to ride a hybrid with flat handlebars. Starting off at the back, I had quickly caught up with her and seen how nervously she was applying her brakes. When her back wheel inevitably locked, she swerved, slammed on the front brake and went, rather innocuously it has to be said, over the handlebars and on to her side. Fortunately, as she got to her feet and back in the saddle, she seemed more embarrassed than hurt. Portentous omens, nevertheless.

During the nine days that Michaela rode with us on the tour, the poor girl seemed to attract more calamity than the bowler-hatted bobbies Thomson and Thompson from *Tintin*. By the time we reached Avignon in Provence, Michaela had crashed twice, was stung by bees or wasps at least three times, and chased by dogs on innumerable occasions (the second of which resulted in her being bitten on the leg and upended into a ditch). If being a cycling cynophobe wasn't enough, she also managed to get sunburnt on the one day when the sun properly came out to play, and needed to enlist the help of the mayor of a small French village after taking the wrong turn and veering 20 kilometres off course. For someone who was merely attending a nursing conference in Malmö and had decided, at the last minute, to throw in a spot of bike riding at the end, this was terrible bad luck. That said, she sought solace in the safety of the support van on fewer occasions than Suren, which either says a lot for her fighting spirit, or spoke volumes about Stag-do Suren's risible stamina.

At the bottom of the hill we made an early pit stop at the cafe in the centre of Montseny. With a storm brewing (as well as some bitter Spanish *cortado* coffees), everyone else was happy to ride back up to the hotel and call it a day. But I had not come all the way here to ride an opening day that was effectively the same mileage as my daily commute in London. Sure, this was a marathon and not a sprint – with more than three weeks and two and a half thousand kilometres to go – but I had to set out as I intended to continue: to test myself and ride more than the daily suggested itinerary. I also wanted to tackle as many routes as the pros may have done – and Sam assured me (erroneously, as it turned out) that just around the corner lay a classic climb from the Vuelta.

So, setting the tone for the remainder of the trip, off I went on a mad solo mission to take on the Turó de l'Home, a beast that boasts a maximum gradient of 13 per cent and whose initial, gentler slopes are often used in the annual Volta a Catalunya stage race. Some well-known names – such as local favourite Joaquim 'Purito' Rodríguez – appeared in paint on the increasingly wet roads alongside some less familiar ones. A chap called Rémi had a fair bit of support, judging by the amount of times his fan club had sprayed 'Vamos Rémi!' on the road. As the rain came down harder, I subconsciously became Rémi and with every sighting of his name, I felt by proxy a pat on the back from the author of those messages. After all, how different can my feelings on this climb be from those of my new friend? Although I doubt Rémi had to combat the elements as much as I did that day.

My initial intention was to carry on until I got tired or the downpour was too unbearable, and then turn back. But the further I went, the more determined I became to complete the whole 32-kilometre loop. Rémi didn't give up, so neither should I. In normal circumstances, this would not have been a problem. But I was on my own, without a map, and the weather was becoming biblical.

Little did I know that, some 100 kilometres north in the Pyrenean principality of Andorra, stage 14 of the Vuelta was being played out in equally apocalyptic conditions, in stark contrast to the hot sun of Castelldefels one day earlier. As the American veteran Chris Horner underlined his credentials as the number-one threat to the current leader Vincenzo Nibali, scores of riders – including Nibali's fellow Italian Ivan Basso – were forced out of the race because of hypothermia. The temperature where I was had not plummeted to such depths, but my right knee was starting to sting with every pedal stroke. Like Basso, I should have called it a day. But that wouldn't have impressed my new companions when I regaled them with tales of my derring-do over the dinner table.

Throwing caution to the increasingly blustery wind, I passed through a ghostly wooded segment that offered eerie shelter from the rain but reminded me of the *Blair Witch Project* (although being put out of my misery was becoming more appealing by the second). The road then split in two, with Purito and the others continuing along the well-manicured plateau and my man Rémi heading up the one-way road to the summit. Calling it a road is perhaps generous. Rémi had clearly set off some landmines when he ventured up.

The Volta a Catalunya came this high just the once in 1976 and there have been calls to include the Turó de l'Home in the Vuelta ever since (despite Sam's assertions, it has yet to be used in Spain's premier race). The logistical problem for race organizers is that the summit is both a dead end and dead. There's nothing but a meteorological station and a mud track down the other side. At least, that's all I could see – because by the time I had made it to the top and passed the congratulatory 'Bravo Rémi' painted across the road (I wish they'd get my name right), visibility was down to about 10 metres. It was no doubt a similar kind of fog that, in 1959, caused an aircraft carrying twenty-nine students home to England to crash into the side of the mountain nineteen minutes after departure from Barcelona. All passengers and the three crew members were killed on impact.

This morbid aside would have put my gripes into perspective had I known it at the time. As it was, I just felt rather sorry for myself.

It's one thing riding up a road that appears not to have been relaid since a plane crash back in the late 1950s – but try cycling down such an obstacle course in the rain on a bike you haphazardly assembled a matter of hours earlier. There were so many loose stones and divots I was convinced that a puncture was inevitable. Braking became harder and harder as my hands grew more numb. Throw in my shivering arms, throbbing knee and chattering teeth, and my whole body was a symphony of soreness.

But my sense of humour remained intact and I couldn't help bursting out in laughter at the ridiculousness of the whole situation. I imagined phoning home to tell them the whole thing was off because I had crashed down a ravine on the first day while doing my utmost best to knacker myself and catch a cold. Coming all this way and being bitten by an act of bravado before the real deal had even begun would have been an ignominious way to end my amateur race career – a bit like the obligatory chap who crashes in the prologue of a Grand Tour and is forced to watch the rest of the action on TV from the comfort of his hospital bed (Chris Boardman's tumble in the 1995 Tour springs to mind).

Discarding these downbeat thoughts and buoyed by a passing driver who flashed his lights and tooted his horn (clearly another Rémi fan), I pedal-plodded back towards Montseny while dreaming of a warm bath and a good feed. As soon as my phone regained reception and there was a slight lull in the rain, I pinged off a grovelling text to Dylan, asking him to be a gent and pick me up in the van to save me doing the final climb back to the hotel from the centre of town. My knight in shining armour arrived when I was about three kilometres from the finish. In I jumped, a broken man – my limbs sore, my kit utterly drenched and my bike making all manner of peculiar noises.

'Good effort, mate. How do you feel?' asked Dylan.

'Too shattered for someone about to start a bike ride to Rome tomorrow' was about all I could manage.

As chuffed as I was to have made it to the top of the Turó de l'Home and to have put a large tick next to the first of many challenges, it was at a huge cost. For my temperamental right patella to be inflamed so early on was of huge concern.

Clearly keen to get our rooming relationship off to a cosy start, Terry had already started running a hot bath for me. I peeled off my kit, had a shave and then spent a few taut minutes trying, without success, to take a dump. Perhaps I had pushed things a bit too far today, I thought. In a bid to show up the oldies, the impetuosity of relative youth had stumbled at the first hurdle.

Pre-dinner drinks quickly rid me of any regret for it became clear that I had been cast as some kind of hero for my wet-weather climbing exploits. A glass of local Cava was thrust into my hand as I entered the lounge to a round of applause, and as I answered a flurry of questions, it felt like a post-race press conference with me assuming the role of stage winner. Everyone was stunned when I told them I had only taken up cycling relatively recently. They were equally stunned when I came clean and told them I was hoping to write a book about my experiences.

'That means you are all potential characters and that I am guaranteed at least a dozen sales,' I joked. In hindsight, this was probably a mistake – and could well have explained why some of our group took a while to open up to me. Having crossed the world to test their cycling skills, see the scenery, sample the local delicacies and make new friends – the last thing they probably bargained for was to be cruelly caricatured by a gangly Pom.

Our hotel for the night, the Sant Bernat, lived up to its name by the presence of two resident Saint Bernard dogs who roamed the grounds like a couple of docile bears, their smell often preceding them. Confusingly, both near-identical dogs had the uncanny knack of never appearing in the same room together. The upshot of this was that every nook and cranny of the Sant Bernat was seemingly populated by one magically omnipresent Saint Bernard. Michaela's canine phobia, allied to the fact that there was a Spanish wedding party going on that night, meant we almost had enough material for an eighth *Beethoven* film (yes, there really are seven).

'If it rains on your wedding day it's supposed to be good luck,' Sharon said, as we all enjoyed our first of a catalogue of colossal dinners together. Served a medley of Catalan bruschetta with goat's cheese, followed by veal medallions and local custard tart, it was undeniably a case of quantity over quality – but there are times when that suits me just fine.

Later, as Terry and I lay in our beds and the wedding band played a cover of REM's 'Losing My Religion', my voluble room-mate, who had put away quite a few glasses of wine for someone who claimed not to be a big drinker, offered his own combined take on the marriage condition and inauspicious meteorological conditions: 'I always heard that if it rains on your wedding day then it actually *won't* last the year. The day I got married, it poured and poured. Yet, somehow, me and the wife are still together.'

I was just going to make some laboured analogy about this being our own wedding night, the forthcoming days our cycling honeymoon and how a divorce may be on the cards before we even reached Rome – but then I heard the first rumbles of Terry's quite broad snoring repertoire. Clearly, in the Reynolds household, earplugs have been the key to a long marriage.

Ever since Lance Armstrong and his US Postal cronies decided to move to Girona for off-season training, the place has been a cycling hotbed. With the French authorities starting to crack down on doping, the likes of Tyler Hamilton, George Hincapie, Frankie Andreu, Michael Barry and Tom Danielson all uprooted to the Catalan town in the late 1990s, and were joined by Armstrong when the American decided to leave his old stomping ground in Nice. This was a time when riders' fridges were most likely to contain foil-wrapped vials of performance-enhancing Erythropoietin (EPO or 'Edgar' after Edgar Allan Poe) alongside their cartons of milk, a time when syringes fitted snugly beside the knives and forks in the cutlery draw, when empty cans of Coke probably contained enough residual testosterone to power the entire Catalan porn industry, and when coat hangers enjoyed greater versatility.

I had heard good things about Girona, a town surrounded by hills as well as flat open plains, making it ideal for varied training rides. My friend Justin, who filmed Dave and me sitting in that electric car back in Castelldefels, had recently moved his family out from Canada to Girona to be closer to the pro riding scene he was reporting on. Dave was visiting to cover the Vuelta, and the pair had filmed some snippets of the old town – basking in sunshine – that made Girona look pretty special.

But for me Girona will always be remembered as a town of torrential rain, roadworks and red traffic lights. We passed through the cycling Mecca towards the end of our first full day in the saddle just when the heavens had decided to open. This was the kind of rain which, had it fallen in the UK, would have forced all the train networks to cancel their services, grounded flights at Heathrow and inundated the Somerset Levels. Large and strangely tepid drops fell like liquid javelins with such a speed and density that I had to pull to the side of the road and shelter in the doorway of what I soon discovered – much to my mirth – was Girona's main ONCE outlet.

ONCE is Spain's national lottery for blind people, which is quite ironic, because between 1989 and 2003, ONCE also sponsored one of Spain's leading cycling teams – seemingly taking a gamble by casting a blind eye to a raft of doping offences, many of which didn't come to light until ONCE had sensibly jumped ship. ONCE's star riders included

Frenchman Laurent Jalabert, the 1995 Vuelta winner who uncannily morphed from a sprinter into a climber later in his career, only to have his name published in a list of positive doping tests from the 1998 Tour in a report released days after Chris Froome's 2013 victory; Belgian Johan Bruyneel, the less-than-contrite mastermind behind Armstrong's seven Tour 'wins'; and Swiss maestro Alex Zülle, a bespectacled two-time Vuelta winner whose fighting-fire-with-fire response to riding in the same era as five-time-Tour-winning behemoth Miguel Indurain was, quite naturally, to take shedloads of EPO, which he claimed he did 'to satisfy his sponsors'.

Upon disbanding, Team ONCE revamped into the infamous Liberty Seguros and Würth outfits, themselves heavily implicated in the 2006 Operación Puerto blood-doping scandal. Things didn't fare much better when Astana took over the team licence: the Kazakh-based team were blocked from entering the 2008 Tour because of the antics of local favourites, blood brothers Alexandre Vinokourov and Andrey Kashechkin. This was a blow to defending champion Alberto Contador, who had only just joined the team following the disbanding of Armstrong's old Discovery Channel outfit. The Spaniard had already been given the 'ONCE-over' by authorities in the 2006 race when the Liberty Seguros team was kicked off the Tour – and would later miss the 2012 race following his much-publicized positive test for the powerful anabolic agent Clenbuterol. Poor Bertie, a career stalled by the unlikelihood of lightning striking the same place TWICE.

Having left behind the Girona headquarters of the visually impaired Spanish lotto, I caught up with fair-weather pedallers Richard and Suren, who were taking refuge in a sheltered petrol station forecourt. I had been last to leave our lunch stop at the rather grotty town of Anglès – aptly described by Dave as 'a bit of a shit hole' when I'd quizzed him about our route through Catalonia back in Castelldefels – and so had been playing catch-up on the long, flat slog into Girona as the storm clouds gathered. Richard and Suren, whose relative youth had got me excited one day earlier after my initial fears of being team leader to a group of fossilized domestiques old enough to have parented grizzled German veteran Jens Voigt, were, it turned out, not as accomplished on the bike as Suren's expensive kit suggested. In fact, Suren was about as handy as you'd expect from someone who had bought a snazzy hybrid worth two grand on the ride-to-work scheme before duly using said bike for one mere twenty-minute spin in the past year. While Richard was at least a battler who would dig deep on climbs not ideally suited to someone more at home performing Chunk's famous 'Truffle Shuffle' from *The Goonies*, Suren had the tenacity of a lame nag whose horseshoes had been nailed on backwards. In fact, had he been one of Hannibal's elephants then the Carthaginians would no doubt have had him put down.

Hampered by an increasingly gammy knee, I nevertheless dropped both Suren and Richard early on during the ascent of Els Angels in the Gavarres mountain range above Girona. The former would resort to his usual tactic of calling up the van for a lift (the same van whose passenger seat he had become well acquainted with during the course of that first day, particularly when rain fell or the gradient crept above 2 per cent) while the latter chugged along at a pace so slow that I even had the time to fix a rear-wheel puncture without assuming the role of *lanterne rouge*.

There's never a good time to pick up a flat, but halfway up the final climb of the day, when you're isolated and it's raining, and just moments after popping a blackcurrant energy gel, is right up there with the worst. The instant pick-me-up powers of the sickly-sweet goo were meant to propel me towards the summit, not aid my tyre de-rimming and right-arm pumping prowess. It was quite a miserable way to cap off what had fast become a rather dank and depressing afternoon.

Els Angels was one of Hincapie's favourite climbs and part of a circuit known as 'The Armstrong Loop' that takes in the peaks around Girona. Coupled with a hefty intake of blood-boosting narcotics, the two American riders would use the climb for short high intensity training during their preparations for the Tour. At the top there is a monastery, which looks out over a series of fog-clad forested hills, and a cafe serving the thickest and most chocolatey hot chocolate. With septuagenarian stalwart Bob already cruising down the descent towards our hotel, most of our group were enjoying a cup of this brown gold. Chilled and demoralized, I lingered briefly before pressing on to the finish as the clouds began to part.

The descent was pretty ropey, with tight bends and a wet road. To add to the trauma, the rainfall had provoked some kind of mass snail pilgrimage and hundreds of these slimy, tiny creatures were making their way across the road at the kind of pace you'd expect from a snail. It wasn't until I heard a couple of crunches that I clicked what was happening. Instantly, I felt pangs of guilt. After all, if you're a snail with a shell measuring less than one centimetre in diameter and you had managed to be in the right place at the right time to avoid the wide tyres of many a speeding car, then it has to be pretty rotten luck to have both your house and its contents splattered across the road by a bicycle wheel roughly two centimetres wide.

Can Bassa, the fourteenth-century farmhouse we were staying at for the night, was part of a cluster of honey-coloured stone buildings that made up the charming hamlet of Madremanya, perched on a small ridge amid the surrounding green hills. Peering out of a window with just a towel to cover his modesty, Bob, fresh out of the shower but clothes-less until the belated arrival of our support van (no doubt looking for Suren somewhere), greeted my arrival with a line I am sure he had been working on for quite some time.

'Did you see the old guy collecting animals for his ark?' he asked, while showing off impressive biceps for a man of seventy.

'You were collecting animals today?' I replied, provocatively.

'No, Noah!' said Bob, before my quip belatedly hit home and he shook a fist in mock castigation.

In his *History of Rome*, the ancient historian Livy wrote that Hannibal 'ate and drank not to flatter his appetites but only so much as would sustain his bodily strength'. Burning off anything up to five thousand calories a day, sustaining our bodily strength for us riders meant we pretty much had carte blanche to eat anything we fancied. Being a greedy bugger, this delighted me. Over the next few weeks as we passed from Spain, through southern France and into Italy, our evening meals became more and more decadent as we gorged on local delicacies with the kind of hunger that Hannibal so stoically resisted. If Hannibal got through the day on bread and water – the kind of 'paniagua' diet that has become the metaphorical cornerstone for clean riders in the professional peloton – then we were doped to the gills on all manner of buttery, creamy, saucy, high-protein and carbohydrate-heavy culinary classics.

Although their leader held back, the vast Carthaginian army certainly needed a good feed too. Their favourite dish is said to have been a piglet roasted with its stomach stuffed with sausages. Once ready, the hog would have its tummy slashed so that the chipolatas would spill like an enemy's intestines. The rest of the time, their chefs no doubt made veal roulades by initiating an elephant stampede over a pack of calves, or crucified chickens over a hot flame. By comparison, our culinary exploits were tame, but then again we weren't climbing mountain ranges with the risk of being greeted with a mace to the face on the other side.

That evening's dinner at Madremanya may have been deemed rather poncy by our Carthaginian cousins, but it certainly flattered the appetites that Hannibal so determinedly repressed. Local gazpacho-style soup, salmorejo, came alongside plates of courgette carpaccio with Parmesan shavings and a huge, fresh salad that – most unlike normal Spanish 'salads' – was not pebbledashed with sweetcorn nor drowning in tinned tuna. Our main was a Catalan take on surf and turf: a rustic meatball and calamari stew served in a pottery bowl with peas and rice, which really should have been eaten with our hands. A chocolate brownie with melon and mint rounded things off nicely. An ambrosial feed in a country that can have such a functional view of cooking was an unexpected treat. Only that morning, at our coffee stop in Viladrau, I had taken down a glazed custard-filled croissant with both its ends encased in milk chocolate – probably deemed one of your five-a-day in these parts – and had longed for the pâtisseries that loomed just over the border. Following it up with some rather disappointing sandwiches at lunch in Anglès had me thinking the gastronomic leg of this ride would only get going on the other side of the Pyrenees, but that meal at Can Bassa instantly put paid to this theory.

'I can't see how any meal or hotel can beat this place,' I told Terry later in our room as I prepared for that night's snore storm.

'You'll be surprised,' Terry replied while applying some prescription anti-grunt tape to prise open his nasal cavities (apparently his snoring has been a lifelong problem but is now 'on the mend'). 'I thought the same at this stage last year but I found the bar being raised constantly. Every place is so incomparable and they all stand out in their own way. Just you wait until you see the castles and monasteries on the horizon. It's not as if I came back for the cycling.'

Earlier that evening, while enjoying a drink overlooking a field of sad and wilted sunflowers, Sam had gone into archaeologist mode and explained how these very plains were no doubt the ones over which Hannibal marched with his army of 90,000 men, 12,000 cavalry and 37 elephants some 2,230-odd years ago.

'Thirty-seven elephants? I read that there were thirty-eight,' said Ted, Sam's former lecturer at university. Ted had the most enticingly refined Australian accent, so mellifluous on the ears each time he opened his mouth (a rarity for Australians).

'I'm pretty sure it's thirty-seven,' replied Sam, the pupil fervently standing his ground against his old master.

'Right,' said Ted.

'There's the Aussie education system for you. No wonder you're no longer any good at cricket if you can't even count,' taunted Suren (who by now had finished the stage after the van deposited him a few kilometres away from our destination so he could ride home like a conquering hero). If only he knew then what awaited the English cricket team at the hands of the Australians . . .

When Hannibal opted for the arduous land route to Italy – where potential pitfalls lurked at every step – it was chiefly because he did not have much choice, what with the Carthaginian navy – once the pride of the Mediterranean – reduced to a mere handful of seaworthy vessels following defeat in the First Punic War. While the once-prosperous city-state was a former mercantile juggernaut that evolved from a thriving Phoenician colony, Carthage and her fleet had deteriorated so much that when Hannibal's father, the venerable Hamilcar Barca, decided to take his illustrious Barcid clan to the Iberian peninsula in search of the natural resources needed to boost the Carthaginian coffers, he had to eschew naval transportation and instead march his army along the coast of present-day Morocco before crossing the Strait of Gibraltar in borrowed boats.

Hamilcar hated Rome with a fervent intensity that he passed on to his son, who is said to have sworn eternal enmity to Rome at the sprightly age of nine (when most other boys are going through their eternal-enmity-towards-girls phase). Not only had Rome stolen Sicily from Carthage, scuppered her fleet and enforced some serious reparations, the burgeoning Mediterranean power had also rather sneakily swiped Sardinia from under their rival's noses, before adding it retrospectively to the terms of the original treaty. To make a cycling analogy, this was the equivalent of a Tour commissaire rewarding the current yellow jersey with a massive time bonus three days after a stage victory, whereby kicking the faltering reigning champion in the gonads while he was down (not to mention stealing his lunch-filled musette).

With Hannibal and his two brothers – the 'Lion's brood' – by his side, Hamilcar's conquest of the Iberian peninsula was so successful that the war indemnity was quickly paid off and Carthage's grip in the Mediterranean was on the rise. Freud would have had a field day with Hannibal's fondness for elephants, for the young warrior watched as his father was drowned while riding into battle on the back of an elephant in 228 BC. With Hannibal still not old enough for a driver's licence (or 'pachyderm permit', perhaps), his brother-in-law Hasdrubal the Handsome took over from Hamilcar, quickly signing a treaty with Rome whereby Carthage would not expand north of the Ebro river provided Rome did not move south. Hasdrubal's reign was short-lived, however, and in 221 BC he was assassinated by one of his servants, presumably for some elephant-related felony.

Now 26, Hannibal vowed to continue his father's project by conquering the entire Iberian peninsula before taking the war with Rome to her own soil. While consolidating Carthage's influence south of the Ebro, Hannibal sent scouts ahead to the Gallic tribes that inhabited the Po valley to gauge whether or not they would entertain the idea of a Carthaginian uprising. Fearful of Hannibal's growing influence, the Romans themselves made an alliance with the Iberian city of Saguntum, making it a protectorate despite its clear location south of the Ebro.

Perceiving this as a violation of the treaty, Hannibal lay siege to the city, which fell after eight months.

Although Hannibal now had two hundred elephants at his disposal, their trumpeting trunks and flapping ears weren't much good in the face of the Saguntines' weapon of choice: a type of oversized javelin which was covered in a flammable liquid before being set ablaze and thrown down on the attackers. One such javelin pierced Hannibal in the thigh when he strayed too close to the city walls. Like Tour de France riders who crash at an ungodly speed, rip their body to shreds, then carry on, Hannibal did just that, though presumably with a bit of a limp. With Saguntum surrounded and resources dwindling, its inhabitants resorted to desperate measures. Having exhausted their supply of sausage-stuffed piglets (or whatever their own local delicacy was), they were forced to feast upon the bodies of their dead relatives. Once they had licked the last bones dry and Hannibal's army was battering down the gates, the locals built a huge fire in the main square, threw their wives and children into the blaze, then jumped in themselves. Those who were still alive when the Carthaginians arrived were either slaughtered or enslaved.

Soulless Saguntum now under his command, as well as a vast army and an area larger than 200,000 square kilometres (filled with natural resources and silver-bearing mines akin to free-flowing Las Vegas slot machines), Hannibal's influence was growing as quick as his thirst for blood and world domination. We're talking Lance Armstrong levels in the early noughties. Shrewdly, Hannibal sent all the spoils of war back to Carthage. So when Rome sent a delegation over the Mediterranean to demand justice, the Carthaginian government refused to repudiate Hannibal's actions – just as Armstrong's sponsors would initially stand by their man.

And so, in 218 BC, began what Livy described as 'the most memorable war in history'. It was time for Hannibal to pack his trunks and head over the mountains. Taking the overland route may have injected an invaluable element of surprise to proceedings, but it was a tactic fraught with risk. A bit like a cyclist supplementing an attack on the first climb of a mountain stage by doing it on a tricycle while dressed as a clown.

In Armstrong vernacular, what Hannibal was doing was clearly 'not normal'.

My right knee wasn't feeling particularly normal either. Incipient twinges had marred some of my long training rides but already, less than two full days into our journey, mild discomfort had graduated to considerable pain. Before setting off from Madremanya I made some alterations with the height and angle of my saddle, but that only appeared to make things worse. Rubbing salt into the wound, my Garmin GPS (on to which Sam had meticulously uploaded every day's route) had a bit of a meltdown early in the stage just after Dylan had dropped back to see to Suren, who was probably contemplating a return to his perch in the van, and I'd overtaken Michaela, who had stopped to push her bike across a busy intersection. Resorting to the trusty combination of road signs and common sense, I chased down a rider up ahead whom I wrongly believed to be in our group. (In my defence, the man was old and had grey hair, so the rules of logic had him down as one of our own.) There followed a 15-kilometre detour after I stubbornly refused to backtrack and find the right road.

Arriving at the seaside town of L'Escala considerably later than the others, the sight of Justin sipping coffee in a dayglo luminous yellow kit made me momentarily forget my throbbing knee. He and Dave had driven over from Girona to join us for an afternoon on the bike. Dave made up for his companion's atrocious dress sense by sporting one of the slick white jerseys with pink hems that Paul Smith had designed for the previous Giro d'Italia (the race Bradley Wiggins made a right meal of – primarily, it seemed, because of persistent rain and the organizers' audacity to follow climbs with downhills). I was somewhere in between my friends in the fashion stakes, having ditched my brown-and-lime monstrosity for my signature chic Cinzano kit. This was a seminal moment in our friendship for I had never seen either of them in Lycra before, an oddity given cycling was what brought us together in the first place.

We had all met for the first time in the flesh at the London Bike Show earlier in the year. Back then, Justin was 'Johnny Gunn' – one half of an online spoof cycling news programme with larger-than-life fellow Canadian Aaron, the self-styled 'Ripp Finklemann'. As my own *Blazin' Saddles* alter-ego, I contributed to their shows with regular Skype interviews which I'd conduct in various disguises to preserve my anonymity. Aaron himself was a man of many faces, having made ripples in the cycling community as the 'UCI Overlord', a parody Twitter persona that poked fun at Pat McQuaid, the then-president of the International Cycling Union, the sport's governing body best known by its French acronym. Soon, both Justin and Aaron were the driving forces behind the satirical cycling website *Cyclismas*. I was one of numerous guest columnists, while many pro riders and key figures – including Garmin-Sharp manager Jonathan Vaughters – got involved with articles and video interviews. Sponsors leapt on board; the money started rolling in. Dave entered the fray to manage marketing and quickly negotiated a deal with Trek and the charismatic cyclist Jens 'Shut up legs!' Voigt for a series of sketches, which Justin produced.

Keen to strike while the iron was hot, Aaron sold his cafe in Nova Scotia and Justin wound up his massage therapy business. They decided to move their families closer to the action – and they were en route to a new life in Girona when we all met in London at the bike show.

Just as *Cyclismas* was going stratospheric, it all sensationally fell apart. When Paul Kimmage, the former *Sunday Times* journalist, was sued for defamation by the UCI after Kimmage implied that McQuaid's predecessor, Hein Verbruggen, had helped cover up a positive drugs test returned by Lance Armstrong back in 1999, Cyclismas hosted an online defence-fund to help pay his legal bills. Almost $100,000 of donations arrived from around the world, a reported $60,000 of which apparently went missing. Fingers were pointed at Aaron. He always maintained his innocence, but at the same time seemed incapable of proving the exact whereabouts of the money. Eventually he claimed he needed to retain the funds because he was in a bitter legal dispute with the owners of *Cyclismas*. Concerns also surfaced about a potential tax liability due to an error in the way the fund had been set up. It became the biggest irony of ironies: the man who spent his every waking moment flagging up cycling's lack of transparency suddenly seemed about as opaque as Lance's urine.

Almost overnight, Aaron's empire shut down. UCI Overlord ceased to tweet. All contact between him and all his former colleagues and friends – including myself – simply ended. The last thing I heard from him was a very brief email in which he told me that everything was a 'big misunderstanding' that had resulted from 'poor communication'. He then promptly deleted me as a friend on Facebook and that was that. Justin and Dave had often come across him in Girona, where he had become persona non grata.

Despite having since set up a website promising to refund donors, Aaron is still embroiled in a complicated legal case with both Kimmage and the owners of *Cyclismas*, who did their best to rebuild their reputation and distance themselves from a man, rightly or wrongly, suspected of fraud.

As for Dave and Justin, their friendship grew during those testing times and they started creating topical and humorous video content for their own website, *Road Reel*. While any future collaborations with Aaron may be less likely than a steamy tryst between Lance and Betsy

Andreu, they still share their old friend's doggedly sceptical views on doping. And from our coffee catch-up at L'Escala and our recent Vuelta chin-wagging at Castelldefels, it became quickly apparent that both Justin and Dave were incredibly cynical about what was happening not so far away in the Vuelta.

Since Warren Barguil's stage win a few days ago, the race had entered the Pyrenees where we all expected leader Vincenzo Nibali to cement his hold on the red jersey. But the 28-year-old Italian – winner of the Giro d'Italia in the spring and Vuelta champion from 2011 – was having difficulty shrugging off 41-year-old Chris Horner. That a rider just one month younger than Armstrong, one of his previous team-mates, could be producing such exceptional staying power in the mountains was a bitter pill to swallow for many fans – especially seeing that Horner had never performed so well before in his career (his previous best finish in a Grand Tour was ninth in the 2009 Tour, aged 38). Seeing the utter dominance of a man old enough to father Barguil and several other riders in the Vuelta top ten was, like Hannibal's ambitious plans, difficult to fathom.

An old man performing in such bullish fashion was, however, a source of much joy and inspiration for Bob, the oldest veteran in our group. I had overheard Bob drooling over Horner and now, in the presence of Justin and Dave, I felt a little provocation was in order.

'Hey, Bob,' I said as he ambled over, 'we were just talking about your man Horner . . .'

'Incredible, huh? It's absolutely amazing what he's doing at his age,' beamed Bob, revealing what Terry (a retired dentist) described as his 'film star smile' (most people carry cash in their pockets; Bob effectively walked around with $20,000 stashed in his mouth).

'Truly unbelievable,' deadpanned Dave, forcing me to flash my own wonky, slightly beige, £100-a-year dental disaster.

'I don't get it. He's never been *that* good and yet here he is within striking distance of winning a Grand Tour,' I said, teeing things up.

'Well, he's always been a strong climber and this year he's fresh and lean,' Bob replied, oblivious to the cheeky insinuations. 'He didn't actually start competing properly until he moved over here when he was 30. He was riding in the US for small teams until then. The common perception is that he didn't want to dope and so stayed away from Europe.'

'Then changed his mind,' Dave said, with delicious ambiguity.

After coffee we went to the nearby ruins of Empúries, once the most important Greek colony on the Iberian peninsula. Hannibal led his vast army here on his way to crossing the Pyrenees, soon after allegedly founding the city of Barcelona (which takes its name from his Barcid clan). The locals of Emporion (as the bustling trade colony was then called, and from which derives the word 'emporium') were so afraid of Hannibal and his elephants that they let the Carthaginian warrior stay as a guest of honour and replenished his army's supplies. Being summer, there's no doubt that some soldiers would have taken a dip in the glistening waters of the Mediterranean and, seeing that this was our route's first and only encounter with the sea, there was no way I was going to let the opportunity of a swim on the Costa Brava pass me by. With Justin recording with his GoPro camera, I stripped off and treated the holiday-makers to the sight of a pasty Brit plunging into the sea in nothing but a pair of tight black underpants and a bulbous helmet (left on purely for comedic integrity).

A video of my striptease, swim, subsequent shower and stretching – all speeded up and played along to a jaunty Benny Hill-style jingle – soon found its way on to the introduction of Justin and Dave's next online show. My star must be on the rise, I thought, as I unleashed my rangy torso, curly chest carpet and nascent tan lines to the unsuspecting masses. 'Saddleblaze strips to reveal his helmet,' ran the obligatory header.

Livid with the idea of Hannibal's men displaying similar levels of holidaying horseplay on their shores, Rome finally declared war on Carthage and ordered an army of around 25,000 infantry and cavalry to cross the Mediterranean under the command of general Gnaeus Cornelius Scipio. This Scipio was brother of the consul Publius Cornelius Scipio, father of the great Scipio Africanus, who would later become Hannibal's longtime nemesis (the LeMond to Hannibal's Hinault, so to speak). It goes to show the contempt with which the Romans viewed the enemy: not only did they commit such a small force, they faffed around so much that when Scipio finally arrived at Empúries the Carthaginians were already long gone.

Led by Hannibal, his two brothers, Mago and Hasdrubal, and his nephew Hanno, the enemy was already heading over the mountains into modern-day France. Not all of the Carthaginian lieutenants were from the Barcid clan; the Roman historian Polybius also mentions Hannibal Monomachus and Mago the Samnite. Not much is known about the latter, but the former was a renowned advocate of inflicting total horror on the Romans, starting with a blanket sacrifice of all their children (had there been a Roman equivalent of *Chitty Chitty Bang Bang*, Monomachus would have been ideal for the role of the Child Catcher). The bloodthirsty warrior also felt that Hannibal should teach his army to eat human flesh so that they would become accustomed to the taste should such dining arrangements be necessary during the Alpine crossing.

To make matters even more confusing in the name stakes, one of the great Barcid opponents back in Carthage was a chap called Hanno – not to be confused with Hannibal's nephew Hanno, or a previous Hanno who was son of yet another Hannibal back during the First Punic War, or, for that matter, Hanno, the pet white elephant of Pope Leo X, which must have been the only constipated elephant in the expansive history of constipated elephants to die from the highly niche treatment of gold-enriched laxatives. Like their blue-blooded Scipio-centric Roman counterparts, you could say the Carthaginians had problems coming up with original names.

Unfortunately – or perhaps fortunately, given the outcome – there were no gold-enriched laxatives in our support van's medical kit. Being unable to shed some bib-short ballast was wreaking havoc on my mind. For the entire Spanish leg of our tour – the best part of three days in the saddle – I was about as bunged up as a former President of the UCI allegedly trying to brush an alleged Texan's alleged failed drugs test under the alleged carpet. Despite the lavish array of Catalan delicacies passing through my lips to fuel my forward momentum, nothing was balancing out the equation on the other side. Either my body had risen to the challenge and found some way of performing total gastric absorption, or my colon had pre-empted the French border and gone on wholesale strike, forcing me to sweat out clear liquid faeces.

This all reminded me of that time I found myself discussing bowel attacks in a hotel bar with Greg LeMond . . .

The rear end of the triple Tour winner was very much on my radar ahead of my debut sportive in the French Alps. I couldn't, after all, spend two hours in the company of cycling immortality without quizzing him about *that* notorious incident with Bernard Hinault.

Winning his first 'Grande Boucle' in 1986 was not all plain sailing for Greg. In his first years as a pro, LeMond made such leaps and bounds that rumours had actually surfaced about doctors having inserted a kangaroo muscle into his thigh. The American soon became the first rider in history to sign a million-dollar contract by joining French team La Vie Claire and agreeing to help rival Hinault to his fifth Tour scalp. Twelve months on, the man they called 'The Badger' seemed to confuse his previous promise of returning the favour with a policy of systematic attack. Not only was LeMond metaphorically shat on by his French team-mate, he also had to deal with a sudden bout of diarrhoea some 60 kilometres from the finish of stage 10 to Futuroscope.

'It was a bad peach,' Greg grinned as I listened and the photographer snapped away. 'My stomach started turning and then –' he paused to make an evocative gargling noise – 'there were a couple of rumbles. All of a sudden, I'm like, holy shit! I asked a team-mate for a hat to stuff down my shorts but it was too late. It just went *boom* like a shotgun blast.'

Any mere mortal equating an embarrassing back-door incident to a shotgun blast might be accused of over-egging the pudding – or, as the French so deliciously say, throwing a de-frocked granny into the nettles. But when it comes from the mouth of someone who, months after the sorry scene, was actually blasted by a shotgun to within seconds of his life – well, you have to give him some credence. Some thirty-five lead pellets still pepper LeMond's heart, liver and lungs. In my book that gives him licence to egg as many puddings and sting as many grannies as he likes.

'My Lycra shorts expanded about an inch or two,' he continued. 'Then it went straight down my legs.' Unfortunately for fans of a masochistic bent, this episode was not caught on the new Technicolor TV cameras – nor, alas, was the sequel when, moments after the stage finish, LeMond made a beeline for his team's motorhome in order to finish off what he had begun almost two long hours earlier. Here, in the surprise absence of a loo, he improvised by digging a hole in a box of Bernard Hinault promotional postcards before pulling the evacuation cord.

'His box just happened to be open and in the perfect position,' Greg gushed. 'I shat for about an hour and a half. It was so painful. I remember like it was yesterday.'

Funnily enough, in an otherwise sensational season for LeMond, there was a third (pronounced the Sean Kelly way) shitty occasion amid those sweet-smelling bouquets of flowers. One that involved an Alpine cow trough. But that's quite enough for now.

My own two brothers being absent on the approach to the Pyrenean foothills, I had to make do with a couple of surrogates in Justin and Dave. Leaving their car by the sea in L'Escala, they agreed to ride along for 50 kilometres until we hit the lunch stop in the sleepy hillside town of Darnius. Their presence did wonders for my morale, which was somewhat in limbo – the excitement of being on the open road somewhat tempered by fears that my knee injury could well put a cap on how long this adventure would last. Almost instantly after clocking my bike earlier on, Dave had shaken his head and made numerous tweaks – lowering the saddle, shifting it slightly forward and tilting the angle down so that it was flat (for some reason, I had the front pointing to the sky like a victorious Usain Bolt). Dave was convinced that these alterations would, in time, bring about total riding comfort. The problem was that the initial damage had already been done.

Although my right knee displayed no visible exterior wounds, the internal suppuration was putrid. Every downward pedal stroke produced a searing pain through my patella – making me crave long, gradual downhills. To compensate I used my left leg much more, in turn transferring some of the stinging to my left knee. Crocked in both joints, riding out of the saddle became nigh on impossible. Just as children learn not to put their hands into flames, I knew that dancing on the pedals would fire up a disco inferno. Adding insult to injury, this inability to ride out of the saddle meant zero respite for my persecuted perineum. Locked into the saddle, my undercarriage became as swollen and leathery as a dead cow's tongue stung by a bumblebee. No amount of nappy cream could affect the requisite emollience, and I felt as if I'd crossed a desert perched upon the coarse hump of a limping camel. The prospect of riding for the next three weeks with pain pretty much everywhere from the waist down was not exactly something I welcomed with open arms (which was just as well, seeing that riding without at least one hand firmly clenching the handlebars was at that point still beyond me). That my elderly riding companions were jollying along without any visible signs of hardship or displeasure was a cruel irony that caused me further embarrassment.

To throw yet another curveball into this equation of unyielding grimness there was the parallel concern – less pressing though notable nonetheless – of what to do with all the trapped wind that follows the lavish accumulation of picnics and roadside snacks. Farting, in my books, is not something that should be done with one's bottom firmly rooted to the saddle. Not only does the presence of a narrow and protruding object block the airways and provide scope for friction (whereby increasing the dual possibilities of blowback and backdraught), the uncouth aesthetic pleasure that one derives from letting rip while stretching the legs is something to be savoured, however lowbrow an activity.

So, yes, I was suffering across numerous planes. In my head, violins screeched an irksome cacophony. It was frustrating not being able to compete – or even keep up with – my friends as the road started to edge upwards. I was at the lowest ebb of the entire tour. I never expected to joust effortlessly with an uphill prodigy like Justin or a wily old-timer like Dave – but my total impotence as we hit the nursery slopes of the Pyrenees mirrored the travails that Hannibal himself faced while passing through the same region.

In the two months between seizing Saguntum and entering Gaul, Hannibal lost around 13,000 troops after facing numerous hostile tribes in Catalonia. The foothills proved particularly costly and Hannibal was forced to take some drastic measures. First, he decided to leave his brother Hasdrubal in command of 11,000 troops to deal with any lingering hostilities as well as to hold the mountain passes and protect his rearguard. This – as self-designated leader of our group – I echoed in bidding farewell to my kindred spirits Justin and Dave. A further mishap happened for Hannibal when 3,000 conscripts from a recently subdued tribe decided to scarper, forcing him to send home a further 7,000 men whose loyalty was questionable and who looked as if they would be more of a hindrance than a helpful addition to the cause. In this respect, you could say our own group followed Hannibal's lead a few days later in Carcassonne, where we put both Suren and Richard – two men whose dedication to our combined cause of reaching Rome by bike was undeniably dubious – on a plane back to Blighty.

Although achieved through clenched teeth and a gallimaufry of painkillers, riding with Justin and Dave had still been a real pleasure. Having yet to strike up a close rapport with anyone in our group, being able to goof around and chew the chorizo fat with two fellow bike enthusiasts reminded me of my winter training sessions with Ray in Gran Canaria.

After crossing the flat and fertile planes of the north-easterly tip of Catalonia, we had risen into the hills and an area of outstanding isolation and mystical beauty. The narrow road wound through the woodland of La Jonquera that was ravaged by wildfires fifteen months earlier. A cigarette butt tossed through a car window is thought to have been the cause of the fires, which claimed two lives and affected some 14,000 hectares of land. A corresponding blaze at nearby Portbou also took two lives when a father and daughter, cornered by the flames, jumped from cliffs into the sea in a tragic inversion of the scenes at Saguntum. While the black tree trunks with their wispy, charred branches were a stark reminder of what happened, green grass and bushes had grown back and juxtaposed quite splendidly against the bright blue sky and puffy white clouds. It was a reminder how something beautiful can come from moments of complete tragedy. It was also the first of many 'wow' moments that would define the next three weeks.

Justin, Dave and myself decided to take the slightly longer route to our lunch stop, enabling us to gaze out over the sparkling waters of the Boadella reservoir. It is no reflection on their company that my parting memory of my friends that day will be the foul stench of dog turd. But alas, while picnicking with the others in the town square of Darnius, both Dave and I trod in the offending muck and spent much of the break presuming the other person had experienced some kind of Greg LeMond moment. Before leaving, an avuncular Dave oiled my creaking chain (no euphemism here) and Justin gave me a bag of sweets (he lives next to Girona's Haribo headquarters) – parting gifts from a duo who played a huge role in the start of my first Grand Tour.

A solo mission to find some ice for my knees meant I was once again left to my own devices as I caterpillared in isolation up the stinging climb of La Vajol and out of Spain. At the summit the road disappeared as the border neared. With neither Spain nor France prepared to tarmac the pass – and no local mayor living in the vicinity – there was just a rugged dirt track linking the two countries. We had been warned by Dylan and Sam that a bit of walking would be necessary. Typically, I misread the GPS and got lost. After what seemed like an eternity pushing my bike along increasingly unwelcoming terrain and uttering all manner of Wiggins-endorsed profanities, I joined a tarmacked road and heard the beep of my route being reconfigured. It was *avec plaisir* that I freewheeled down a breathtaking gorge and sped into France.

# CÉRET TO AVIGNON

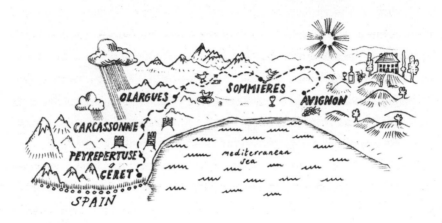

THERE'S NOTHING LIKE A FERAL DOG with a willy like a skinned salami to create a scene. The mangy black mongrel was loitering around the car park of Céret and edging closer to a white fluffy creature which had brought her master out for an afternoon stroll under the tall plane trees of the sleepy town. While the mutt had yet to open his picnic hamper, so to speak, the man was clearly agitated by the lingering presence of the stalking canine deviant. On numerous occasions he interrupted his conversation with an old lady to shoo away the stray, sometimes swinging a leg as tempers began to fray.

Then came the lunge – which wouldn't have looked too out of place on a dance floor in Newcastle. The two dogs locked together amid yelps (from the bitch) and howls (from the beast). The attacker latched his hindquarters around the poor white terrier while the owner kicked out and shouted a stream of obscenities ('*Putain! Merde! Arrête!*

*C'est dégueulasse!!'*). A jet of spray was launched into the air as the two animals were forcibly separated, the offender bent double as if his pelvis were dislocated.

With the irate owner running after his fleeing pet, the black dog lingered, hobbling around in circles in a cowering wreck as if in a trance. Then something I wish I could erase from my memory bank. Passing by I noticed the quivering dog's inflamed member: alas, uncannily reminiscent of the merguez sausages we scoffed back over the Spanish border, in a place where dogs were still man's best friend.

Trust the French to put on a good welcome. And that wasn't all. Within seconds of joining the busy main road at the bottom of the winding descent from Spain, I had been forced on to the verge by a driver probably blinded by the lime fluorescence of my gyrating glutes. Clipping the ledge of the hard shoulder with my tyre, I lost balance and was sent sprawling on to my side. Luckily no vehicle was trailing – otherwise I'd have added to the trip's fine array of unexpected roadkill (crackling caterpillars had joined crushed snails since entering France). It was hardly a Hoogerland – but enough to shake me up.

With a small graze on my leg the only perceptible injury, I went on my way, cursing the ineptitude of Gallic driving. Reaching round the back of my Cinzano jersey to rub my flank, my fingers touched something sticky, sweet and red. Thankfully, not blood, nor excess vermouth from my unofficial sponsor, but, rather, the contents of an energy gel that had exploded in my pocket on impact. I pulled into the side of the road to clean myself up and straighten my wonky handlebars, before riding on to the dog denouement.

As far as crashes go, this was pretty tame – right up there with my uphill tumble in the Megève sportive where, unable to unclip in time, I rolled on to my side to avoid a collision with a strong-smelling Teuton of some rotundity who had slowed considerably after a sudden gearing issue. Fortunately, though, nothing in my amateur cycling career had yet come close to the horrific moment when, aged 15 and in a post-GCSE cider-fuelled stupor, I rode into a Cornish pothole at top speed, was thrown over the handlebars before landing heavily in a heap, my left hip bone tearing through its surrounding flesh to create a grit-filled gash so wide it could not be stitched. (For years I told my friends the scar was the result of a shark-related incident.)

Despite the shoddy welcome, Céret proved a delight. Wandering its narrow streets and taking in the colourfully painted rickety buildings, I could easily see why Picasso, Braque and most of the Cubist gang decided to follow Catalan sculptor Manolo and call the place home. That's not to say the locals had wonky faces, square breasts and noses where their eyes should have been (come on, we weren't in Tasmania). Just, simply, that it was a very pleasant place which had such a hold on me that I questioned my sanity choosing to live in a city as hectic, noisy and cycling-unfriendly as London. But then I remembered the salami dog cock and thought W9 wasn't so bad after all.

The first French phase of our tour would take us over the Pyrenean foothills, through the interior of the unspoilt Languedoc-Roussillon region and into Provence, where the opening leg of the ride concluded at the Papal city of Avignon. Rugged and beautiful, the backwaters of the Languedoc are a cyclist's paradise thanks to quiet, rolling roads, stunning scenery and challenging climbs – not to forget some serious gastronomy. With focus usually falling on the Alps and the Pyrenees – rather than what lies in between – the Tour de France seldom puts in a decent shift in these parts, and when it does pass by, the route usually hugs the Mediterranean coast or blows on the big towns that we were trying to avoid.

For Hannibal, too, the march from the Pyrenees to the Rhône was fairly transitional: many of the Gallic tribes he encountered had heard neither of Rome nor Carthage, and were very much in awe of the sheer size of the marching army – which now stood at around 50,000 soldiers and 9,000 cavalry (not to mention those immense grey behemoths with trumpeting arms in place of noses). By showering with gifts a conglomeration of tribes that had gathered near present-day Perpignan, Hannibal was able to pass by largely unmolested – but hardly unnoticed. Supposing his soldiers marched three abreast, the Carthaginian train would have stretched out for some 40 kilometres. It would have taken an estimated four hours for each individual to cover the daily average of 15 kilometres, meaning that when the pace-setters arrived at the stage finish at 11 a.m. only a third of the army had left the previous night's camp, the stragglers not even setting off before 3 p.m.

And yet Hannibal still managed to shield his progress from the Romans and their scouts. For the invading army to go about a mass march across unknown territory with all the inconspicuousness of a rider ghosting into the top ten of the Tour without ever appearing on the front of the peloton was testament to Hannibal's powers as a commander. Like us, he shied away from the coast to ensure that the enemy were in the dark as to his whereabouts. The tactic worked, with the lackadaisical Roman army under the two Scipio brothers procrastinating in northern Italy so much that they had only just set sail towards Spain.

Free from opposition (with the exception of the odd disgruntled driver), we too were able to build up a bit of momentum. Having been on the road for a few days, certain group dynamics began to emerge. Bob and Bernadette, tenacious old-timers both happier on the bike than off it, would usually gun ahead at the first possible chance, eager to test out their legs and set a tempo that Ted and Camilla would easily follow were it not for a multitude of pâtisserie pit stops. In Bob, Bernadette found the perfect partner – someone competitive enough to ride clear but gallant enough to act as a wind shield when called upon. Ted – the closest thing our group had to a friendly bear on wheels – lacked the speed and natural talent of Camilla, but he was powerful on the flats and the two combined in the best tradition of chalk and cheese: one as a windbreak in the valleys, the other as a metronome in the mountains.

Sharon, bless her soul, fell into her riding partnership with Terry in the same way that someone might find themselves shoehorned into an arranged marriage. That's not to say that they didn't grow to love and respect each other over the course of the ride – just that Sharon didn't seem to have much choice in the matter. She accepted the way things were with the stoicism of someone who had read the small print and realized that, well, perhaps this was exactly what she signed up for. In an alternative universe, Sharon might just as well have joined forces with Michaela: they were, after all, both Australian, roughly the same age and worked in the health sector. But in the event of any alliance, Sharon would have found herself twiddling her thumbs for long stretches – not to mention subject to frequent attacks by dogs and bees. Instead, she sought out a father figure in Terry who, in turn, relished being mothered. After all, Terry often seemed to be a little boy trapped in an old man's body. 'Oh, Sharon, you are good to me,' he would say. 'But I know you love it too.'

On the rare occasion that they rode apart, you got the impression that they were still joined by an invisible cord. Sharon certainly wore the trousers in their relationship, and she was often reminding Terry who was boss. This allowed Terry to continue his default position of ever-suffering husband at the beck and call of his indomitable trouser-wearing five-foot wife and her reputed (and no doubt heavily exaggerated) reign of tyranny. Displaying the kind of pain-numbing sensibilities better suited to an anaesthetist than a radiographer, Sharon had a knack of being able to tune out and ignore Terry's grumbling as she nursed him up hills and through rolling valleys. They were an unlikely partnership but one of the journey's most enduring duos.

Next up in the natural order of the road was Richard, who may or may not have been riding with Suren depending on whether Suren was in malingering mode (which was quite often) or showing some bite (which was not). Unlike Suren, Richard had actually done some preparation for the ride, buying himself a road bike and even booking some surreptitious sessions with a personal trainer. It certainly showed. While his friend often jumped in the van citing 'an old football injury', not once did Richard, after his wet opening day capitulation, throw in the towel – even after a heavy fall that followed his, quite inexplicably and with illusions of grossly misplaced grandeur, letting go of the handlebars for the first time in his life while trying to remove his rain jacket at top speed.

'It looks easy when they do it on TV,' he muttered from the warm tarmac, clearly having underestimated the coordination required to pull off such a manoeuvre.

Keeping up the rear with a smile – and every day wearing matching club kits – were steady-Eddies John and Kay. Although the weakest of us full-Hannibal conscripts, the Wollongong wonders kept willingly spinning away in their own world. They loved cycling and were enthralled by the scenery, often stopping to take photos. John, who I clocked early on as a dead ringer for legendary Welsh crooner Tom Jones (no one else agreed), had a tendency to wear his reflective rain jacket come rain or shine. A day didn't pass when the red light atop his helmet was not flashing away, giving the impression that he was some kind of sloth-like machine, like a persistent Duracell Bunny stuck in slow motion.

So where did I fall in the road hierarchy? To be honest, nowhere. Being the youngest and in possession of a pair of metre-long legs that worked on the pedals like pneumatic pistons powering a high-spec Wankel engine, it was of no huge surprise that I was stronger than a group of riders whose average age was a quarter of a century my dearer. Even with my stained-glass knees (nice and smooth to look at but immeasurably fragile), I often found myself effortlessly riding clear of my companions. I was forced into an early rethink of tactics, targets and alliances. Firstly, I vouched to clock up more than 100 kilometres every day, which often meant zipping off on impromptu detours to make up the numbers. I also got into the habit of starting from the back of the field, which, by picking off my 'rivals' one by one (or two by two, as was so often the case), is precisely how I clocked the group dynamic so well.

Bob, on the other hand, probably rode the entire Hannibal without sharing more than a few pedal strokes with the majority of his co-riders. He perhaps had no idea that Tom Jones had a flashing helmet, that Terry had a propensity to veer into the middle of the road, or that Sharon had an admirably languid pedalling action. And he may not have noticed the uncanny similarity between Bernadette's riding style and that of his hero Chris Horner, another ageing American performing concurrent miracles on a bike. One thing he certainly did understand, though, were the motivations behind his own tendency to stop and remove an item of clothing as soon as he started to struggle on a climb when in the presence of a rider creeping up in his wake; a ruse that fooled no one.

If Sam and Dylan had devised routes of geographical beauty and historical splendour, it's not to say they couldn't be supplemented by regular detours. A mere hunch that something of interest lurked around a corner was usually enough for me to defy the despotic beeping of the GPS and venture off-piste. Hills were there to be climbed, towns to be seen, views to be savoured and rivers to be crossed. Above all, the bike was there to be ridden.

In some instances, my innate curiosity didn't even require cycling that extra mile. On stage five to Carcassonne, as we passed through the tiny village of Missègre, I would spot an enormous bust of a bull staring out on to the main street – one that far outdid in enormity all previous bull bust sightings I have accumulated in my life. Standing 1.5 metres tall and weighing 2.5 tons, the horned sculpture marked the twentieth edition of the Missègre fair in 2003 and was donated to the town by a local sculptor who spent 200 hours forging the bovine icon from local crimson Languedoc marble. This quizzical taurus head was really rather splendid – certainly worth the photo I took of it seemingly dwarfing a green tractor in the background.

Oddly enough, no one else, despite my encouragement, stopped. Perhaps they weren't as easily awed as I by animal carvings – for no one had shown much interest in the crazed wild boar hacked from a tree trunk back over the border in Spain. Nor would they stop for the series of sculpted creatures – from bears to owls – that we passed one day in the Alps, nor even for the giant bronze elephant effigy in northern Italy. It became quickly apparent that my other riding companions did not like to stray too far from the beaten track. Either that, or the problem was me.

The day after my cow encounter, we stopped for coffee at the small town of Caunes-Minervois – located at the foot of the rugged hills where the bust's marble was quarried. A farmers' market was taking place just around the corner but no one dared join me for a quick gander (given this was a French market, ganders would be very much on display – most notably in liver form). When I came back laden with spiced bread stuffed with dried fruit – which I duly doled out, like Hannibal diplomatically bidding to appease the hostile tribes – the gesture was met with less enthusiasm than had I proffered slices of Céretan salami.

Often, Terry wouldn't recall half of the things I had seen during the day. Sometimes it even felt as if we had covered an entirely different route. 'I just look down at the tarmac,' he said once, before qualifying the bleak statement: 'If I started looking around then there's no way I'd get to our destination every day.'

These words put the whole tour into perspective. While I was in search of every possible stimulus on two wheels, for Terry every day was a constant battle just to keep going. His priorities were at the other end of the spectrum to mine. We all had our own personal quests and motivations, not to mention ups and downs. My mistake was that I, perhaps churlishly, took other people's desire to concentrate on the principal task in hand – riding from A to B – as indifference to our surroundings.

These chance encounters of mine were not restricted to bestial busts that could not talk back. Nor was it merely stray dogs who had a habit of exhibiting themselves in public in my presence. For it was while riding a solo mission that I encountered the self-styled 'Baron de Synclair' relieving himself, admittedly in true doggy fashion, against the back wheel of his car.

Our first full day in France had seen us canter through the vineyards north of Céret before climbing up into the hills of the Fenouillèdes. A bright start had quickly given way to persistent rain. Grappling with rain jackets, we passed some intriguing sandy rock formations known as the Orgues, which would have looked like a selection of crumbling chimneys and organ pipes designed by Gaudí had they not been shrouded in dank greyness.

Once past the tiny village of Trévillach we joined an even smaller, single-track road that took us over the summit of a testing climb. Through the rain you could just make out a lake in the valley below, which was where our lunch stop overlooking the Roman aqueduct at Ansignan was located. Having distanced the others, I careered downhill until I saw a sign for the aqueduct. It looked worth a pop so I duly defied the orders of my Garmin. At the end of a heavily potholed track I came to a makeshift car park in a clearing. It contained one car, beside which a balding man with spectacles was taking a leak.

Not wishing to intrude upon his moment (after all, there is an unwritten rule among TV cameramen to avoid filming cyclists answering a call of nature), I averted my gaze, whipped out my map and contemplated the aqueduct. I saw that our lunch spot was in fact on the other side of the valley, beyond the town of Ansignan and on a layby beside the road overlooking the fine structure. A door slammed and an engine started. The man was heading for the exit when he stopped and wound down his window.

'*Bonjour*,' he said. 'Could I help you? You are perhaps lost?'

'Don't worry, I'm fine. Just on a bike ride and thought I'd take a look at the aqueduct,' I replied.

'Sorry, you caught me in an embarrassing moment. I was just taking a leak.'

'Oh, really. I had no idea.'

'I assure you, I didn't come here especially to have a pee,' he assured me. 'I am a local amateur historian and this aqueduct fascinates me. Fascinates me.'

'It is rather magnificent,' I admitted, before adding once again (for this seemed his way of speaking), 'magnificent.'

'Perhaps you'd like to hear some of my theories,' he said in a forthright manner that suggested I had very little choice in the matter, before promptly turning off the ignition. Beads of sweat – or perhaps rain? – trickled down his pink forehead and gathered in the bushy eyebrows above his beady eyes.

'Let me introduce myself. I am the Baron de Synclair. Now let me ask you a question. What is the most famous picture in the world? In the whole world.'

I hesitated for a while. 'The . . . *Mona Lisa*?'

His smile clearly indicated that I had answered correctly. 'And what is located behind the left shoulder of *La Joconde*?'

'Erm, I'm not sure. A river?'

'Close. An aqueduct,' he said with pride, while leaning out of the window of his car. 'To be more precise: this aqueduct.'

He proceeded to explain just why the aqueduct in Da Vinci's masterpiece was not – per the traditional view – that of Val di Chiana near Arezzo, but instead the aqueduct of Ansignan. His explanations seemed to involve a series of riddles, anagrams and numerical sequences. At one point he was even talking about the thirteen moon cycles in a year representing the number of small arches of the aqueduct. He prattled on for so long I was worried that he may need to get out for another pee. If so, I'd probably join him.

'If you arrange the letters that make up "Mona Lisa" in a different order you get *mois à l'an* – months in the year – and I am convinced Da Vinci meant that as a sign.'

'You're certainly a man after Dan Brown's heart,' I said, finally getting in a word edgewise.

'I'm worse than Dan Brown,' he cackled. 'I'm a total crackpot! A crackpot!'

This clearly being the case, I decided it was time to take my leave. Besides, I was feeling rather peckish and the others would be wondering where I had got to.

'Look, I won't keep you any longer,' he said, perhaps sensing my unease. 'But you must go on my website.' He handed me a business card. 'Your French is very good for a German. What is your name and what do you do?'

'I'm actually English. But thanks. I'm a writer of sorts. My name is Felix. And you are, Monsieur . . . ?'

'Just call me the Baron. I'm sorry, your accent sounded Germanic. Perhaps it's because you are so tall and have a bike. Lots of Germans come here to cycle. It's great you are a journalist. These issues need to be written about. But don't steal any of my ideas. I have enough to make Dan Brown tremble. Tremble, I say. You know, I have done some writing for the local paper before—'

But thankfully the arrival of Camilla and Ted, who had also ventured off-piste, saved me from hearing about the delights of the *Ansignan Gazette*.

With Dave and Justin now sharing their Haribos elsewhere on the other side of the Pyrenees, the closest I got to replicating that camaraderie (besides my bonding with the Baron) was with Dylan and Sam. Taking alternating days behind the wheel and on the bike, our virtuoso tour guides got their fair share of Lycra action and were always up for a bit of saddle sparring. The obvious problem was that they often had to hold back a little and check on the back markers. But every now and then circumstance allowed them to blow off some steam and give me a run for my money.

This was the case following our picnic lunch in Ansignan when Sam and I pulled clear of the others on the small climb to Saint-Arnac. It was our first proper chance to bond since Barcelona and the setting was suitably glorious: after an open plateau we found ourselves on a ridge overlooking the valley with Château de Quéribus looming in the distance beyond the red-roofed, vine-ringed village of Maury. Spectacularly perched upon a sheer cliff – like a thimble balancing precariously on a thumb – Quéribus is one of the Five Sons of Carcassonne, a group of castles in Languedoc strategically placed to defend the old French border against the Spanish (the border was moved back beyond Céret in 1659). These castles are often given the modifier Cathar because they acted as places of refuge for the Cathar resistance against the Catholic Church in the thirteenth century. Quéribus was the last stronghold before the remaining survivors fled in 1255, and it wasn't hard to see why.

'Blimey,' I said. 'We're heading up that way?'

'And some. Me and you are going to the base of the castle.'

Above Maury the rising road was visible, cutting across the side of an opposing ridge from right to left, before doubling back on itself and soaring upwards across the side of the rock face towards the castle. With an unforgiving headwind, the first segment of this 6 kilometre slog was fairly brutal, with our immense effort in no way proportional to the paltry progress we made. But following the tight hairpin, the same gale that had been blowing us back became a merciful tailwind. Propelled to the top, we then had a choice: take the 2-kilometre slip road up to the castle, or carry on towards the next valley and the stage finish. Sam kept to his word and led me on to the extra climb, which snaked upwards to top out at an almost comedic 22 per cent. He exploded first, those hefty thighs of his no match for my long, lithe pistons. Having dosed up on post-prandial painkillers, my knees were merely simmering away in pain. This was welcome progress from the stabbing sensations of those opening days in Spain. Not only could I muster up a few out-of-the-saddle bursts, I even managed to slalom to the top with a morale-boosting extra gear in reserve.

A group of French tourists applauded my arrival, and that of Sam a minute later. While two garrulous men admired my bike, Sam zipped back to meet the others as they reached the intersection (no one else, bar Camilla, was crazy enough to attempt the climb). The castle itself was only accessible by a ten-minute walk up a winding path cut out in the stone, dashing any hopes I had of taking in the view back towards the storm clouds that had hampered our progress earlier in the day.

Perhaps the next castle, at Peyrepertuse, would be more friendly to a cleat-wearing cyclist?

Our hotel was in the village of Duilhac, at the foot of the seemingly unassailable spine of rock on which the castle rises in gravity-flouting majesty, surrounded by sheer drops of hundreds of metres. Quite how anyone managed to build such a structure – especially over a thousand years ago – is anyone's guess. A single road zigzags its way up to the castle entrance. While not as consistently steep as the knock-out ascent to Quéribus, it's almost three times as long. The climb was an optional extra – and not even Sam was up for recording a Cathar double. Having been overtaken by the rest of the field while at Quéribus, I expected everyone to be well on their way to turning on the hotel showers by the time I reached the foot of the ascent.

If I could pick one person from our group whom I would not have expected to see spinning a low gear up the extra climb, it would have been John. Primarily because, at 68 years old and owner of a generously barrelled chest, he was not only the second oldest but also perhaps the least ideally suited to uphill riding. The late afternoon sun was beginning to peer through the parting clouds as I drew level and said hello, making a jaunty comment about our current plight. There was no reply – and not for the first time since we embarked on this four-week odyssey. I initially put it down to tiredness or perhaps even dislike towards me, the whippersnapper journo, but later that night I would notice for the first time the hearing aid in John's left ear. He had simply not heard me. Worse, perhaps he thought that *I* hadn't acknowledged *him*.

On I ploughed as the afternoon sun became hotter and the sky clearer. When stopping for a photo of a sweeping hairpin I noticed, in the distance, John pushing his bike up the hill. He never actually made it to the top – probably because he belatedly realized that there was no hotel awaiting him at the summit, just the awe-inspiring ruins of an ancient castle, for he was there entirely by mistake. He had been dropped by Kay, his riding partner, on the initial climb, and then taken a wrong turn when entering Duilhac. Not hearing the warning beeps from his Garmin, he pressed on in the belief that the arduous ascent was taking him towards a hot bath and cold beer. A querying text message from Kay – presently enjoying both beer and bath – made him realize the error of his ways.

Oblivious of this mishap, I continued the challenge. A couple of ladies running down the hill offered encouragement, saying the top was nearby. They lied. There were still a number of tight bends as the gradient ramped up further. But the reward made it all worthwhile: a sense of achievement enhanced by breathtaking views back across a rolling green valley now entirely basking in sunshine. Peaks and jagged ridges made for numerous horizons, the rooftops of Duilhac could be seen at the foot of the mountain, while Quéribus gracefully soared in the distance as a reminder of the earlier triumph. It's hard not to laugh out loud in such a situation. It was one of innumerable episodes over the entire course of our journey where gargantuan effort was rewarded with a set of geographic and meteorological fortuities that felt as if they had been delivered down from above as a giant pat on the back.

Like Quéribus, the actual castle at Peyrepertuse is reached by quite a dicey path and the girl on the ticket desk discouraged me from attempting it in cleats. I was not so gutted because I had recollections of coming here years ago on a family holiday, so I coasted down to Duilhac, stopping to take the odd snap as proof of my Cathar conquest. Down at the bottom, the first of two shuttle runs up to the castle was just leaving the hotel. So it all worked out well: I could enjoy a celebratory beer then head up in the second van. In the commotion, I forgot to switch off my Strava – the GPS programme cyclists run through their smartphones which both maps and times their rides – and proceeded to break all the existing records on that final bus-assisted climb to the top, leading to a raft of congratulations from some Strava followers for my end-of-the-day king of the mountains award. It would be months before someone flagged this up as counterfeit, but I enjoyed the glory while it lasted.

We gathered at the lookout of the highest tower and shared a glass of wine as the sun set over the largest and most impressive of the Five Sons of Carcassonne. Just two of our number were absent: Bob, who had scaled the castle the year before (and no doubt needed to carry out a quick autologous blood transfusion in his hotel room to beef up his shopworn figure ahead of the exacting days ahead) and Michaela, who didn't have a head for heights and so kept to the lower keep (where no doubt a hornets' nest was primed for disruption).

Once we had ridden through the pastoral perfection of the valley north of Peyrepertuse (where sheep dogs worked the French way and led their shaggy counterparts – as opposed to chasing them, *à l'anglaise*), our ride to Carcassonne the next day took us through the hippy-friendly town of Rennes-les-Bains (where a mobile butcher, Chez Seb, arrived as we were drinking coffee – much to Bob's annoyance – amid jolly musical jingles to sell sausages and steaks with all the fanfare of a sea-side ice-cream van), alongside the boxy castle of Arques (outside of which Richard bit the tarmac after his rain jacket calamity) and past the watching eyes of that bull bust at Missègre.

We were rewarded with a long, gradual and fast downhill run after our chilly picnic lunch, which we ate taking refuge in a grand stone garage in the centre of rustic Villardebelle, just as the most beautiful female farmhand in France came to fill up the water tanks on the back of her 4x4 (the precision with which she reversed said vehicle and avoided myriad bikes and bodies was perhaps as commendable as her flawless complexion. If only there was a Chanel-sponsored reality TV programme for the farming sector, she'd be a star in no time).

Bolstered by this rare sight of human bucolic beauty, I bounded clear of the others and ploughed on through what looked like a regional hunt. One bearded man in camouflage gear loitering on the side of the road resembled a bored jihadist more than anything else. Meanwhile, old men with their rifles resting on the ground sat on various stools dotted around the woods looking like landlocked fishermen waiting for a catch. Give me foxes and hounds any day – this hunt was even more half-arsed than France's attempts to win its own national bike race over the past two decades.

Beyond lay Carcassonne, which is essentially a Disney-style medieval theme park filled with a lot of Germans, Chinese and Russians, surrounded by a traffic system as bike-friendly as your average cycle path in central London. Nevertheless, we all arrived in one piece before cracking open some celebratory beers in the garden of our hotel just outside the turreted fortress walls of the old Cité. It was both Richard and Suren's last evening on the tour, while we were welcoming a new arrival, Eleri, the president of Ted and Camilla's cycling club back in Sydney. Eleri had come straight from the week-long Haute Route event in the Pyrenees and so had a fair few climbing kilometres in her legs. She was to prove a great foil over the next four days.

For their boozy farewell dinner, I was sat at Richard and Suren's end of the table with Dylan. The trio described by Ted as 'The Inbetweeners on Wheels' were in fine fettle, with Suren eager to ramp up what he had considered to be a rather tame leg of his international stag do.

'I was assured by my former friend Dylan that there would be lots of stops, lots of opportunities to use the van and lots of opportunities to re-enact the famous British pub crawl,' he said with exaggerated pompousness while stirring his piping-hot onion soup, which brimmed with Gruyère and croutons. 'It's all turned out to be lies.'

'How so?' retorted Richard. 'You've had ample opportunity to use the van. In fact, I'd say I've ridden four hundred kilometres to your one hundred and sixty.'

'That is an outrageous slur,' replied Suren with faux concern. 'You are unfairly portraying me as a slob. It's just an old football injury that I'm starting to feel.'

'That is a load of bollocks,' Richard taunted. 'You've never played football in your life – certainly not enough to pick up an injury that will stop you cycling.'

'The real reason why you've struggled so much,' said Dylan, entering the fray, 'is that you did no training. You bought a bike over a year ago and still haven't used it. You've spent most of the time sleeping in the van.'

'I'd love to see your phone records from the tour,' Richard chipped in, 'because every five minutes you're calling Dylan or Sam for assistance.'

'But I envisioned a pub crawl on a bike with a bit of fitness thrown in!' Suren protested.

While this debate went on I tucked into my slab of foie gras with toast and salad, before polishing off the remnants of Suren's discarded onion soup, cheesier than an eighties ballad. My main course was the kind of hearty cassoulet (white beans, two confit duck legs and a coarse sausage) that would later wreak havoc with both the aromatic and atmospheric conditions of mine and Terry's room. Unaware of the impending doom, Terry was in his element. Having positioned himself strategically close to the red wine, he regaled the table (much to Dylan's chagrin) with the story of how he ended up in a police station after getting lost during last year's stage to Carcassonne.

'I was going uphill and clearly the wrong way so I turned round and rode to the local police station. I soon felt like I was in a porno. The policewoman absolutely blew my mind. She was heavily made up, had lovely curves, a tiny belt and, of course, a truncheon. She had the whole lot. It was wonderful,' Terry beamed with intemperate abandon.

'How long did you have an erection for?' asked Suren, instantly lowering the tone, if that was possible.

'I haven't had one of them for thirty years,' said Terry with a hint of regret.

'Too much information, Dad!' Dylan cringed.

'She was very helpful and I didn't want to leave,' continued Terry. 'She could have kept me there for ever, locked me away and indulged herself. Instead she went into the back room and sorted all my problems out. One year on, I still dream of that policewoman . . .'

One year on, it wasn't Terry getting lost but the ever-suffering Michaela. It was stage six, the longest so far, and spirits were as high as the sun in the bright blue sky. Since our departure from Barcelona the weather had been pretty variable, with sunny patches punctuated with heavy showers and some decidedly chilly segments that were – to coin a phrase from Bob – 'colder than a well-digger's butt'. Leg and arm warmers and rain jackets were very much the norm – except for hardman Ted, who didn't approve of such extravagances. The temperature could have been in single digits with a biting, bone-chilling wind and a steady icy drizzle – and Ted would be there, unflinching, in nothing but his shorts and jersey.

'I've lost one arm warmer and so don't see the point in using the other,' he told me when I raised the point of his superhuman tolerance to the cold. 'Leg warmers I just don't subscribe to because if ever they slip down it looks like you're wearing some kind of pervy French maid's outfit,' he reasoned.

We started the day on the Voie Verte – a grit-covered cycle path built on a disused railway track that ran alongside the Orb river and through the Espinouse mountains. Gently easing us into action, it was far more appealing than the busy main road; in short, ideal cycling terrain for Michaela, who perplexingly chose to start the day in the van. Perhaps she was privy to the pitfalls present in the form of wooden barriers crossing the path at every road intersection. The experienced Eleri, of all people, must have been daydreaming as she almost rode head first into one of these obstacles, only just applying the brakes to avoid a nasty collision. In fact, given the chaos of the subsequent busy roads around the grotfest that was Bédarieux (where a clueless girl in the local bakery served us something quite vile masquerading as coffee), it was a wise choice of Michaela's to wait until we joined a narrow, quiet slip road that rose into the hills at the 30-kilometre mark.

It was a glorious climb through fields of horses and thriving woodland. Halfway up, the road forked, which is where we guessed it must have happened. Turning right, I rode with Eleri and Camilla towards the summit, where Sam and the van were waiting with water and bananas. Bob and Bernadette, wisely eschewing the morning's 'coffee' stop, were somewhere out ahead, riding over a rusty brown volcanic plateau towards the sparkling Lac du Salagou, where late-season tourists were out on kayaks and canoes. Michaela, meanwhile, must have taken the left-hand turn in the road, which would have carried her over another summit and down into the corresponding valley. By the time we regrouped in the sleepy town of Saint-Félix-de-Lodez (where I celebrated my namesake with numerous photos and my fourth pain au chocolat of the day), it became clear that no one had seen – or heard from – Michaela in quite a while.

'Perhaps she's found a nice policeman to help her out,' said Terry.

While Sam retraced our steps in the van, we pressed on to our lunch break beside the Grotte de Clamouse, an extensive system of dolomite caves on the western wall of the Gorges de l'Hérault. Sam had already dropped off everything we needed for a typically lavish picnic, after which two by two everyone rejoined the road to ride through the gorge. Dylan and I were left guarding the cool box when the phone rang. It was Michaela. She was with the mayor of a town some considerable distance away. Not wanting to worry anyone, she had tried to find her own way back on course but had merely got more lost. She spoke no French and so made her way to the nearest town hall to ask for directions. Before she knew it, the entire village was out in force to help her on the way. Could someone possibly pick her up in the van?

The mystery solved, Dylan and I were free to press on. We hid the picnic things behind a bush and clipped into the pedals. Having passed two lakes where swimmers were making the most of the warm autumn sun, I had my heart set on having a dip. We found an ideal spot just beyond Saint-Guilhem-le-Désert – one of the numerous villages we had passed laying claim to being 'the prettiest in France' – and then stripped down to our shorts and plunged in. Dylan went first, his dive as impeccable and splash-free as you'd expect from someone who appeared to be wholly competent at pretty much any sport he took his hand to. Somewhere back in Britain, Tom Daley probably suffered a convulsive shock as I sullied his profession with a dad dive of such ineptitude that it gave my own children good reason to remain unborn for at least another decade. Dylan captured photographic evidence of my wonky-legged flop which could be used in schools the world over as an example of how not to enter water.

Still, the river was wondrously refreshing. When Dylan dashed off to chase down the others and fulfil his guiding duties, I was happy to wallow in the waters and make the most of the glorious isolation, before riding solo up the stunning Hérault valley and through the Cévennes National Park, where the green leaves on the trees had started to turn orange and yellow. One day later, underneath the outstanding Pont du Gard – an ancient, three-tiered aqueduct so magnificent it made Jean-Jacques Rousseau wish he'd been born a Roman – I went for another swim, this time under the gaze of the rest of the group (not to mention the myriad tourists who had come to see the grandiose feat of Roman engineering – and, unexpectedly, my own grandiose feet).

Unfortunately, there were signs up forbidding diving, which meant I had no chance at redemption. 'They probably heard about your last effort,' quipped Terry.

By now, Terry and I had grown quite used to each other's company. We had quickly established a system of co-habitation loosely based on the ships-at-night principle: that's to say, he was a huge oil tanker, not often seen after dark, but always heard. It didn't take me long to learn that he was a man of habit – as unbending as the hard-on he claimed he hadn't had for thirty years.

On arriving at a new hotel, instinct led him straight to the bathroom to check whether or not it was equipped with a bath. A mere shower would be grave cause for concern. Hopefully with the taps running, he would then head to the cupboard to liberate an extra pillow before unpacking the contents of his bag. Then came his post-ride bowel movements, played out amid sighs of pure rapture. Once he had managed to flood the bathroom in condensation, Terry would wash his kit in the sink (he only had two alternating sets of shorts and jerseys), find somewhere to hang it, and then emerge from the steaming room wrapped in towels.

A snooze would ensue – often preceded by a half-hearted attempt to read a page or two of Darwin's *On the Origin of Species*. God knows why he chose this for his bedtime reading – surely his daily travails were a big enough reminder of man's constant struggle for survival. Once asleep, Terry's nasal noises were often so bombastic that he'd even wake himself up – although this only happened during his pre-dinner naps; during the night it was left to me shouting 'TERRY!' to rouse him from the subliminal conducting of his own nocturnal windpipe orchestra.

For a retired dentist, Terry seemed remarkably slapdash with his teeth, never flossing and often leaving red wine and chocolate stains to fester on his fangs overnight. Every evening he would set his alarm for 7 a.m. the next day. Every morning said travel clock would go off (having ticked ferociously throughout the night) anything up to half an hour early, leaving him bemused and me grouchy. Perhaps it was lucky Terry got up early because his morning routine usually ran for the best part of an hour. It involved showering, shaving and packing; complaining that his kit had not dried properly; the liberal application of chamois cream (thankfully behind closed doors) before his emergence at the breakfast table at least 15 minutes ahead of anyone bar Bob, who habitually rose with the sun.

Although Terry had three decades of mossbacked conservatism on me, deep down I appreciated that I, too, was unduly heavily set in my ways and that we were perhaps more alike than I cared to admit. Our daily soap opera kept everyone entertained and was played out in a range of hotels and locations of astonishing calibre and diversity. In the southern French leg alone we stayed in the backstreets of Céret, below the towering castle at Peyrepertuse, a stone's throw from the fortress at Carcassonne, beside the medieval Pont du Diable at Olargues, and in an old nineteenth-century carpet factory in Sommières, overlooking the calm river Vidourle. Each establishment had its own story and I found the charming simplicity of the Fleurs d'Olargues perhaps the most appealing. Run by a Danish couple who scoured the whole of France to find the ideal setting for a guest house and restaurant, the Fleurs d'Olargues has just a handful of rooms with shared bathroom facilities.

Terry and I lucked out with a huge, bright, airy room with creaky floorboards and a king-sized bed that used to belong to the grandmother of the guest-house manager, Joan Abrahamsson, who moved from Copenhagen with her husband Anders eleven years ago. They also run a separate restaurant across the narrow cobbled road that links the south bank of the river Orb with the rickety hillside town via the Pont du Diable, or Devil's Bridge. Their son Casper is head chef. All fruit, vegetables and salads are grown in the garden beside the river, with meat locally sourced and fish from the nearby Mediterranean coast.

Sitting outside in the late-afternoon sun, enjoying a beer on the terrace, I felt more relaxed than ever before. Behind the blossoming pear and apple trees, the thirteenth-century single-span bridge has somehow survived the test of time; nestled on the side of an otherwise forested hill, ancient buildings jut out at different angles, crowned by a thousand-year-old belfry which rises into the sky; the only sounds the rustling in the leaves and the flow of the river below.

'You have the best view in town,' I told Joan as she came out with another beer.

'We have the best view in southern Europe,' she corrected me.

Her accent and Danish candour reminded me of Denmark's most famous cyclist, Bjarne Riis. The 1996 Tour winner had his title taken away from him after admitting to doping in 2007, before being written back into the record books in 2008 (albeit with an asterisk).

When I'd interviewed Riis for Eurosport ahead of the 2012 Tour it was during a period of acute turmoil for his team. Saxo Bank's star rider Alberto Contador had been slapped with a two-year ban for the illegal fat-stripping steroid Clenbuterol, whose presence in his blood back on the second rest day of the 2010 Tour in Pau he famously blamed on that contaminated piece of Basque steak. The Spaniard won that Tour with his former team, Astana, and he'd already agreed to join Riis's outfit for the coming season when his positive test came to light. There followed a year of limbo in which Contador appealed his ban before having it upheld by the Court of Arbitration for Sport. During the prolonged case, Contador was cleared to ride. He won the 2011 Giro and then – once his second appeal was postponed – finished fifth in the Tour. In February 2012, 'El Pistolero' finally met the firing squad and was handed a retrospective ban. Deprived of his main man for the first two Grand Tours of the season, Riis was effectively twiddling his thumbs until August's Vuelta. Although his contract had been annulled, Contador was still training with Saxo Bank and was expected to re-sign once he'd served his time.

Given the precariousness of the situation, Riis was not prepared to answer questions about a rider who still vociferously denied any guilt.

But while the doping antics of Albuterol Clentador (as many had taken to calling him) were off limits, those of Riis himself were not. After all, our interview preceded a public Q&A coinciding with the launch of his book, *Stages of Light and Dark*. In a frank yet measured confession, Riis's book opened the lid on his own use of performance-enhancing drugs – so he had to expect at least a gentle ribbing.

'Bjarne, you are a man of many nicknames. How did "the Eagle of Herning" come about?' I asked.

'A nickname is something you get, it's not something you take,' he replied (take note, Marco Pantani). 'A Danish journalist called me that once after a win in the Tour in '93 when I was up there with the big guys and it stuck. Fine, I think I have to live with that, it's not something I can change.'

Most cycling fans know that Riis's other moniker was a reference to his haematocrit – the volume percentage of red blood cells in the blood, an indication of EPO usage – during his heyday. During interviews with riders in the wake of the Festina scandal of 1998, when the entire French team were thrown off the Tour when their soigneur, Willy Voet, was caught with a car boot filled with drugs, it was suggested that had the Festina riders been doped to above 50 per cent, then Riis must have been doped to at least 60 per cent. Riis's more notorious nickname stemmed from this hearsay.

'What about your other name, "Mr 60 Per Cent"?' I probed.

There was a small silence as he fixed me with the kind of glacial stare that you'd expect from someone named after a bird of prey.

'I think that's a stupid name,' he replied.

Changing the subject as quickly as possible, I moved on to the first question I saw on my list: what kind of food did you used to eat before the races when you were a pro? Given the context of the previous grilling, perhaps not the best thing to ask.

'Probably the same as what the riders have today. You know: rice, pasta, omelette. But that's not my favourite food to eat. What I like more than anything else is a good, juicy steak. Nice meat.'

The temptation was too much to resist. Mr 60 Per Cent had teed me up with an inch-perfect pass.

'But presumably not a steak from the Basque country?'

The silence was even more awkward than the last one. Had the cameras not been rolling I think he might have swung a punch.

'That's actually not funny,' he said.

'No, it's not,' I capitulated.

If it was *Blazin' Saddles* who asked the question, it was a beetroot-red Felix Lowe who was reduced to gutless acquiescence before swiftly moving on to the next question. To be fair, Riis carried on with utmost professionalism – even if he wasn't interested in naming a hypothetical all-star fantasy cycling team ('Can I just say Alberto nine times?'). Once we were done, I did approach him to apologize for putting him on the spot. 'Ah, it's OK,' he said with a laugh. 'It was just a bad joke, I think.'

Here's the thing: even if Bjarne had found the line vaguely funny, he was not in a position to show it. He had gambled by bringing Contador to Saxo Bank and the double Tour winner's ban had put his team in a very delicate situation. His contract torn up, the best all-rounder of his generation was free to sign for any team come August. Without Contador, who went on to win the Vuelta later that season, Riis's one-dimensional Saxo squad would probably have not picked up enough UCI points to merit automatic inclusion in cycling's top division the following season. The sponsors would pull the plug and the whole ship could sink. Looking back at that interview, Riis was on a total Contador charm offensive, claiming he was the 'most talented rider I have ever seen' and that he still felt that the Spaniard – and not de facto winner Andy Schleck – was the rightful 2010 champion. Given that Schleck rode for Riis back then, that's quite a statement.

Later that evening, Riis's humour would shine through a little when taking part in the Q&A. Asked how he had managed to transform himself from a stage hunter to a GC rider back in the mid-1990s, his response was initially delivered with a straight and considered face. 'I trained differently and much harder. I lost a lot of kilos. I got older and stronger in my head.' Then, following a pause, came the punchline: 'And, yeah, there was the EPO.'

Bjarne Riis's assertion that his diet was 'probably the same as what the riders have today' was echoed years later in another controversial Danish rider's warts-and-all autobiography. Michael Rasmussen was on course to win the 2007 Tour before being kicked out by his Rabobank team for lying about his training schedule amid mounting claims of general doping nefariousness. A two-year ban pretty much ended the career of 'The Chicken', who continued to deny all accusations levelled against him before holding a press conference in January 2013 in which he admitted to using pretty much every performance-enhancing drug known to man during his career.

In his subsequent autobiography, *Yellow Fever*, Rasmussen tells an anecdote from the start of a Tour stage in 2005 when both he and Lance Armstrong were lining up at the front of the peloton in their respective polka dot and yellow jerseys. 'He looked at me with a teasing expression and asked: "Well, what did you eat yesterday?" I just looked at him and replied, "Probably the same as you."'

Rasmussen would have probably hated riding our pseudo-tour. Not only did our soigneurs Dylan and Sam turn up with a van completely devoid of PEDs, we were also eating enough food in one day to keep the emaciated Dane alive for a week. Renowned for being freakishly concerned about his weight, Rasmussen apparently used to count each grain of rice before eating and would pour water, not milk, in his breakfast cereal. When, three months earlier, I had asked Greg LeMond if I should show such culinary restraint during my approaching ride, the American didn't mince his words.

'No! You only live once, man,' he laughed. 'Perhaps don't push it as much as the old guys – they used to drink brandy from their bidons – and that will affect you – but otherwise don't hold back.' He then told me a story that – months later – made me feel less guilty about enrolling upon a systematic programme of performance-enhancing calorie intake that essentially amounted to a legal drip-feed of decadence.

'I remember racing the Giro one year. Think it was 1990. We were on the Marmolada climb and it was covered in snow,' he said with a twinkle in his eye. 'After the finish we rode back down and I was with four guys. I hit the wall. Zero food or water. So we resorted to giving out our hats to the Italian fans to get some of their stuff. But the only food they had was sausage, cheese and beer. By the time we got back to the hotel we were all drunk. I think we fell asleep at eight p.m. that night, stuffed with Parmesan, sausage and beer. The next day I got in the breakaway and rode good – so you never know.'

With Greg's blessing I was gorging away pretty much all day. Breakfasts would be a chance to fuel up on croissants and pains au chocolat, baguettes with butter and jams, slices of cheese and ham, and bowls of cereal, yoghurt and fresh fruit. In Carcassonne the buffet was particularly lavish, and complemented by soft-boiled eggs, which might have explained why the Hotel Montmorency mascots (chocolate Labrador Cerise and basset hound Elliot) were so outrageously fat. Waddling around the breakfast bar in search of titbits they so clearly did not need, Elliot and Cerise made the most obese canine combination known to man. The hotel staff actually fed them with a carefree vigour similar to that of French farmers forcing grain down the throats of geese (the thought of canine foie gras actually made me rather nauseous as we rode off that morning).

For the most part, our Languedoc lunches consisted of extravagant picnics in picturesque settings – with Dylan and Sam each day trying to outdo the other by bringing another addition to the table, be it a fourth creamy goat's cheese, a new variety of salami or perhaps a couple of fruit tarts for dessert. One of the most memorable picnics was also the coldest: on a rocky outcrop atop the 886-metre Col de Salettes after an invigorating climb through a forest which I started way off the back and finished just shy of catching Eleri after gobbling up the others one by one. Local fresh fruit were an important part of the diet, too. We enjoyed succulent figs near the Pont du Gard, bought from a man on the side of the road for €3 a sack. Mindful of Maurice Garin, the first ever Tour winner in 1903, and his cherry-induced bout of indigestion on the race's first ever stage (a seventeen-hour schlep from Paris to Lyon), I went easy on the famous cherries of Céret.

If there was a certain level of fuel-restocking functionality surrounding our breakfasts, lunches and mid-stage snacks, then our dinners were habitually an exercise in pure gluttony. Burning on average four thousand calories a day in that opening week in France, I had to up my daily food intake by more than 100 per cent. For someone with a fast metabolism who loves pretty much everything about eating, this was heaven. Sometimes our evening meals would reflect the journey we had done that day – like in Céret where my peculiarly alluring prawns-and-roast-chicken combo was named 'Mer et Montagne' as if to echo our ride up from the Costa Brava and over the Pyrenees.

But the pick of those opening week dinners was easily chef Casper's set-menu bonanza at the Fleurs d'Olargues. To get the taste buds going we were first treated to an amuse-bouche of swordfish galette on a crispy Oriental-style salad with ginger honey. Then came a quite stupendous starter: scallops marinated in olive oil and lemon on a bed of broad beans, peas and mint puree (all from the riverside garden). Keeping the green theme going, we then sprinted as fast as Mark Cavendish through a vertiginously designed tower of mint mash, crispy garden vegetables, succulent filet mignon du porc and a truffle and sage sauce. Capping the meal off in some style came individual plates of four puddings – four! – featuring a chocolate mousse with fifty-year-old Armagnac, an almond cake with cardamom and blueberry, an orange, peach and apricot posset with a gingerbread finger, and finally (my favourite) a lavender-infused crème brûlée. I could have married Casper then and there.

For its unbridled culinary licentiousness, however, our meal after the seventh stage in Sommières deserves special mention. It was the day that I pulled off the famous 'Duck Double': two slices of warm duck terrine wrapped in fine filo pastry and served with various accompaniments (including a zesty herb jelly) followed by the pièce de résistance – strangled duck fillets (apparently this means of death makes the meat more flavoursome and tender). It came with a truffle fluff, roasted figs and a spicy chocolate sauce – a type of Gallic sweet-and-sour, if you will. Preposterously good is all I can say. Anything that you eat where the mode of slaughter has an effect on its taste has to be applauded. A dish worthy of Carthage. Poor Terry was already down on his luck that night after being charged €28 for two pints of shandy. Having ordered duck twice in the opening week and on both occasions been presented with something tough and leathery, he ordered the cod this time and really missed out. Seeing his envious eyes drooling over my plate like Elliot and Cerise waiting for breakfast scraps almost made me feel guilty for giving him such a hard time about the snoring. Almost.

As I was enjoying a restrained pudding of melt-in-the-mouth poached pear, nougat ice cream, almond cake, chocolate sauce and raspberry coulis, adorned with – heck, why not? – a meringue stick and caramel ring, it dawned on me that my duck double could well have been a *canard* trifecta. For before dinner we had done some wine tasting in the shady grounds of the Auberge du Pont Romain – and one of the rather avant garde canapés had been a duck foie gras macaron. In a young mallard's nightmare I'd become a type of Freddy Krueger figure – devouring their kind in as many ways as possible, even crafting them into the kind of poncy cake that usually adorns the windows of glitzy Parisian pâtisseries.

Back in Spain, Chris Horner was busy taking the Vuelta by storm. As we rode across rural Languedoc, the 41-year-old was chipping away at Vincenzo Nibali's overall lead on a daily basis. By the time we had arrived in Olargues, Horner had gone off-script to cut the Italian's lead to just three seconds after attacking on the steepest ramp of the final climb of Peña Cabarga. Nibali, the Giro champion, was stunned.

'I know that when I am almost 42, I won't still be racing. It's as if Chris has an extra gear compared to the rest of us,' Nibali joked with reporters. In the hours preceding my duck double in Sommières, Horner turned this three-second deficit into a three-second lead in stage 19, breaking clear of a breathless Nibali on the final climb of Alto Naranco to take the red jersey for the third time in the race. With just one more mountain stage remaining, Horner was on the verge of becoming the oldest ever winner of a Grand Tour.

No one was happier about this unexpected turn of events than fellow aged American, Bob. As we sat on a bistro terrace in Castillon du Gard enjoying a warm lunch before pressing on to Avignon, Bob glowed when I brought up the topic of Horner.

'What he is achieving at the moment is outstanding for an old fart like me,' said Bob. 'It's not that he's American, it's that he's so old that makes me happy. If Nibali were 42 and Horner were 28, I'd be rooting for Nibali.'

Despite the sixteen bikes on display in his man cave – and the one hundred cycling kits he claims to own – Bob came late to cycling. In 1990 he listened to his wife and gave up his first passion, mountaineering.

He had lost too many friends to fatal accidents in the Himalayas – not to mention one buddy who was forced to have the highest ever haemorrhoidectomy in history (according to Bob, an ophthalmologist from Harvard carried out the operation with his eyes closed). Instead he channelled his energy into his expanding business empire, which involved the mass production and patenting of power sources required for disposable medical equipment. One of the company's biggest money-spinners was the aforementioned prostate-cooking butt plug. These made Bob a very rich man. But also a very fat man. Over the years he ballooned worse than Jan Ullrich in the off-season. So Bob took up cycling. And twelve years later, here he was: a lean, sinewy, riding machine.

Like Horner, Bob's strong current performances owed a lot to being injury-free. 'Last year I cycled this route off the back of a knee problem and it was hell,' he said as the waitress brought our orders. 'I couldn't wait to get off the bike every day. This year I'm much lighter and stronger. I feel just great. I'm enjoying it more because my fitness level is higher. I'm riding the best I ever have in my life at 70. Isn't that brilliant?'

While we ate – me: a sumptuous salad with cured ham, cheese, fruit and grilled vegetables; Bob: lentils and a piece of grilled salmon whose crispy skin got the thumbs-up when he passed it over – Horner and Nibali were preparing to do battle on the Vuelta's final mountain-top showdown, the gruelling Alto de l'Angliru. Did Bob think Horner had enough in the tank to keep Nibali at bay?

'It's never easy when you're that age because you can be hit by mother nature's collapse at any time,' he said. 'But my guess is that if he's three seconds ahead then he will hang on and he'll win both the stage and the race.'

Bob almost got it spot on. Horner didn't take the stage win – that accolade went to a Frenchman exactly half his age – but in finishing second, the American distanced fourth-place Nibali and increased his overall lead to 37 seconds. With just a processional stage to Madrid remaining, Horner had entered the history books. For me, Horner's emergence as a geriatric force on two wheels had caused a bit of a quandary. I should have welcomed the news that I still had a decade to get to the top echelons of professional cycling. But covering this sport makes you rather cynical and I couldn't help but think that Nibali was being a trifle flippant with his 'extra gear' comment.

On the Vuelta's first rest day long before we set off from Barcelona, when Horner returned to the top of the standings for a second time following his second stage win of the race, I had written a measured piece for a website entitled 'Should we be excited or worried by red-hot Horner?' The gist was that here was a man performing not only better than he had ever done, but better than much younger riders in their prime and, at a time when the spectre of doping loomed once again, doing so in a race which had so far been filled with anomalies. With eleven more stages remaining, many of which were particularly brutal, I'd be 'highly surprised' if Horner made a sustainable bid for the red jersey, I wrote. He would concede the lead in the individual time trial (he did) and then slip down the standings (he didn't). Talk of doping, while understandable given the climate, was surely premature and unfair. 'A man pressing 42 can perform well over 10 days,' I concluded. 'Should Horner still be up there come Madrid, that's when the alarm bells should start ringing. Then we would have a real problem.'

It was a perfect example of fence-sitting, but I genuinely believed Horner would not be able to sustain his challenge, whereby freeing me – or anyone else – from having to speculate about his training methods and that 'extra gear'. The problem I encountered after the Vuelta was simple: the piece I wrote intended to outline the case for and against Horner while stopping short at planting my flag in either camp. But by winning, Horner had planted the flag for me. A couple of weeks later I received an email from a disgruntled reader who took issue with my 'outspoken' column. 'How do you feel now that Chris has done the impossible and won?' he asked. 'Trash-talk is not called for but I think it's a pity that you are still probably doubting that it even happened and will use your pen to further criticize when in reality it's you that deserves the criticism.'

When I outlined the concerns regarding Horner to Bob, he was happy to show his fellow countryman the benefit of the doubt.

'Good grief, I hope he's clean. I really do,' he said, showing genuine concern. 'It's a great tale – the first American to win the Vuelta and an old dude, to boot.'

The seven Tour wins of Lance Armstrong was also a great tale. 'I'll say to the people who don't believe in cycling, the cynics and the sceptics: I'm sorry for you. I'm sorry that you can't dream big. I'm sorry you don't believe in miracles.' Those were the words of Armstrong on the podium in Paris after the last of his wins in 2005. Is it any surprise that both fans and reporters find it hard to believe in the miraculous exploits of a former team-mate of a man like this, coming good in his fifth decade on the planet? Horner has categorically denied all accusations levelled against him – but what's a rider's word these days? If you haven't failed a test, why *would* you throw it all away and come clean?

I still don't know where I stand. The fact that Horner's RadioShack team did not offer a contract extension to a Grand Tour winner suggests that they had concerns too – and not just with the reported $1-million contract he was demanding. In the end, Horner was given a lifeline by Lampre-Merida, the Italian team whose track record could be questioned quicker than you can say 'Mantova doping investigation'.

My own daily cocktail of drugs (paracetamol laced with codeine and ultra-strong ibuprofen, not to mention the temazepam for my nocturnal battle against Terry) may have made Michaela, a renal specialist, roll her eyes in teacherly concern, but it was certainly working wonders on my morale, which had been as low as my bottom bracket. Since hurting my knees back in Spain, I had ridden most days in moderate-to-acute pain. The mornings were the worst, with the first couple of hours before our coffee stop particularly hellish. As well as strong espresso and pastries, my daily elevenses were a chance to stuff my knee warmers with ice cubes and chuck a few more pills down my throat. Three days into my regime I noticed that my tongue was becoming swollen and sore. A quick Google search that night showed that this was one of the side effects of codeine, a drug which shouldn't be taken for more than three consecutive days because of its addictive nature. How something that creates that much discomfort can also be addictive flummoxed me. But I wasn't prepared to find out.

For some professional riders even the use of non-banned medications like these are frowned upon. When Welshman Geraint Thomas completed the 2013 Tour de France with a fractured pelvis he did so with only the help of a few paracetamols and shots of coffee – refusing the controversial (but legal) painkiller tramadol, whos widespread abuse in the peloton has been blamed for a spike in race-day crashes, putting Thomas's Team Sky, among others, under the spotlight. For his part, the young American time-trial specialist Taylor Phinney is one of a minority of cyclists who shy away from both caffeine pills and painkillers, once claiming he 'felt uncomfortable fooling my body into feeling something that it wasn't supposed to be feeling'. To counter that, I would probably say that I would have felt more uncomfortable leaving my body to feel what it was actually feeling. Phinney nevertheless argues that if you're taking painkillers to mask the natural effects that riding a bike is having on your body, then you are essentially taking pills to enhance your performance. I see where he's coming from, but I wasn't taking these pills to enhance my performance, merely to get it near to a level at which every pedal stroke was not mired in agony.

These ethical quibbles aside, as we neared Avignon and the end of the first phase of the tour I was relieved to be approaching what I felt was a fair representation of what I could achieve on a bike. Pain-free I was not, but then again, cycling is not meant to be easy; no endurance sport is. And after that al fresco chat with Bob over lunch in Castillon du Gard I was ready to nip off on one of my extra loops – both to get my kilometre-count into three figures and to make the most of the Provençal sunshine.

Crossing the summit of our only climb of the day in pole position, I left the planned route and headed north along a deserted road flanked either side by low-lying trees and the famous Garrigue scrubland. A break in the branches to the west showed in the distance the majestic l'Hertus cliffs from the Pic Saint-Loup wine region which we traversed on our approach to Sommières a day earlier. I then rode through a hidden valley presided upon by an ancient tumble-down castle – Le Castellas – above the pretty town of Saint Victor la Coste. It was a Saturday and there were lots of weekend riders out on the road, each one happy to raise a hand or utter a 'Bonjour' in passing.

And then I saw it – rising from the green sea of rolling vineyards like a stone shark's fin. Mont Ventoux. The Giant of Provence. The Bald Mountain. On this beast of a climb, Tours have been won and lost. And on this windswept 1,911-metre beacon that dominates the Provence skyline, I was soon going to face my first real test on two wheels.

But first there was a night in Avignon to look forward to – including yet another mind-bogglingly exquisite meal: marinated sardines on a bed of mustard potatoes, with an anchovy and caper paste, followed by a rare chunk of tuna with a gingery sauce, finely chopped tomatoes, spices, lemongrass and coriander, served with a carrot and chickpea hummus.

Before we'd entered Avignon and been bamboozled by its confusing one-way system, narrow streets and weekend road closures, there was the small matter of crossing the Rhône. For us, thanks to a modern bridge on a quiet road ten kilometres north of town, it was just that – a small matter. But when Hannibal came up against the river obstacle it was less straightforward.

Crossing the Rhône was Hannibal's greatest challenge since setting out from Spain. Not only was it a vast expanse of water, but waiting on the other side were hostile Volcae tribesmen, goading the Carthaginians, banging their shields with their swords and generally being rather unpleasant. Hannibal's plan was simple: he sent his nephew Hanno to cross the river 40 kilometres upstream with a unit of crack Spanish troops with a view to catching the Volcae out with a classic pincer movement. Once Hanno and his men were in position, they made a smoke signal and Hannibal started to send his own troops over the water on rafts. The Volcae came to the river bank to meet Hannibal but were surprised by the coordinated rear attack and fled. The battle won, now came the small matter of getting the elephants across the water hazard.

Polybius says that Hannibal's men built huge rafts and covered them with soil to make them look like an extension of the land. The Carthaginians then lured the herd on to the floating islands with the use of a female elephant before detaching the rafts. Angered by being duped, the elephants panicked and caused the rafts to overturn. The elephants then supposedly used their trunks as snorkels and walked along the river bed to the other side. Such poetic imagery is all very well, but Polybius was clearly oblivious to the fact that elephants can swim. Indeed, writing seventy years later, Livy states that the lead male was driven into a rage and into the water by his driver, who then jumped in and used himself as bait, swimming across the river with an angry pachyderm in pursuit. The other elephants simply followed the lead of the herd's big cheese, and voilà.

Once the elephants were accounted for, the rest of the Carthaginian army – now down to 38,000 infantry and 8,000 horsemen – could follow. Hannibal then sent his crack Numidian cavalry to scout the surrounding areas. It just so happened that Publius Cornelius Scipio, the Roman consul, had simultaneously landed in Massilia (modern Marseille) and had sent his own horsemen north on a reconnoitre mission. The ensuing skirmish was the first battle between Rome and Carthage in the Second Punic War – and the Numidians proved more crap than crack. Fleeing back to camp, they alerted Hannibal of the impending danger and Hannibal started to march north. Now realizing that Hannibal intended to cross the Alps, Scipio decided to head back to Italy and prepare for war, sending his brother Gnaeus on to Empúries to try and cut off the Carthaginian supply lines in Spain.

What Hannibal didn't do next – quite sensibly – was head to the top of the nearest, biggest mountain so that he could get a better view of the retreating Romans. Wisely, he steered well clear of Mont Ventoux as he made his way into the Alps. But no cyclist can come this close to such a mythical beauty and spurn her advances. Tomorrow may have been Sunday and our first scheduled day of rest, but the Ventoux was there to be ridden.

# MONT VENTOUX

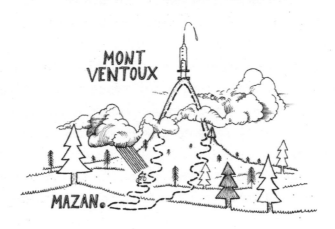

WHEN I TOLD MY UNOFFICIAL MENTOR that I was planning to ride Mont Ventoux on the first 'rest' day of the tour his smile had suddenly disappeared, filling up those trademark dimples with fleshy, palpable concern.

'Don't do that,' Greg LeMond had said, imploringly. 'Hell, no.' He actually looked at me as if I were crazy.

But here I am, gingerly edging towards Bédoin, the gateway of Mont Ventoux, and three hours of largely unmitigated torture. The sun shines on rows of vines flanking the road but the summit of the Bald Mountain is capped in a toupee of grey, threatening clouds. The 22-kilometre ascent from Bédoin that I am about to embark upon is the route the Tour de France has used on the fourteen occasions the race has ventured up Ventoux since its first ever visit in 1951, where the riders used the slightly gentler approach from nearby Malaucène.

'When the Tour came here a couple of months ago the riders had a rest day afterwards. This is my rest day,' I tell imaginary viewers inside my phone as I record, rather jauntily, the first of four to-camera pieces of the afternoon.

'I've got the Café du Cycliste purple top. I have the official *Blazin' Saddles* lime green shorts,' I say, panning down to reveal what looks like a sack of spuds moving fairly suggestively around the protruding black pan handle of my saddle.

'I've got the leg warmers on, because it's quite chilly – or it will be chilly, up there – and some blue Santini arm warmers. So I'm going to be a bit of a rainbow today. There might even be a bit of a rainbow up there because it's sunny . . . [dramatic pause] . . . and wet. And up top it's going to be cold. They're saying four degrees.

'But I'm looking forward to it,' I conclude, perhaps a bit chipper for someone fast approaching cycling's equivalent of squaring up to a drug-fuelled Mike Tyson and his infamous fake penis.

This morning, all those keen for a Ventoux rendezvous were shuttled up from Avignon to Mazan, a pretty Provençal hillside town where the actress Keira Knightley held her wedding a few months previously. Following the example of Keira's guests, most of us are staying the night in the eighteenth-century Château de Mazan, once home of erotic philosopher extraordinaire the Marquis de Sade.

It seems fitting that our day of unrelenting uphill punishment should commence where the world's most famous aristocratic sexual libertine wrote of sadistic rides of a very different sort. Given its length, unforgiving spanks and distinct sting in the tail, the Ventoux is, after all, tantric sadomasochism on wheels. Six of us have decided, using our hearts, not heads, to have a stab at the climb best known for its barren, wind-battered moonscape of a summit. Camilla and Eleri have signed on as a final swansong before returning Down Under with Ted (who is sensibly sitting this one out). Bernadette is also game, while new arrival

John, a retired civil servant from Melbourne, is hoping to add the fabled climb to his rapidly expanding list of European conquests (he joins us for the second leg of the tour after a week in the Italian Alps, where he snared the holy trinity of the Stelvio, Mortirolo and Giau passes. Incidentally, John booked his passage on phase two of our ride because of a tweet I posted a few months ago, which essentially makes him a *Blazin' Saddles* groupie. I'm not yet sure how I feel about this. Had John been a leggy blonde and not a 50-year-old man with chapped lips, excitement levels would have been higher).

Finally, another Australian, Alan, has arrived as part of a large group of strong Sydney cyclists who will be riding through the Alps next week with Dylan as their guide, following a day behind the rest of us. Bob had hoped to join us on his wooden steed but he has a problem with the rear derailleur. 'I'm not too pooped,' he said back at the hotel. 'I rode all three different ascents of Ventoux on one day back in 2006 so I know the carnage that you have in store. I only wanted to do it this year if I could take the Renovo up for a photo.'

As we were making our final preparations Camilla dutifully informed us all that the Italian scholar Petrarch climbed Ventoux in 1336, to which Eleri – clearly preoccupied with the task in hand – replied 'Wow – that's a solid time!' before enquiring which team he rode for.

Impatient and unimpressed with my faffing around, the others soon left Mazan without me. Save for the steady stream of Sunday cyclists out to carve a Ventoux-shaped notch in their own bedposts, I'll be riding the biggest test of my amateur career alone. It's no big deal. You only ever really ride a climb like Ventoux alone anyway, even when in the presence of others.

My morale in Bédoin is curiously high for someone in line for a severe pummelling. I grab a bite to eat from a *boulangerie* – just as much to delay the inevitable as to fill up on calories – and then make my second video of the day. This one has a culinary theme.

'Here's my food pouch,' I say with perhaps too much pride, revealing a not-so-discreet pocket attached to my top tube and stem with Velcro. I'm fully aware that such accessories are to bikes what bum-bags are to humans – humiliating, irritatingly useful and a sure-fire way to avoid a bonk. 'Inside there's a wrapped-up pain au chocolat liberated from breakfast and a bag of Haribo – both fairly essential.'

'I have two water bottles,' I continue, panning down to the Felt's dual bidon cages. 'One with a special energy tablet in. Then I have this,' I say, whipping out a brick of cake from my back pocket, 'which is pure rocket fuel.' A banner on the front of the packet lavishly boasts of 6 per cent fig content, whereby underlining its credentials as the 'wife beater' of fruity snacks.

'This is basically legal Pot Belge,' I elaborate, making reference to the famous cycling elixir of the 1980s and '90s: a heady mixture of cocaine, heroin, caffeine and amphetamines that would help pros 'unclog the motor' during winter training rides (not to mention boogie on the dance floor until the early hours). 'It's great stuff.' (The cake, that is; although I would probably swap it in a flash for a hit of Belgian Stew right now.) 'I got it from a market the other day. I had the apricot variety and it got me to Sommières when I was feeling a bit ropey.'

'And I have some gels,' I say, holding up two tubes of sticky blackcurrant magic potion. 'So it should be fine,' I add breezily, as if eating loads of sugary crap is all there is to climbing one of the toughest ascents in professional cycling. 'The next time I'll speak will be halfway up. Chat to you then.'

Just as I'm clicking into my pedals my phone buzzes and I receive a text from my brother Alex informing me that his wife has gone into labour. 'Wonderful news,' I reply. 'Fingers crossed and good luck – it's great that she's showing some solidarity ahead of the turmoil I'm about to face.' After all, scaling Ventoux is probably the closest thing I'll get to giving birth on a bike.

In an equal display of solidarity, the weather is getting worse and it looks like the waters have broken from those stormy clouds on the horizon. Inside my stomach butterflies flutter alongside a mulch of pizza, apple tart and peach ice tea. Mont Ventoux is renowned for its climate extremes and its exposed peak acts as a weathervane for western Provence. World-record wind speeds of 320 kmph have been recorded on the summit, which in between being buffeted by the Mistral gales is either baked in sun or covered in snow. These meteorological unpredictabilities make me a trifle nervous as I finally begin my quest to come of age on this fabled cycling nerve centre.

It was sweltering temperatures as high as 32 degrees Celsius that accompanied Chris Froome's triumphant win here a couple of months earlier during the centenary Tour. A group of ten escapees – five of whom were French – arrived at the foot of Ventoux with a small advantage over the peloton. The riders had already notched up a staggering 220 kilometres before rolling through Bédoin, which puts my menial 10-kilometre warm-up from Mazan into perspective. It was on this early, timid section of the climb that Sylvain Chavanel gave the French crowds some short-lived cheer on Bastille Day with a dig off the front. Chavanel's attack did not result in the home nation's first stage win of the 2013 Tour, but it gave the veteran the edge over his compatriot Thomas Voeckler in the annual two-way tussle to become the French housewives' favourite, a position occupied for so long by 'Tricky Dicky' Richard Virenque, victor on Ventoux in 2002.

With an average gradient of 4.5 per cent, the first 6 kilometres hardly necessitate a change of underwear. The key here is to ride within yourself precisely so you can follow through later on. At this point the burden is more psychological than physical – especially with the mountain looming to your left and the not-so-distant rumbles of thunder getting ever closer. There are numerous riders on the road but none who are keeping a similar pace to me. I pass them one by one, often offering a jovial '*Bonjour*' as I carefully disguise my mounting heart-rate and pretend to be breathing as if I were merely out for a stroll. These mind games and rival-baiting offer a small victory of sorts.

Over-drinking coupled with nerves means I soon feel the urge to pee, which I stubbornly resist because of the good rhythm I've managed to establish. Yet emptying my bladder would clearly be better than the constant drip-feed that seems to be permeating my shorts and making my balls start to tingle. It's as if someone has surreptitiously applied a small dollop of Deep Heat to my scrotum. I can't stop conjuring up warped images of a goldfish bowl in which my privates jangle around like a fish gasping for water. Seeing that I've yet to master the skill of saddle-bound urination – such an act requires the kind of flexibility, balance and dexterity that I clearly lost during my teenage growth spurt – I stop to relieve myself on the side of the road.

After a rare hairpin bend at the village of Saint-Estève the gradient ramps up quite considerably. In my place, Chris Horner would no doubt be rampaging up these 10 per cent slopes with a smile on his face and a trail of destruction in his wake. But on the day I ride up the Bald Mountain, the follicly challenged Horner is currently coasting into Madrid to be crowned winner of the Vuelta. (After which he will jump on a plane back to the States and, following a misunderstanding with the authorities, miss the compulsory end-of-race doping control.) In his absence, I'm doing my best Horner impression, cobbling together long bouts of out-of-the-saddle riding while being threatened by no one. It's quite invigorating – although for the most part the riders I'm reeling in are either overweight, female, elderly or all three of the above.

One aspect that makes Ventoux stick out from other more traditional Alpine climbs is its lack of tight bends, the switchback at Saint-Estève being the first and last until a couple of compact corners in the exposed finale. It's as if the mountain has taken a pair of hair-straighteners to the one remaining strand that grows from its flaky scalp – but botched the job: for there are, mercifully, just enough crimps in the road to break up the uphill monotony and help us riders set some targets in our respective skyward skirmishes. Zooming around some of these bends and building up some serious pace on the long straights are numerous cyclists on their way down, many of whom shout an encouraging '*Allez*' as they whoosh past. It's not their speed that I clock so much as their attire, which seems for the most part more suitable for polar exploration than a late summer Sunday afternoon bike jolly in Provence. More of a concern are their pinched red faces. Many of them seem rather wet, some even visibly shivering.

What the hell's happening up there?

At the start of the summer only 200 of the 900 starters of the annual Granfondo Ventoux sportive made it to the exposed summit. Gale-force-nine winds made most riders rue their super-light carbon-fibre frames, while even the best leg warmers in the business were no match for temperatures of minus four. Skidding around on their cleats like runaway curling stones, grown men were clinging on to their bikes with frost-bitten hands to stop them being blown off the mountain and into some far-flung Provençal valley. At least one rider was hospitalized after being whisked over the parapet; others were treated for hypothermia; most turned round, said 'Sod this for a laugh' and headed back to Malaucène, where the temperature was a clement 19 degrees.

I'm just recalling a recent *Cyclist* feature on this turbulent sportive when the first drops of rain start to fall. I'm on to the claustrophobic wooded section of the climb where cedars, oaks and pines fight for a place on the side of roads like frantic spectators eager to get closer to the action. Gusts of wind blow rogue branches in my path, like the stray arms of fans running alongside the race. It's not yet chimney pot-shattering stuff, but the tree-lined path uphill has become something of a wind tunnel, making progress that bit more stuttered. That extra gear given to me by emptying my bladder has now been taken back.

What you don't appreciate while watching pulsating Ventoux stage finales on television is that there's so much riding to be done before the bare and barren summit. Everyone remembers the duel between Armstrong and Pantani in 2000 or, more recently, Chris Froome and Nairo Quintana – but not for what happened here in a forested section so dense that TV image quality is often fuzzy and distorted. It was here that Quintana, the Colombian Tour debutant with a birth certificate that makes a mockery of his crinkled-as-an-elephant's-knee face, attacked the main pack – including yellow jersey Froome – in pursuit of the few remaining escapees up the road. Just two months ago he rode solo through this very same rocky chicane that I'm now tackling in increasingly heavy rain.

I'm not even halfway up and the pounding rain is so monotonous that I'm beginning to understand what Chinese water torture is all about. I stop to throw on my rain jacket and have an energy gel. On the back of a blackcurrant burst, I soldier on. But it feels like I'm riding the wrong way up an escalator as I fight the current of this river road. The French have a delightful expression for making very little progress: *pédaler dans la choucroute*. I now understand the subtleties of cycling in sauerkraut.

Soaked through and stinging, there's no way that I'm going to post a competitive time on Ventoux despite feeling every part the recreational king of the mountains. The fastest ever ascent here belongs to Spain's Iban Mayo, the only professional rider whose name sounds like a condiment for international bank accounts. Mayo set a blistering time of 55 minutes and 51 seconds in an individual time trial in the 2004 Dauphiné Libéré, bettering a fifth-place Lance Armstrong by almost two minutes. Given Armstrong's ineffably vigorous doping diet throughout that decade, plus the Spaniard's own EPO bust in 2007, we can safely presume that Mayo's blood was also thick as ketchup at the time. In fact, looking at the list of fastest Ventoux ascents over the years, the first rider whose time doesn't raise eyebrows is that of fourteenth-place Frenchman David Moncoutié, a self-confessed loner nicknamed 'The Postman' whose edgiest characteristic was a penchant for homeopathy. Six riders in the psychedelic free-for-all that was the 1999 Tour – including Armstrong and two US Postal cronies – finished above the 58:31 time set by Moncoutié, a rider for whom accusations of doping can be laughed off on the grounds that they would actually make him vaguely interesting.

All this talk is immaterial when it comes to my faltering bid to join the greats, as I look down at my Garmin and realize that I've now been trundling along for just over an hour and I've only just passed the 8km-to-go stone on the side of the road. So far, I've been taking my inspiration from the retired Italian rider Eros Poli, who, during a stage in the 1994 Tour, was able to build up a sufficiently large buffer on the flat approach to the climb that he managed to stave off the peloton in spite of a relatively shoddy climbing speed that went hand in hand with his lofty six-foot-four frame. Poli's initial gap of 25 minutes in Bédoin was whittled down to just six minutes over the summit, but he managed to stay out ahead on the descent and take the win in Carpentras. Besides this uplifting story, I will always hold a space in my heart for someone who, when asked how he would like his epitaph to read, answered: 'Here lies Eros Poli, famous for being tall and coming last in the Giro d'Italia.'

The rain on the tarmac amplifies the roar of cars as they stutter past in second gear with enough regularity to question my own choice of transportation. It was around here, as the trees start to thin out, that Australia's Richie Porte catapulted his Sky team-mate Froome clear of rival Alberto Contador as the main favourites pursued danger man

Quintana during the Tour. The rain eases up as I approach the Chalet Reynard cafe, a popular stop-off for Ventoux cyclists and the spot where the third trail up the mountain, from Sault, joins the 'classic' route. I'm keen for some hot caffeine by a roaring fire but I know stopping would be folly – like popping into the pub for 'a cheeky pint' before returning home to fill out tax returns. Besides, the weather is clearly on the mend. In fact, is that the warmth of the sun I can feel on my back?

'We're about—' deep breath – 'five and a half kilometres from the top,' I gasp to the camera, swaying shoulders mirroring my steady pedal strokes as the noise of car engines fades in and out. Fatigue is etched across my face but I seem upbeat. My helmet, which is covered in rain drops, half obscures the luminous glare of the sun, refracted through a thinning layer of cloud. Every now and then, and in sync with my nodding head, bright rays appear from behind my red right ear and dazzle the screen. Over my left shoulder you can see a wispy cloud melting into a patch of blue sky.

'We've gone through the forest section. Just near the top of that it started to rain really heavily.' Sniff. 'Big time.' My puffy eyes are mostly on the road, but every now and then I look down at the screen – usually to emphasize a phrase. The unflattering nature of the low camera angle may be something to do with the main focal point being my infeasibly large nostrils. Is this really how most people view me as I tower above?

'I managed to put my jacket on without stopping.' Sniff. 'But to zip it up—' looks to the camera – 'I had to stop. I popped a gel because, er, I thought I should do. Mainly for this open bit here. As you can see . . .'

The screen pans across to reveal a rather bleak sight: the exposed side of a mountain covered in brownish scree and peppered with green bushes and the odd pine tree. Grey clouds scud across the sky ahead. In fact, that bit of blue seems to be a mere break in the gloom. Across the road someone has used paint and a very large brush to communicate his or her belief, right or wrong, that Roman Kreuziger from Contador's Saxo Bank team is '#1'. The number one what, I'm not sure. If it's 'emaciated Christian Bale lookalike', then they're on the money.

'Yeah, the sun has come out, which is good.' Cue sudden gusts of wind. 'But it's quite cold. My knees are holding out. I took a codeine and a paracetamol and an ibuprofen so that's the extent of my doping today.' As for my other legal leg-ups: the fig cake has yet to be eaten, although the pain au chocolat is long gone. My sweet intake is not so high today because the Haribos in my special pouch are sticky with rain water and also much harder to chew than usual, because of the temperature. Eating sweets has become a tiring process – much more detrimental than the combined effects of taste, energy and distraction are advantageous.

'These guys up in front—' deep breathing as the camera turns to show a handful of riders about 50 metres up the road, riding in what must be one of the highest bike lanes in the world – 'I overtook already. But I stopped to take a photo. It was hard to get the phone out because I've had to wrap it up because of the wet. But I'll overtake them again,' I say, matter-of-factly, before delivering a little personal appraisal. 'No one has overtaken me yet while I've been cycling. I'm proud of that. I've only overtaken, which is good.' Sniff.

'Right.' I look to the camera as another gust of wind crackles in the background. 'I'll see you at the top. No,' I add, just as a large stream of snot appears from my right nostril before being hastily inhaled back inside, 'I'll see you at Tom Simpson's memorial.' Off camera the tip of my tongue heads up into my bristly upper lip and seeks out some of the bogey residue. This personal, organic energy gel provides the requisite fillip for a series of unseated surges that in turn allow me to warm my nether regions with some class-A mountain flatulence. No one said climbing the Ventoux would be pretty. Or smell good.

Before Tom Simpson's memorial, which stands at the spot,

1.5 kilometres from the summit, where the British rider collapsed and died during the 1967 race, I finally face some stiff competition. It comes in the form of a rider in a stripy black-and-white top who creeps up behind me twice as the gradient drops to around 7 per cent. On both occasions I manage to put in a little dig to open up some daylight between us – but he's a persistent bugger and makes the most of my sudden desire to forage for sweets. It's like Froome versus Quintana all over again – except watered down, played out in slow motion and viewed through a Willy Wonka prism.

Vitalstatistix, the plump chieftain of Asterix's Gaulish village, would not like it here. Not because of his ample rotundity: there are plenty of portly Danes and generously girthed Germans with barrel chests and thighs like hams spinning away in a low gear, albeit in a state of frenzied delirium. No, the real reason Vitalstatistix would hate what I'm experiencing right now is that he's always harping on about the sky falling on his head. And that's precisely what seems to be happening on Ventoux. We may be above the tree line and done with those showers, but that famous panoramic view of Provence, which has only just lifted her skirt and given me a surreptitious flash, is now about to be chastity-belted up by the same fast approaching roof of clouds that still obscures the summit.

As I slow to take in this uncanny phenomenon, my rival draws level. I take consolation from the fact that his ego will hardly be flattered by overtaking an Eros Poli lookalike in lime green shorts riding one-handed while taking photos of the view with sticky fingers, snot running down his face and – wait a minute! – are those flakes of pain au chocolat clinging to his leg warmers? No doubt embarrassed at the sudden realization of his own apparent ineptitude, my adversary manages to open up a little gap over me, the rangy chancer. A big mistake, for it stirs the sleeping giant inside.

It's the first time anyone has passed me on my maiden ascent of

Ventoux – and even though it was purely on a technicality, I want to put things right. Entering the clammy cloud, I reduce the gap with a few stinging surges. His head down and legs grinding out a rhythm, my opponent doesn't notice the memorial on the side of the road. I salute Simpson and promise to pay my respects on the way down. But there's business to be done. And just like Froome a couple of months earlier, it's here that I make my decisive attack. As the gradient ramps back up to 10 per cent nearing the final kilometre, I zip by and – growling inside – restore the natural order of the mountain.

By now the conditions are quite preposterous. The fog is so thick that cars coming down the mountain can only be seen by their headlights before suddenly breaking into vision less than 50 metres ahead. Descending riders, too, emerge from the mist but they're riding at a pace that's scant reward for the severe effort they've made to haul themselves up the 1,911 metres to the summit. The yellow-and-black-striped poles that mark the edge of the road at times of snowfall are extremely useful in giving me a vague idea of the direction in which I'm meant to be pedalling. Alongside the calcified white rock which covers the bald pate of Ventoux and gives the erroneous impression, from afar, that the mountain is perpetually covered in snow, are, well, piles of snow. Despite this being September, the generous drizzle falling inside this misty gloom is indeed turning to ice and gathering in stacks of slush that crackle under my wheels.

Although the end is metaphorically in sight, I still have yet to glimpse the red and white tower of the large, concrete weather observatory that stands atop the summit. Capped with a large TV antenna, it is exceedingly unfortunate for a sport so mired in doping controversies that this structure resembles a giant syringe. Given that the edifice was built in 1968, one year after Simpson's life came to an end amid a flurry of brandy, amphetamines and misplaced assertions to 'put me back on the bloody bike', perhaps *unfortunate* is not the best word. For what is unique about the final 6 kilometres of Ventoux is that, thanks to the lack of twists and turns in the road, you can normally see directly where you're headed. And making professional cyclists ride as fast as they can towards a giant syringe does somewhat seem to give out the wrong message to the youngsters.

Deprived of this ethically dubious carrot, I press on regardless. Operating with a scope of vision that fails to extend beyond 10 metres is not how I imagined my maiden schlep up Ventoux to conclude. But it's certainly adding to the mystical allure of the place. Some might feel hard done by with the cards dealt out by the weather gods, but I look at it another way: it's a boon to know that I've battled pretty much all the elements – wind, torrential rain, sleet and a runny nose – and still come out on top. In fact, that a mountain renowned for its rum meteorological conditions has decided to throw the whole kitchen sink at me on the day I decide to ring its doorbell should be seen as a compliment. Like a Jehovah's Witness, I keep coming back for more.

It's nevertheless hard to reconcile my current Ventoux experience with anything I've seen on TV, chiefly because I can hardly see what I'm experiencing right now. Is this really the same mountain where Froome cemented Kenya's first Tour victory with a Bee Gees-style jig over the finish line? Or where Armstrong, in yellow, and Pantani, in pink, went shoulder to shoulder before the American eased up to gift his rival the stage win in 2000? Back then riders were still allowed to discard their helmets on the final climb of the day, and Pantani's hairless head was as shiny and white as the stones scattered across the brow of the mountain. But didn't that gesture provoke a war of words, eh?

'At the time I thought it was the right thing to do because I respect Pantani and the last twelve months for him have been tough,' Armstrong said of his manoeuvre, with a nod to the '98 Tour-Giro double winner's barren year after being kicked off the subsequent Giro for a dangerously high haematocrit. (Given his own efforts to keep his

EPO-induced haematocrit levels down for the drugs testers at the time, Armstrong had good reason to show Pantani some respect.)

The troubled Italian was not happy, though. 'Pantani does not need Armstrong to give him victory,' he said, betraying his haughty proclivity for the third person.

Armstrong struck back by calling Pantani 'Elefantino' and saying he was 'showing his true colours'. Quizzed why he was using Pantani's old nickname – the one he despised – the Texan said: 'I call him '*Elefantino*', not '*Il Pirata*', because the last time I checked you're not supposed to give yourself nicknames. I can't just say my name's Big Tex.'

Re-watching that duel between Big Tex and the Pirate propels you into a bygone era of cycling. Armstrong shields the sun from his eyes with a trusty pair of Oakley sunglasses but Pantani's purist aesthetic means both his rival and the global public can peer directly into the squinting eyes of this Gandhi on wheels – a bizarre sight for those used to seeing Nosferatu lurking in the shadows. Without helmets to hide beneath, both riders have their guards down, their faces true portals to their pain. Having ditched the trademark bandana, Pantani has consciously pared back the very layers he so intentionally cultivated to hide behind. Both riders grimace and gurn their way up, trading blows and visibly suffering the consequences of each strike. What's more, there's so much colour – from the riders' jerseys, the spectators on the side of the road, the white rocks reflecting the sun's unrelenting rays and the deep blue sky. It was a glorious Technicolor of an ascent, in stark contrast to my own monochromed mumble of a climb. Sure, through the fog my fluorescent green shorts are alerting my presence to oncoming cars, but my own field of vision is as hazy as the mist that is enveloping my accomplishment.

But, look! Here is the final steep swing to the right – and I'm now on to the closing straight. At least I would be if I knew where the bloody hell I should go. The road splits in two. I go right and it seems to take me along a bypass beyond the observatory. I'm almost on my way down the other side to Malaucene when I find a slip road back to the top. My time of 1 hour 53 minutes is nearly an hour slower than Mayo's record – but then again, he had clement weather and a favourable tailwind; he was also a professional cyclist with access to panaceas a bit more advanced than a bag of Starmix.

Froome's winning time here in the summer was exactly 59 minutes, which bettered the Texan–Elephant combo of thirteen years earlier but was only enough for twenty-third place in the Ventoux hall of fame. Both he and Quintana were so exhausted they needed oxygen masks at the finish. A sign of a cleaner era in cycling? Perhaps. While many figures were quick to point out that spectacular performances could be achieved without doping, Froome's convincing win did remind people of the Armstrong era. The difference? 'Lance cheated. I didn't cheat. End of story,' according to the yellow jersey. Sky were urged to release Froome's power data in a bid to put all these accusations to bed. When they did just that in the week following the Tour, it only fanned the flames. In cycling, *c'est la vie* and *plus ça change* ring true.

There's no oxygen mask waiting for me, although the wind is so ferocious I can just open my mouth wide, face the gusts and let the lungs fill up naturally. Anticlimactic is an understatement. There's no view and the only distraction is a shop selling souvenirs such as replica milestones – a tad cumbersome for the descent. The chap I beat is on his phone and, through the gale, is trying to explain in a very plummy British accent, no doubt to his wife, that, don't worry, he's on his way home. He acknowledges my presence, grudgingly. I get a game Belgian to take a snap of me underneath the summit sign astride my top tube, green thighs spreadeagled – cycling's equivalent of posing for a snap with your arms holding up the leaning tower of Pisa. And then it's back on the bike because it's frightfully cold and, to be fair, there ain't much of a party vibe up here.

As I nip around that final bend, two riders on their way up have a look of anguish on their faces as they shout out, 'Which way?' I shout something typically unhelpful like 'I went right but you can also go left!' and in barely a couple of minutes I'm pulling over at the Simpson memorial to remember my side of the bargain. The shrine is surrounded by cycling knick-knacks left behind by fans – water bottles, caps, inner tubes and the like.

'*Blazin' Saddles* here at the Tom Simpson memorial,' I tell the camera, getting in character. I have droplets of water clinging on to my stubble and my right eye squints in the bright glare of the clouds overhead.

'I've actually stopped on the way down because I was having a bit of a duel with an English guy on the way up. He overtook me while I was taking a photo—' sniff – 'while riding and having a swig of water. Actually, I think I was eating a sweet – a Haribo – and it got me a bit breathless. I had to overtake him and so I thought I'd pay my respects on the way down. It's very misty and cold. My fingers are freezing as I hold this. I'm going to pan round so you can see what I mean. You can barely see the bottom and we're right up in the clouds. But there's a break every now and then – and look, here's a car . . . '

I turn the camera round to show two cars driving by and into the fog up ahead, rotating the camera until it returns to the memorial and the trinkets adorning the steps in front of the granite plaque. Bizarrely, there's a rather racy black-and-white shot of a blonde model amid all the signed stones and plastic memorabilia. It strikes me only too late that I should have had a rummage around those countless ex-votos adorning Simpson's grave. If ever one were to chance upon a vial of Pot Belge then surely it would be here. People leave kisses for Oscar Wilde, metro tickets for Serge Gainsbourg and spliffs for Jim Morrison. Surely it only follows that cycling groupies would bring amphetamines for Tommy?

'I'm tempted to leave my Ragpicker cap but it's quite dear to me,'

I say. 'Tyler Hamilton actually complimented me on it when we met at a talk in London. I suppose I could leave my bidon but it seems somewhat disrespectful to offer Tom Simpson, of all people, a bottle that isn't filled with brandy . . . Right, time to head on down for a coffee. Over and out.'

Having exited the cloud and passed the sweeping corner where fans, presumably from the Netherlands, have scrawled the names of all seventeen Dutch riders from the last Tour, I'm just approaching the Chalet Reynard when I catch sight of someone who looks like an extremely pained version of Eleri riding up the mountain. She's followed by a figure with an uncanny resemblance to Melbourne John, were he ten years older. He's even borrowed John's garish kit. All in all, there's enough evidence to convince me that they are not lookalikes but the real people. It's baffling because they left Mazan well before me, and I procrastinated with a strung-out lunch-cum-multi-media-presentation in Bédoin, yet I have no recollection of passing them on the way up. It all becomes clear when I enter the cafe and see Bernadette, Camilla and Alan huddled around a table, tucking into a huge, communal crêpe slathered with Nutella. I offer my congratulations.

'We haven't made it there yet,' says Bernadette. 'We got lost before we even started the climb.' It turns out that all of them, except Alan, took the wrong exit out of Bédoin and rode halfway along the lower road to Malaucène before realizing their error. This detour, funnily enough, saved them from being rained upon on the way up. Eleri and John decided to press on while the other girls had nipped in for a break when they spotted Alan, who had already made it to the top, warming his fingers around a mug of hot chocolate. Being Australian and macho to the extreme, Alan is in full summer kit, bereft of both leg and arm warmers. His lips are blue and his body is twitching in a series of chilled spasms. We decide to team up for the descent while the others head off in the opposite direction.

I don't know Alan but there's every suggestion that he's a dab hand at cycling. His Giant bike must weigh less than one of his bulging thighs, while he's got a special, expensive-looking saddle with a front tip that, either for reasons of aero-dynamism or to grant extra overhang for his crown jewels, droops suggestively as if in need of some Viagra. Perhaps this is the kind of seat that particularly well-endowed men use to avoid unnecessary frottage? Or men who wish to give that impression. Whatever the case, it has the word 'Pro' emblazoned across it and no doubt cost more than Alan's return flight to Sydney. Once we get riding, proof of his prowess becomes apparent when he effortlessly glides clear on the descent. There I am, admiring the quite beautiful effect of condensation evaporating off the road in the mid-afternoon sun, which has thoughtfully decided to put in another appearance, and he's storming ahead, throwing caution to the lessening wind and – oh my God, he's overcooked that bend! Alan veers right into the path of an oncoming car and needs to ride off the road and into a layby to avoid a collision. Phew, that was a close one.

Now most sane people would use this episode as a stark reminder of how fortunes can change in a flash. Alan was no doubt showing off a bit, pushing things a smidgin too hard, as any alpha male would do when trying to impress a rookie. The crazy thing is, Alan could have pretty much done anything this side of crashing to impress me on a descent. I don't do downhill riding. I'm a pansy with the bike-handling skills of Raimundo Rumšas's mother-in-law on a wet day and without her stash of EPO (which is her own, of course, and not in any way that of her professional bike-riding son-in-law, whose form has suddenly gone through the roof). Seeing Alan almost go through the windscreen of a car should have been an invitation to wear out my brake pads even more than I'm already doing.

*Me posing in my garish Hannibal kit ahead of the first proper stage.*

*Team Hannibal (L–R): Bob, John, Kay, Bernadette, Sharon, Terry and Eros Poli.*

Wax on, hair and tan off.

The misty approach to the Turó de l'Home climb on my warm-up ride.

Regrouping at a roadside church during the opening stage in Catalonia.

A quick dip in the sea at L'Escala.

Vermouth o'clock: overlooking the Boadella reservoir near Darnius.

Trees ravaged by a forest fire line the open road ahead of the Pyrenean foothills.

The lofty ruins of the Cathar castle at Peyrepertuse.

The huge marble bull bust at Missègre.

Fat dogs Cerise and Elliot at Carcassonne's Hotel Montmorency.

Taking in 'the best view in Europe' at the medieval town of Olargues.

Chilly picnic atop the Col de Salettes in Languedoc-Roussillon.

Spotting my name on the road signs.

Belly flop into the Hérault: Tom Daley, eat your heart out.

Mont Ventoux looms on the horizon beyond the vineyards of Provence.

*Clouds gather over the Giant of Provence ahead of my 'rest day' ascent.*

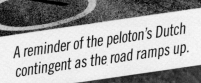

*A reminder of the peloton's Dutch contingent as the road ramps up.*

*The view wasn't the best from the cloud-clad summit.*

*Paying my respects to the late Tom Simpson on the way down.*

A lush valley in the Drôme.

Entering tunnels in the Gorges des Gats,
where Hannibal was ambushed.

Freewheeling down the sweeping descent of the
Col de Prémol in the Alpine foothills.

The clouds break over the Église Saint-Ferréol at Dutch Corner.

Sheep hamper my progress on the barren Col de Sarenne.

Celebrating my daring double ascent as night falls.

Narrow switchbacks on the treacherous descent of the Sarenne.

Instead, quite inexplicably, the competitive spirit in me suddenly thinks it's a chance to show him what I'm made of. Knowing that he's now behind me, I actually speed up, edging above 70 kmph. Worse still, I decide that on today of all days – during this long, slippery descent with limbs both chilly and weary – I will finally try and face my fear of riding on the drops.

Shifting your hands to the lower part of the curved handlebars is meant to give you more control. It's how all accomplished riders tackle descents because the brakes are more responsive and you can improve aero-dynamism. But I've always found cornering hard in this streamlined position. I feel more vulnerable and I get the jitters. Because this is Ventoux, where big bends are minimal, I can understand my logic at giving it a go. But I've clearly forgotten about that hidden chicane in the rock-walled gully midway through the forest section. I exit the first bend still carrying too much speed from the long straight, and on seeing a tight and enclosed corner I panic and squeeze tight on the brakes. My back wheel locks and I'm almost thrown from my bike, like a cowboy in a rodeo. Somehow I manage to keep my balance but I'm still going too fast. A sudden instinctive clenching on the brakes has the same result, locking my back wheel once again.

I've seen this happen before in professional races – most vividly when Joseba Beloki was catapulted from his bike in that famous accident which saw Lance Armstrong take evasive action by riding off the road and through a field. Nine times out of ten, when the back wheel locks at speed, the rider is dispatched into a world of pain (Beloki broke his femur in two places, not to mention his elbow and wrist). If you do survive the sudden jolt then often a crash happens when you skid as you try to correct your course while still travelling at speed. Perhaps it's because I witnessed a similar episode just minutes earlier with Alan, but I don't do the natural thing. Instead, I ride out the hairy moment, maintaining a straight line as if responding to a car skidding on ice. It's a massive stroke of luck that no vehicle is coming up the hill as I ride across this blind corner, over the other side of the road, and into a pile of rubble that has gathered on the roadside. I come to a standstill just inches in front of a sheer rock face. Somehow I'm unhurt and, even more surprisingly, I haven't knackered my wheels. In fact, if I just get back on to the road now I might even be able to pretend to Alan that none of this happened, because he still hasn't emerged from the chicane himself.

This whole chain of events is played out in less than ten seconds. Ten seconds which could have turned a triumphant day into utter hell. Ten seconds which could have ended my Grand Tour before even reaching the Alps proper. I ride on, both shivering with the cold and trembling with nerves.

'What happened there?' Alan asks. Dammit, he noticed. 'You entered those corners way ahead of me. Were those your skid marks?' It's the kind of question I'm used to being asked in a very different context. I can only nod in the affirmative.

The remainder of the ride back to Mazan with Alan is a less frenetic and more contemplative affair. Having come so close to derailing my forthcoming march over the Alps and on to Rome I find myself thinking of Hannibal, who sensibly gave the Ventoux a miss. The previous night, Sam had given us one of his historical crammers by reading out Livy's description of Hannibal and his martial attributes. Hannibal and I were clearly not cut from the same cloth. For instance, Livy talks of the perfect unison of the young general's 'power to command and readiness to obey'. I'm pretty useless at doing either, not least taking orders from Sam or Dylan as they try to rein in my constant tardiness and propensity to ride off and do my own thing.

But me and Hannibal certainly shared some qualities. Livy speaks of his 'recklessness in courting danger' and his 'superb tactical ability' – both of which I have displayed on the bike today. Hannibal was 'indefatigable both physically and mentally' and 'able to endure with equal ease excessive heat or cold'. Mont Ventoux certainly forced me to prove my worth in these domains too. Hannibal was able to 'sleep anywhere, even with the common soldiers on the ground'. But would he have coped sharing a tent with Terry? I think not. While 'his clothing in no way distinguished him from other young men of his age [. . .] his accoutrements and horses were eye-catching'. Likewise, to many bystanders my daily donning of Lycra makes me inseparable from the other riders of our group – although it has to be said, the toxic shorts and rusty top have not gone unnoticed, while my own generously proportioned steed, with its sweet pouch and saddlepack, is a bit special.

'Mounted or unmounted he was unequalled as a fighting man, always first to attack, always last to leave the field.' Well, this has me down to a tee. Once, like Hannibal, I shrugged off an early injury in Spain (my shoddy knees to his speared thigh), I proved to be a belligerent bike rider, attacking my rivals with gusto (and often from a strategically sound position to their rear). And with all these extra loops, more often than not I'm last to arrive at our destination.

It was with a sense of both accomplishment and relief that I rolled back into the Marquis de Sade's old back garden and bade farewell to Alan, who was returning to Avignon to meet up with the other riders on his corresponding tour. I was not staying at the château with the majority of our group, but instead at the nearby Hôtel le Siècle (probably where Keira Knightley's poorer guests shacked up after the wedding). On spotting me hanging up some dripping jerseys out of the window, Martin, the manager of the hotel and owner of a nose that could have hosted its own ski-jumping competition, urged me to bring down my dirty kit so he could wash and dry it properly. We got talking.

When the Tour came to town earlier in the summer, Martin's hotel had been filled with race officials with the exception of one Belgian couple who had booked their room months in advance, before the 2013 Tour route had been announced. On the day of the race, the road to Ventoux was closed very early because of the 800,000 fans lining the route, somewhat throwing a spanner in the spokes of the couple's plans to head up the mountain. 'The organizers pulled some strings and allowed them to ride up to the summit in the broom wagon so that they could take in the atmosphere,' Martin said. '*C'était un bon geste, n'est-ce pas?*'

The couple would have become very familiar with one rider's backside that day. Before the race had even reached the foot of Ventoux, Frenchman Jonathan Hivert had already spent a couple of hours riding behind the peloton. While Mark Cavendish and the other sprinters finished the stage in the gruppetto some 32 minutes down on Froome, Hivert came home on his own another 18 minutes later, having spent most of the afternoon simultaneously fending off the advances of the van and fighting against the current of inebriated fans making their way down the mountain in the belief that the show was all over.

'It was difficult for my morale. I did what I could, I hung on in to arrive within the limit just ahead of the broom wagon,' Hivert said, adding that it was 'going to be a real struggle to make it all the way to Paris'. Seeing that this was Bastille Day, it must have been all the more testing for Hivert, who already had rather tortuous memories of Ventoux: three years previously, on the Tour's last visit up *Le Géant*, Hivert was once again the day's lanterne rouge, trickling over the line a comparatively fast 26 minutes behind stage winner Juan Manuel Gárate. That day, the stage was around 80 kilometres shorter than stage 15 of the 2013 Tour, where the hardest and longest climb of the race came at the end of the race's lengthiest stage since 2000 – the year Armstrong beat a top ten of similarly juiced men in Lycra to Paris in an era that could only be described as golden were you referring to the urine samples that should have all come back as positive as the south end of a magnet.

By my reckoning, Hivert would have completed his 2013 Ventoux ascent just four minutes quicker than me, which underlines my coming of age as a cyclist. Indeed, it makes me almost as good as the Tour's worst climber on a day in which he gave me a 200-kilometre handicap. That's almost as flattering as riding the Paris–Roubaix route only slightly worse than the slowest Euskaltel rider in the peloton.

Spirits were high that evening as we enjoyed yet another banquet. The archaeological trio of Ted, Camilla and Eleri had moved on to new pastures, as had the hexed and vexed Michaela, but our dwindling numbers had been bolstered by Melbourne John, as well as another Australian, Roddy, a well-spoken cycling fanatic and corporate lawyer based in the United Arab Emirates. Both men would be with our group for the next week as we ventured over the Alps and into Italy. A trio of bruschetta with crab, gazpacho and tomato sorbet on a bed of crumbs got us started. Over exaggerated boasts of Ventoux heroics, we then tucked into our main of juicy cod fillet with pumpkin puree, baby girolle mushrooms and fig compote.

'We deserve this, don't we, Sharon?' said Terry, by now nicely sozzled.

'Did you take on the Giant as well?' asked Roddy, somewhat surprised.

'Oh no, don't be ridiculous. The only giant we took on was of the ice-cream variety after a leisurely afternoon ambling around Avignon. You have to make the most of your rest days – unlike these sadomasochists,' he said, pointing towards myself, Melbourne John and Bernadette.

Our conversation developed and that evening we covered quite a spectrum of topics, sweeping from the difficulties of endurance training in the UAE during Ramadan and the incorporation of figs into pretty much everything we'd been eating over the past few days – from breakfast jam right through to mountain snack and main course garnish. At some point, no doubt after too many a glass of local plonk from some place called Châteauneuf-du-Pape, Roddy regaled us with the idiosyncrasies of the sandy place he called home. 'There's a rampant homosexual scene in Dubai,' he said, apropos of nothing, before swiftly adding, 'so I've been told. I have never encountered it myself.'

My attention was ripped from a slightly underwhelming chocolate-themed dessert by a vibration in my pocket which relayed the welcome news that I had become an uncle for the second time. Normally you wouldn't want anything coming between you and a *mi-cuit au chocolat* but when a half-baked chocolate pudding is, well, full-baked and totally lacking the desired gooeyness that makes a truly marvellous *moelleux*, then one's allegiance doesn't half dwindle.

Besides, dessert was of no huge concern for someone whose second nephew was brought into this world on the day he so heroically scaled Mont Ventoux. I lay in bed that night comparing the contrasting sporting achievements of myself and my sister-in-law. While I had laboured away for the best part of an afternoon, pedalling through monsoons and metaphorical treacle, she had negotiated a few twists and turns of her own during an equally long and undulating slog. Our eventual crownings were followed by severe after-pains and we both no doubt lost a fair bit of weight – her sudden 9.8-pound shedding was admittedly really quite impressive. She did spend the whole day with her feet up in bed, though, so I reckoned I probably shaded it on balance. We're not all made to be hardcore extreme athletes, I mused as my unrestful rest day was finally put to rest.

# MAZAN TO BOURG D'OISANS

'SCHTOP, SCHTOP, SCHTOP!' THE SHORT, plump man with closely cropped hair and a black shirt sounded as if he were auditioning for the lead role in a Dutch beer commercial. 'Do you have no reshpect? I cannot believe what I am seeing.'

What he was seeing was Roddy's custom-made red and white Dario Pegoretti steel steed resting neatly against the front bumper of his matt black Range Rover.

'Do you think this car was made to have a bike against it? It'sh fucking unbelievable that yoush can have no reshpect like this.' As he splenetically rumbled forth, his South-east Asian trophy wife stood in the background, more concerned with filing her nails than entering the fray. Roddy, meanwhile, was on the other side of the Château de Mazan car park, filling up his water bottles.

'And schtill. . . none of you is moving the fucking bike,' he continued, his voice getting higher and his face redder. 'It'sh unbelievable! Schtop what you are doing and sort out this disreshpecht. Doesh my car look like a wall? Do I look like I don't care a fuck?

'Yesh, about time,' Mr Grolsch said as Sam – the only one of our group not in stitches – liberated the car bumper from the heavy burden of the bike. The vehicle had a Swiss numberplate, which was odd because the guy didn't sound Swiss, nor did he strike me as a purveyor of neutrality. 'The funny thing,' Sam told me as he pushed the bike away, 'is that this is probably worth more money than his set of wheels.'

Without any attempt to smooth things over, the man and his lady friend (I reckon she had been hired for the weekend; surely no one would be married to such a specimen) got in the car and slammed the doors. Having driven to the exit, he realized that he needed to press a button to open the double gates. Rather sheepishly, he looked at me.

'Unbelievable,' I said. 'Do I look like a porter?' Before he could get away I offered up some friendly advice: 'Schtop, schtop . . . You must do up your seat belt. Reshpecht the road!'

Roddy later admitted that he knew it was a mistake to rest his bespoke bike against the car – but part of me sensed that it was a subconscious decision to align something of extreme worth with something else in the same price bracket. My own scratched, muddy Felt frame leant against a soft pine bush, while the others had propped their bikes against the wall or our van. It seems logical that Roddy would have seen the pristine bumper of the scratch-less 4x4 and deemed it a worthy resting place for his pride and joy.

Like Melbourne John, Roddy also had an indirect link towards yours truly. It was while visiting friends in London earlier in the spring that he had picked up a copy of *Cyclist* and read the Last Gasp column where I sought out training tips from a personal coach. Off the back of the article, Roddy had contacted the same foul-mouthed London-based coach for advice on training out in Dubai. Together they came up with some kind of routine to get Roddy back into shape ahead of his week with us in the Alps – although this had been somewhat derailed by his demanding work schedule as a corporate lawyer, not to mention his living in a place where the only thing remotely resembling a hill was a man-made indoor ski park.

Although out of shape and slightly tubby (fair game for a man of 50), Roddy certainly looked the part. Besides his pristine Pegoretti and brand new race wheels, Roddy wore a pair of top-of-the-range cycling shoes in which he never took more than a couple of steps: as soon as he dismounted, they would be whipped off, leaving him to potter about in socks. Roddy was also a man of style, eschewing modern trade team jerseys and only sporting vintage classics from yesteryear: the iconic La Vie Claire kit in the Piet Mondrian-inspired rectangular red, blue, yellow and grey colour system, from the 1980s; a bright orange San Pellegrino jersey with a white sash; a black-and-white Carpano kit with the Italian flag. Judged on attire alone, Roddy was a Grand Tour winner (although Bob gave him a run for his dirhams with a limited-edition Black Dog outfit, including matching socks, which was unique in its peculiarity).

There's a wonderful yet rather embarrassing series of photos of me posing with new boys John and Roddy at our coffee stop in Sault on the first official morning of the Alpine leg. Roddy stands (in his socks) on the right in his La Vie Claire get-up and full leg warmers (coming from Dubai, he suffered bitterly from the cold and was still recovering from a bout of flu, which may or may not have been an excuse for his constant strife in the saddle). John grins on the left in his replica Orica-GreenEdge kit from the Australian team's first season back in 2012.

(In the short time I've been a rider I have always observed one rule:

never wear the kit of a current professional cycling team. By decking himself out in the green, yellow and black of GreenEdge, John, bless him, allied himself to the portly chaps in full Team Sky garb doing laps of Richmond Park in London. Making matters worse, he still earnestly wore one of the long-since-parted yellow Livestrong bracelets so ubiquitous during Lance Armstrong's duplicitous reign. Tut tut . . . Unless, of course, John was an unlikely master of irony.)

Finally, I'm standing in the middle, towering over both newcomers, my slim waist more or less in line with the top arc of their respective mini-paunches. I'm wearing a dark blue kit with pink, green and white horizontal stripes – an outfit designed by my photographer friend George, who has a side project producing his Ragpicker brand of cycling attire – stylish, but considerably cheaper, than the Rapha gear that adorns the shoulders of most fair-weather City-boy cyclists. Stuffed down my leg warmers are a couple of cubes of ice numbing both my sore knees. In my right hand is a can of iced tea. And pointing directly to said chilled beverage is . . . my willy. For yes, through the thin Lycra shorts you can see the (some would hopefully say generous) outline of my todger, standing to attention at around 10.30 a.m. The picture articulated the overriding problem with wearing bib shorts that are not black: they're about as effective in covering up one's trouser truncheon as a couple of strips of cling film.

Unintentional exhibitionism bore down on me for the entire duration of the tour. It led to the kind of constant stress that would have sent some professional sportsmen trotting home with their tail between their legs. There are few worse things than interacting all day with a bunch of people knowing that they can all see – and no doubt, behind your back, are speculating on the unfortunate visibility of – your privates. Worse still was the 'performance-enhancing' effect of such a phenomenon when played out inside my baggy lime green shorts. Like Harry Potter's cloak, these shorts boasted powers of invisibility. Sadly, it was the shorts themselves that were near transparent, not their contents. They were exactly the kind of shorts I had feared others in our group might wear, and was grateful that they had not.

Whatever happens in later life, there's a photo that Bob took of me from one of our opening days in Spain that will come back to haunt me. Shown on TV, the picture would have to appear after the watershed. Not content with displaying my flagrant groinal delineation (2 p.m. this time), the photo also showcases, right on the tip of the bendy bulge, a spot where the green of the shorts has become darker – the kind of spot that could well have been made by a post-urinary seepage of the sort whose absorption wouldn't have showed up on black Lycra (the colour of choice for all sensible cyclists).

Photos of this ilk were regrettably two a penny, so to speak. Photoshop's red-eye correction tool became the only possible, sadly retrospective, course of action. It was the male equivalent of being a lingerie model with a permanent case of camel toe. I felt solidarity with female celebrities caught, in flagrante delicto, exiting cars while flashing their undies, or worse. For something that was an all too apparent reminder of my manhood, it was curiously emasculating.

Taking up cycling had sadly seen off the days where my genitalia were my penetralia. I tried everything to combat this on-going budgie struggle. The uncomfortable 'downward wrap' approach; the 'bundle it up in a ball' tactic; the 'straight up and pull the jersey down' stratagem. None of them worked. In the end I had to resort to simply holding my hands or, better still, my helmet – my *cycling* helmet – in a position of diversional integrity.

Once, I brought up this little issue with Terry and he just laughed. 'I would love to be in your position,' he said. 'Be proud. If you have it, flaunt it.' Which is all very well until you hobble round a corner in your cleats and find yourself amid a group of children roughly waist height and then have to beg tacit forgiveness from their parents by a meek and apologetic look in your eye as the youngest of the kids – the one afraid of green snakes – starts to cry.

By any account, Monday mornings don't get much better than a breezy ride along a vertiginous corniche overlooking a limestone canyon that the world seems to have forgotten. I thought of my friends back at home on their morning commute, at that moment possibly crammed into the Tube or taking on deadly HGVs and double-decker buses on Boris Bikes through central London. For me, the prospect of the working week as we set off from Mazan on the scenic road to Sault was an appealing one: my office would be the Alps and my desk a bicycle. There'd be no Prêt sandwich wolfed down for lunch while replying to emails and overdosing on the *Mail Online*'s sidebar of shame; instead there would be sizeable picnics overlooking cliffs and peaks and meadows, discussing the ocular fodder of the previous few hours while trying to ensure that my bib shorts didn't ruin the appetite of my companions. Put simply: life was good and couldn't have been further from the usual framework of busyness, deadlines, noise, crowds and routine.

Often – while creeping down Oxford Street on a Saturday or queuing up for an easyJet flight to Las Palmas or, perhaps, when stumbling upon a 'reality' show on TV – I am reminded of Jean-Paul Sartre's wily assertion that 'hell is other people'. Well, it's a bit late now, but perhaps Monsieur de Beauvoir should have considered extending his existence beyond the absurdist realms of his Rive Gauche coterie and taken in the glorious isolation of the phenomenal Drôme Provençale and Vaucluse regions of France, where sweet-smelling lavender fields stretch out to bring a linear purple hue to lush valleys between mountain ridges and rolling hills.

In Sartre's eyes, the Gorges de la Nesque that Monday would have been rather heavenly – not simply because of a grandiosity that bordered on the biblical, but for the presence of just one other soul: a smiling old man with silver hair out on his daily morning spin. That he had silver hair was of no doubt for he was not wearing a helmet, these being quiet roads devoid of traffic. The only vehicle we passed along the whole of the gorge belonged to a gardener, who we later saw meticulously trimming a hedge with Lynchian verve next to a small honey farm, the only building on the entire 18-kilometre stretch of road.

Through his bushy moustache, the old boy bade me '*Bonjour*' before effortlessly peeling away on the gradual gradient on a vintage Merckx single-speed. Despite the crisp morning, he wore nothing but a plain regular kit – unlike Terry, who by now took to the start each morning in skiing gloves and jacket; or Bob, whose pasty old mountaineer's legs, criss-crossed at the knees in 'magic tape', remained perpetually under wraps, despite his bold assertions of being 'climate neutral'. Like most keen cyclists of his age from the countries we visited, the old Frenchman had a pair of tanned, sturdy legs long versed in transporting a tummy that betrayed a soft-spot for his wife's excellent cooking. Later on, before the first of a series of four stone tunnels cut through the overhanging cliff, I passed him on his way back; he had presumably ridden to the end of the gorge and was now freewheeling home to coffee and croissants.

Part of me felt a little embarrassed to be overtaken by a moustachioed grandpa with a one-gear bike not overly dissimilar to those used by the early trailblazers of the Tour at the turn of the twentieth century. But this was effectively his garden path and I was taking it all in, stopping occasionally in failed attempts to capture the canyon's muted splendour with the pixel paucity of my phone camera. Weary from my Ventoux escapade the day before, I still found the mornings cruel on my knees and so habitually rode off the back until I had warmed up and the painkillers had kicked in. Besides, I was trying to think of a joke I could tell the others at the coffee stop in Sault that didn't involve a punchline including the words 'pepper' or 'vinegar', worried that even I might not be able to conjure up a credible ruse featuring a donkey attack (or 'ass-sault').

One day later, as we rode up yet another empty gorge at the foot of our morning ascent of the Col de Prémol, I traded places on numerous occasions with a local rider decked out fully in the old white kit of the Française des Jeux team – the second time after I had slowed to chat to Bob about his two sons back in the States. The climb was getting steeper and a light headwind had now become pretty blustery.

'Do you reckon I can catch him again?' I asked Bob, gesturing towards the man, who was now about 100 metres out ahead.

'I know you can,' he replied.

How could I refuse to take up the gauntlet now? So I dug deep and duly swept past the lone escapee for the third time in less than half an hour. We uttered a few awkward pleasantries that soon, at the summit, would be repeated for a fourth time after I had stopped to await my prize from Bob (I had run out of ibuprofen and so Bob – a veritable mobile pharmacy – assumed the mantle of makeshift soigneur until I replenished my stocks).

Since leaving Mazan and the nursery slopes of Mont Ventoux, the Giant of Provence had still cast a shadow on our pedal strokes – just as she had done on the approach to Avignon days earlier. From the top of the Gorges de la Nesque, the white dome of the summit loomed on the horizon – and it returned to our gaze as we edged out of Sault and on numerous other occasions as we rode over successive peaks of the low Alpine foothills. Looking south from the summit of the main climb of the day, the blissfully secluded Col du Soubeyrand (994 metres at 7 per cent), our eyes were naturally drawn to the geological wonder of the Rocher de l'Aiguier, a giant set of parallel rock fins some 90 metres tall and several hundred metres long that rise above the hamlet of Bellecombe-Tarendol like some kind of earthly UFO. But gazing beyond the lavender fields and over the black volcanic formations that characterize the first of many horizons, we saw the tiny upside-down syringe jutting up from what appears to be a snow-clad summit.

Before turning my back on Mont Ventoux for the final time, it struck me that Alan and his friends from the Sydney bike club Velosophy, who were being led by Dylan in their corresponding tour, were probably up there at the very same moment, basking in sunshine and taking in the Provençal panorama a day after the vista no-show that capped my own ascent. With Dylan and Sam separated into two different groups, extra guides with expert local knowledge had been drafted in. James, who came with us, and Mark, who became Dylan's deputy in the second Alpine group, were seasoned resort workers from Morzine, where they skied in the winter and rode bikes in the summer. Given that some of the Antipodean members of our group had no first-hand experience of the Alps, it was a bonus to have someone like James who could regale them with stories from his five years living at altitude.

Hannibal, too, used a similar tactic when entering the Alpine foothills, enrolling a chap called Magilus to act as a guide and ambassador. Magilus was chief of the Boii, a Gallic tribe from northern Italy distinguished by their drunkenness, who boosted Carthaginian morale no end by boasting of the fertile delights of the Po valley and promising Hannibal support from the disgruntled Padane Gauls, who were already rebelling – to devastating effect – against Roman attempts to subdue their region. Hannibal had originally enlisted Magilus's help by sending on envoys to shore up alliances beyond the mountains – in the same way that a team leader in cycling might order his domestiques up the road in a break to pave the way for his own decisive attack. The Boii and their allies the Insubres were renowned for their savage appearance, blood-curdling war cries, and general ferocity – enhanced by their perpetual insobriety. In short: the last thing an invading army would want to have to face after crossing Europe's most formidable natural barrier.

Knowing that the tribes were both accommodating and universally in favour of an uprising against Rome came as a massive bonus for Carthage. Indeed, one of the reasons Publius Cornelius Scipio was so slow to send his army to face Hannibal in Spain in the first place was that he had been caught up trying to put down a rebellion of these very same tribes. And now, having chanced upon Hannibal's army when popping into Marseille to refuel on pastis en route to Empúries, Scipio had decided that his best bet was to return to Italy to defend the Po valley.

Keen to keep ahead of the enemy, Hannibal and his men marched quickly through the Alpine foothills – although it took his army, which stretched out for 20-odd miles, six days to cover the kind of distance we were covering on bikes in just one. At first, things went well, with Hannibal's army managing to reach the foot of the Alps without opposition. One canny piece of diplomacy saw our hero successfully adjudicate a kingship dispute between two warring brothers (think Andy and Frank Schleck coming to blows over who should lead their Trek team). Hannibal took the side of Brancus, the older brother, and helped reinstate him to the throne – a move which garnered him support in both supplies and protection.

But things didn't entirely go the way of the Carthaginians. Shortly after Magilus had returned home to see his Boiis, Hannibal found his army under attack in a region ruled by the fierce Allobroges tribe. It is thought that the ambush happened in what is today known as the Gorges des Gats, which we rode through on stage 11 of our journey, the day after leaving Mazan. It's an obvious place for an ambush: the road (which was probably a mere track back then) hugs the side of the twisting Bez river and is flanked on both sides by increasingly high cliffs. Even at midday, when we rode through, sunlight fights to reach the bottom of the gorge owing to overhanging rocks and numerous narrow tunnels. As you can imagine, it's the kind of road that greets drivers with a series of those red triangular signs depicting rocks of various sizes tumbling down cliffs. It's a shame they didn't have any of these warnings in 218 BC when the Allobroges rolled rubble from above and squashed all manner of living Carthaginian creatures – from unfortunate soldiers to baggage animals and livestock.

Hannibal, however, was playing double bluff. He had suspected an attack was coming and so led some of his best troops out of the gorge and above the enemy's position on a higher pass. From here he positioned his best archers on the overhang. With their backs to the cliff, the barbarians had nowhere to run and were picked off by arrows and stones, falling to their deaths and contributing to the general chasm of doom below. God knows what the neutral tribespeople further downstream thought when their drinking water turned red for a day.

Instead of having to sustain ourselves on an impromptu stew using fresh meat scraped off the rocks, once we emerged from the gorge we had the luxury of a delicious picnic lunch and took up position on a grassy verge overlooking the small hamlet of Glandage, at the foot of the Col de Grimone. The feeding of around 30,000 men was a huge undertaking for Hannibal, whose army relied on the fertility of the land and the goodwill of local tribes to keep the Alpine wolf from the collective Carthaginian door. We, on the other hand, simply relied on our guides to ensure a daily picnic hamper in sync with the lofty standards to which we had become accustomed, helping us to pedal on until our next gluttonous evening bonanza.

So when James – at the eleventh hour and on his first day behind the wheel – was forced to put on a hasty spread when our restaurant plans fell through on stage 10, he was always going to be up against it. Little did he know that over the course of the previous nine days, Dylan and Sam had been consistently raising the bar, adding another goat's cheese here, an apple tart there, perhaps a fourth variety of charcuterie or some fresh strawberries. The standard had already reached quite epic proportions when James – preoccupied with trying to locate Roddy, who was feeling under the weather and needed to hop in the van – was summoned to pick up lunch for the entire group. Cue what became . . . the First Picnic War.

Of course, it didn't help that it was already well past 1 p.m. and we were in a sleepy valley in the Drôme where every town seemed to be shut for the off-season. Nor did it help that James wasn't au fait with our fussy eating habits. When sustenance did arrive, you could almost see Bernadette's nose crinkle up in displeasure at having to even contemplate a ready-made sandwich accompanied by a packet of Bolognese-flavoured crisps. It was clear that there was disgruntlement in the ranks. Had Bernadette been part of Hannibal's army, desertion could well have been on the cards.

Luckily for James (and us), that evening's meal more than made up for any supposed calorie deficit. Our first two nights on the apron of the Alps were spent in La Motte Chalancon and Mens – two small rural towns largely in the middle of nowhere. After a stream of plush accommodation, our beds for both nights were in two simple auberges without restaurants, forcing us, like Hannibal, to seek help from the locals for our evening sustenance. In what was a welcome shake-up from our usual lavish dinners out, we had successive nights eating as guests in people's homes – the first in a rustic farmhouse with a local farmer and his wife, and the second in a wonderfully renovated seventeenth-century manor house owned by a former world record speed skier.

'Just wait until you try the boar stew from the farm we're going to tonight,' Terry told us as we tried to hold down those Bolognese crisps ahead of the Col du Soubeyrand.

'How do you know we'll be having boar stew?' I asked.

'Well, it's what we had last year,' Terry replied, as if logic dictated an omnipresence of boar bourguignon.

'I spoke to the owner,' said Sam. 'It's not boar stew this year, I'm afraid.'

'Oh, no. That's the only reason I came back,' said Terry, gloomily.

'But don't worry, Terry. I mentioned the stew and they may do it as a side dish.'

'Ah, Sam. You made my day.'

Dining at the peasant's table – and a foreigner's one at that – may sound like Nigel Farage's worst nightmare but the expression *table paysanne* doesn't hold the derogatory undertones of its literal English translation. This is how the French describe the arrangement whereby outsiders can enjoy a home-cooked meal in a traditional setting alongside their hosts. In many ways, Benjamin and Angelina Mroz were very much modern-day peasants in that their livelihood largely depended on the land they cultivated and the livestock they raised. If Angèle's cooking was the star of the show then Ben's input cannot have been underestimated. The large wooden conservatory in which we dined that night had been built by Ben last winter while his wife was supplementing their income with a season-long job at a nearby ski resort.

Ben's biggest duty on the farm was to tend to his thirty Limousines cows – although he was probably down to twenty-nine and a half after our carnivorous showing. A warm beef terrine accompanied by a zingy courgette flan and a liberally dressed green salad got things off to a promising start. This was followed by grilled strips of beef (*à gogo* – all you can eat) with some rustic roast potatoes and a hearty ratatouille – not to forget Terry's side of wild boar stew, which certainly lived up to the billing (although predictably debased the air quality of our room later that evening). A local cheeseboard fired further jabs at our almost sated appetite before a prune compote and chocolate brownie delivered the knock-out blow.

Make no mistake – this wasn't haute cuisine. It was good, honest, no-frills food – *à la bonne franquette,* as the French would say – and just what was called for after another hard day in the saddle. Everything we ate at the Table Angèle – besides the local cheeses – was *faîtes à la maison:* either raised by Ben at the Ferme Mroz or grown in his wife's vegetable garden. Glorious in its simplicity, the meal was also superb value for money at just €20 a head. The interaction with local people also broke up the routine of formal hotel and restaurant dining, giving at least James and me – the only French speakers – a different perspective on the region we were riding through. The Mrozes were a lovely, hard-working couple with strong country accents and a staunchly parochial mindset. Seeing that they had not even heard of Mens, our destination for the next day, it would have been no surprise had they admitted never to have set foot in Paris.

Yves and Nanine, on the other hand, were certainly privy to the high society of the capital. In fact, the whole set-up at La Maison de Bonthoux the next evening couldn't have been more different. On entering the well-kept garden of the refurbished four-hundred-year-old manor, a smell of melted cheese waylaid my progression into the main room, where the rest of our group was enjoying an aperitif. Inside a small outbuilding a white-haired man in an apron, blue shirt and chinos was standing over a stone oven where a potato gratin bubbled away alongside a roasting leg of lamb. The aroma was as ambrosial as the sky on the horizon was red. This was Yves, our host for the night, and about as peasantly as Hugh Bonneville.

While watching the sun set over the mountains, we talked about the time he spent in England as a student in his early twenties ('Ah, those were the days – the local women were so *charmantes*'). For six, clearly memorable, months in the Swinging Sixties, Yves lived in Dorking and said he remembered rambling on Box Hill, the slight mound that featured heavily in the London 2012 Olympic road race route (and which since has become a cycling rite of passage for hobby riders in the area). Yves was no stranger to the Olympics: once the world record holder in speed skiing, he played a starring role in the opening ceremony of the 1968 Winter Games in Grenoble, and counts among his good friends the skiing legend Jean-Claude Killy. When I introduced myself properly to Yves he laughed and beckoned me round to the back garden where a large vintage red tractor had pride of place.

Pointing towards two donkeys grazing in the field yonder, he said: 'That's our Félix, over there, with Margot.' It was the first time I'd met another ass called Felix.

We joined the others for a glass of white wine and a nibble of some of Nanine's home-made pissaladière, which, while sounding about as appetizing as a pair of my bib shorts, is actually an exquisite Provençal pizza-style focaccia topped with onions, olives and anchovies. Nanine further spoiled us with an innovative cold soup of cucumber, courgette and guacamole, which was so tasty I had a second helping. We then transferred to the table for Yves's pièce de résistance: the succulent lamb and sizzling gratin, which was cheesy enough to warrant a second and third portion.

Following a call of nature, James remarked that there were lots of old photos of propeller planes up on the walls of the loo. 'Ah yes, it's because I am a qualified pilot. It's just a little hobby,' said Yves, whose other hobbies no doubt included snowshoe biathlon, hot-air ballooning and Arctic polo. That Yves could handle a joy stick was no surprise. Merely talking to the man was enough to ascertain that he was clearly a bit of a *bon viveur* who had probably enjoyed all the trimmings that came with being relatively famous and at the top of his game in an extreme sport which was all about speed and taking risks. Nanine must surely have been the last in a very long line of female admirers. There must have been a time when Yves had to put his speed skiing into practice simply to evade the ladies queuing up round the block. Even now, in his seventh decade, he clearly still had it.

Dessert – a creamy pear flan and some chocolate cake – was followed by a cheeseboard boasting three goat offerings and a zesty Bleu du Vercors. No donkey cheese from Margot, though, which was unfortunate as apparently, preposterous though it may sound, donkey cheese from a particular farm in Serbia is actually the most expensive cheese on the planet: the white, crumbly, Manchego-style 'pule' costs £1,000 per kilo and all known supplies of it belong to tennis ace Novak Djokovic, an unlikely cheese-hoarder if ever there was one.

Serbia is also responsible for a donkey-milk liqueur described by one food critic as blending 'Italian Limoncello with a slice of Roquefort'. In the absence of such a frightful fusion, we settled for a ferociously strong prune liqueur, which burned the back of our throats as Yves and Nanine talked about their three sons. The oldest was a restaurateur, the youngest a ski instructor, and the middle son none other than David Vincent, a former world champion snowboarder, who now, aged 42, lives a quiet life with his family as a beekeeper.

As we said our goodbyes following the meal, we were given a pot of David's honey. It made an excellent accompaniment to the innumerable varieties of goat's cheese that we sampled on subsequent picnics during the high Alps. A sweet touch to the, ahem, fromarginal gains that were the cornerstone of Team Hannibal's pie-in-the-sky approach to cycling.

Talking of picnics, our second-day lunch in Glandage – procured by Sam, whereby avoiding a Second Picnic War – served the dual purpose of showing James just how we rolled while compensating for his previous failure to *couper la moutarde*: a tomato and avocado salad, as well as fresh peaches and olives, complemented the usual array of hams, cheeses, salamis and baguettes (doughy in the middle and crispy on the outside).

'OK, now I see why you guys weren't so excited about my lunch yesterday,' he duly noted. More than suitably replenished, we made our way on to the Col de Grimone – at 1,318 metres, the highest climb of the trip so far for those unindustrious souls who had opted out of Mont Ventoux. (Incidentally, it was also some 400 metres less lofty than the Turó de l'Home climb I had tackled in harebrained isolation on our opening day warm-up back in Spain.) It's a truly scenic climb with a testing maximum gradient of around 9 per cent. I started well back but timed my surge to perfection, reeling in the early pace-setters Bob, Bernadette and Melbourne John with ample time to stop, take some photos, and cross the summit in an invisible polka-dot jersey.

The Col de Grimone has been used just twice in Tour history, most recently in 2002 when Belgium's Axel Merckx, son of the great five-time winner Eddy, crossed the summit in pole position. That day, Merckx crested four out of five summits in the lead but faded on the final rise to Les Deux Alpes, finishing third behind Santiago Botero and Mario Aerts. (Botero's excessive testosterone level was once found to be almost five times the maximum level for normal people, but he was cleared by his national Colombian cycling federation after his doctor, a certain Eufemiano Fuentes, demonstrated Botero's natural aberrancy. As for Aerts, the Belgian was one of fifty-odd riders caught up – but never charged – in the infamous police raids on team hotels during the Giro one year earlier.) Merckx clearly had a soft spot for the Grimone, for he also crossed its summit with a lead of over a minute midway through a 219-kilometre stage in the 2005 Dauphiné before winning solo in Grenoble – his last major scalp before retiring.

While it must have opened many a bike-shaped door, trying to forge a riding career in the shadow of his legendary father must have been as hard as it was for Yves's sons to replicate their father's panache with the ladies. Merckx Junior was no wallflower – during a 14-year career he finished tenth in his debut Tour in 1998, became Belgian national champion and a Giro stage winner in 2000, and took bronze in the Athens Olympics of 2004 – but he was still somewhat eclipsed by a five-time Tour and Giro-winning father widely regarded as the most accomplished all-round cyclist to have graced the planet.

If Eddy was 'The Cannibal' then son Axel was at best a vegetarian who enjoyed the odd ham sandwich. (Those who wish to take into account his links with an infamous pharmacy in Bologna and his subsequent 'suspicious' blood test from the 1998 Tour can probably downgrade his status to vegan; either way, it wasn't as if Axel was anorexic.) Instead of trying to rival his father's exploits, Merckx Junior cannily vowed to make his own mark by achieving things his father never did – such as win the Paris–Tours classic or a stage atop Alpe d'Huez.

He failed miserably on both accounts – his highest finish in the final classic of the season being fortieth in 1996 and his best effort on the Alpe seeing him trickle home almost three minutes in arrears in 2006. But that Olympic medal was a feat that eluded his illustrious father, while Axel *did* become the first Merckx to take second place in a Tour stage finishing in the cartoon capital of Angoulême (a victory of sorts).

Both father and son were – still are – very close to Lance Armstrong. Axel's career started in the same Motorola team as the Texan, and from 1992 to 1996, Eddy, who opened a bike factory in Italy after retiring, supplied equipment to the American team. Indeed, both Axel and Lance shared the same private trainer in the form of a certain Michele Ferrari, the controversial doctor who claimed he was personally introduced to Armstrong by Merckx Senior.

When Armstrong was diagnosed with testicular cancer, Papa Merckx was extremely supportive: not only was he by Armstrong's side when the Texan went for his first ride after leaving hospital, it was Merckx who convinced his friend that he had what it took to become a Tour winner once he was in remission. And when, in August 2012,

Armstrong announced that he would not contest the United States Anti-Doping Agency ruling that he had presided over 'the most sophisticated, professionalized and successful doping program that sport has ever seen', Merckx swam against the current to offer his support, claiming the whole case was 'deeply unjust'.

'Lance has been very correct all through his career. What more can he do? All the doping controls that he has done have come back negative,' Merckx told the Belgian press. He would have been 'crazy' to have done 'something so silly' during his career. For his part, Axel denied that Armstrong's refusal to contest the charges was an admission of guilt. His buddy was merely worn down by the constant allegations, he said. 'He's giving up because enough is enough. It's damaging his image, it's damaging his foundation, and I can see where he's coming from.'

Indeed he could, for Merckx Junior was the director of the Bontrager-Livestrong development team that was founded in 2009 thanks, in part, to Armstrong's long-standing ties with bike manufacturer Trek (Merckx still is director of the U23 squad although Livestrong has since been dropped as co-sponsor). Axel claimed he was speaking 'in the name of my family' when he reiterated his 'respect' for Armstrong. 'He's a friend and he remains my friend, and he's always going to be my friend. I'll stand by him when he's being bashed about.'

But it didn't take long for Merckx *père* to swim with the tide. Just one month later he had become both 'amazed' and 'sick' at the revelations surrounding Armstrong. 'I met Lance many times,' he said. 'He never spoke to me about doping, doctors or other things.' Peculiar, given their shared contact with Ferrari. When Armstrong finally went on the record and admitted doping his way to seven Tour victories to Oprah Winfrey in an exasperating TV interview in January 2013, an 'extremely disappointed' Merckx was in full digging mode – either that, or he was getting a little befuddled in his old age.

'I didn't see it coming,' he said. 'I don't see how he could get to that stage, to lie to everyone and all the time.' Despite his previous assertion that they never brought the issue up in conversation, he said that Armstrong 'often looked me right in the eyes when we discussed doping and obviously he said "no"'. Not mincing his words, the Cannibal claimed he, like so many others, had 'fallen into the trap' of taking Armstrong's word about his training methods. And yet, regarding the doping allegations that surrounded his own career, Merckx went down a familiar road, saying: 'I was clean, I know that. Every day there were controls at races.' Indeed there were – and Merckx tested positive for banned substances on three occasions, the first time resulting in his expulsion from the 1969 Giro (despite his claim that he'd been framed).

I remember bumping into Eddy in Adelaide in 2012 during the Tour Down Under. While fellow five-time Tour winner Bernard Hinault is an ever-present fixture on the podium at the more mainstream races such as the Tour and Paris–Nice, Merckx gamely puts in appearances in far-flung places like Qatar and Australia. Given his track record of being the Pelé of cycling when it comes to bungling a quote, perhaps the downgrading of the Cannibal to the poor-man's Badger for the twenty-first century is understandable. I made this observation in a blog entitled 'Nice guy Eddy' and incurred the wrath of one reader, who likened me to a 'hooligan who pisses on a memorial to a war they were never part of', which I thought was a bit extreme.

While awaiting the start of the evening criterium-style race through the streets of Adelaide that preceded the Tour Down Under proper, I asked Merckx who was his tip to win the season's week-long curtain raiser. His answer was Stuart O'Grady, who was turning out for the newly founded Australian GreenEdge team that was making its debut appearance in the pro peloton on home soil. When pressed on why he felt a veteran rider whose last victory came some four years previously could win this time, Merckx said: 'Because it would make a good story.' Unsurprisingly, O'Grady didn't win – but his team-mate and fellow Australian, Simon Gerrans, did.

What did make a good story, however, was the sudden retirement of O'Grady in 2013 following the completion of his record-equalling seventeenth Tour de France. While hardly a surprise (O'Grady was a fortnight away from turning 40), the Australian's decision was rather controversial for it came on the eve of the publication of a French Senate report detailing EPO use in the 1998 Tour. In the report, O'Grady was named alongside a cluster of riders – including Axel Merckx, incidentally – whose re-tested blood samples were deemed highly suspicious for EPO use. The same day, O'Grady confirmed that he had taken the blood booster prior to the '98 Tour – in which he won a stage and wore the yellow jersey for three days – but had been sufficiently scared by the fallout of the Festina scandal to press the eject button.

In short, O'Grady went down the Bill Clinton route of admitting to smoking just the once, but not liking the flavour, coughing when inhaling, and never trying it again. That's to say, he remained a non-smoker during his time at a Cofidis team fraught with doping innuendo in 2004; there was categorically no puffing on Bjarne Riis's pipe at Team CSC when he was transformed from a sprinter to a super-domestique often seen on the front of the peloton setting a savage pace up fierce climbs for his team leaders; no cigars, even, when O'Grady became the first Australian to win a major classic with a ballsy solo victory in the 2007 Paris–Roubaix. Essentially: giving the performance enhancers the cold shoulder actually enhanced his performance.

O'Grady's carefully measured confession days after Chris Froome's Tour win set the tone for other similar disclosures, most notably from Canada's Ryder Hesjedal, whose unexpected overall victory in the 2012 Giro was feted as a sign of a cleaner era for cycling. That narrative was somewhat skewered when Michael Rasmussen released his book and claimed that he had taught Hesjedal how to inject EPO back in his days as a mountain biker. Although Hesjedal did not confess until the publication of the book the following October, he had been aware that his case was being investigated since the turn of the year – which may explain his rather lacklustre results since being under the spotlight (illness and poor form forced him to withdraw one week into the defence of his Giro crown, while his seventieth place in the Tour was his lowest ever finish on a Grand Tour).

When Hesjedal did eventually confess he claimed he gave up doping after a solitary toke of the metaphorical cigarette. In the past decade – which had seen the Canadian ride at US Postal during the Armstrong era and Phonak during Floyd Landis's stewardship before joining the stringently anti-doping set-up at Garmin – Hesjedal had not used EPO. In winning the Giro nine years after putting his 'mistakes' behind him, Hesjedal was asking the cycling community to believe that he had joined the exclusive club of riders who quit doping in order to win a Grand Tour clean.

To paraphrase Eddy Merckx – all these things do indeed make good stories.

Crossing the Col de Grimone inspired a mixture of excitement and trepidation. The view from the top is nothing short of spectacular, with a lush valley rolling towards a row of pointy, pine-covered peaks. But it's what lies behind these comparatively small triangular-shaped hills, rising up and disappearing into the clouds, that really took our breath away. And if the sight of the Hautes Alpes looming on the horizon gave us the jitters, then it must have roused a rattling din as the collective knees of the Carthaginian soldiers knocked together in panic.

Livy summed up the awe and apprehension of Hannibal's men as they approached the high Alps with this colourful passage: 'The awful vision was now before their eyes – the towering peaks, the snow-clad pinnacles soaring to the sky; beasts and cattle shrivelled and parched with cold; the locals with their wild and ragged hair; everything stiff with frost. All these horrifying sights gave a new edge to their fear.' While we didn't come across too many crazed locals, it was easy to put yourself in the shaking sandals of the invading army.

To enhance my feelings of escapism, I had earlier done something that I rarely do while cycling, and plugged into my iPod as we negotiated the isolated roads of the Drôme valley. But even without the Kenny G sax solo that accompanied my descent of the Grimone I would not have been able to keep it together.

As the trees cleared and I was gifted my first glimpse of the verdant basin below, my first reaction was to laugh and then to hold back the tears. The vast tapestry of green that stretched across the convex lenses of my sunglasses was a staggering sight reminiscent of the kind of grand, nineteenth-century tableaux that you might see hanging in the Flemish Masters landscapes wing of the Louvre. In fact, the arched viaduct that traversed a small hollow below looked a darn sight more like the bridge in the *Mona Lisa* than the Baron de Synclair's aqueduct at Ansignan . . .

Having done an Axel Merckx and crossed the summit in the lead, I was soon near the back of the field after rider upon rider passed me by as I was sucking in my surroundings. When Merckx led the Tour down this same road back in 2002, he rode on with his fellow escapees towards the Isère valley and Les Deux Alpes, passing through the rather sombre town of Mens, which was our destination for the night. We still had 30 kilometres to ride and a rather nasty sting in the tail: an unavoidable section on the main road that ran north towards Grenoble, 'the capital of pettiness' so loathed by Stendhal.

Adding fuel to the fire, this busy stretch of road, which rose steadily uphill on a perceptible gradient and seemingly interminable northern trajectory, was accompanied by a fierce headwind that made cycling about as enjoyable as multiple lashings with an electrified whip. Luckily, James had also slowed on the euphoric descent and so we could trade pulls on the front. For those ghastly few kilometres his vocabulary would have made an arm wrestle between Bradley Wiggins and Gordon Ramsay a kids' picnic of pleasantries. But his heroic pulls were enough to expunge the lingering memory of those ghastly Bolognese crisps.

Once over the ridge, the ordeal disappeared. Free from sharing the road with massive lorries chugging uphill in third gear, I peaked just above 80 kmph on the sweeping downhill as yet another sumptuous valley – nestled between the lofty national parks of Vercors and Écrins – opened out ahead. We ditched the main road and joined a scenic lane towards Mens before I buggered off to do a little detour to ensure that my kilometre count once again hit three figures (having 24 hours earlier broken the 1,000-kilometre barrier since Barcelona).

When we did continue on the same road as Merckx the next morning it was underneath a dull canopy of cloud. So much for the old 'red sky at night' adage: I couldn't speak for the shepherds, but there weren't many delighted cyclists out there as we skulked up the sodden Col d'Ornon en route to Le Bourg d'Oisans, the gateway to the high mountains.

The Ornon is a drab climb at the best of times, a zigzagging affair on coarse tarmac in which each zig and zag (there are three apiece) lasts for the best part of 500 metres. Doing it in heavy rain was a fairly joyless experience which at least one of us (Roddy) avoided by clambering into the van. For those of us who had ambitions beyond an early finish at Bourg d'Oisans, there was an added sense of trepidation for this was the day that the mythical twenty-one hairpin bends of Alpe d'Huez were there for the taking – a prospect, in this rain, about as appealing as twenty-one punches to the gut after a bellyful of Djokovic donkey-milk liqueur.

The Tour had come this exact way for stage 18 two months earlier, the riders heading up from Gap and going through dreary Valbonnais (where we took cover to have coffee, Mars bars and freshly picked strawberries in the only open cafe) before tackling the Ornon and descending down to Bourg. In a historic first for the race, the route then included back-to-back ascents of Alpe d'Huez, separated with an unprecedented climb and descent of the Col de Sarenne.

In a bid to recreate an authentic Tour experience, and show solidarity towards the exploits of my cycling heroes, I had promised myself, my family, my friends, and my fellow Hannibal riders that I would attempt to recreate the gruelling finale of the queen stage of the 2013 Tour. Again, in my current sorry state, this was less appealing than forty-two cracks to the ribs, separated at the midway point by a severe pummelling to the groin.

To make matters even more lamentable, the 10-kilometre descent from the Ornon was in the process of being resurfaced, leaving a fine coating of grit for us to contend with as well as puddles, potholes, fog and dank drizzle. Much later in this whole adventure, when the remnants of the Velosophy bike group joined forces with the Hannibal hardcore for four days in northern Italy, I was to hear stories of downhill bliss and 85 kmph speeds from the Australians shadowing our party. The meteorological lottery that saw their ascent of Mont Ventoux carried out under clement blue skies graced them through the Alpine foothills and on to Alpe d'Huez. This descent to Bourg d'Oisans was one of the highlights of their entire trip. For me, it was hell – and not in the Sartre way, for I did it in complete isolation. No cars were out on this death-trap of a road; no cyclists were crazy enough to brave the elements for a spin on a day as grotty as this; and I had no idea whatsoever where the others were, having decided to put myself out of my misery as quickly as possibly by riding as fast as I could to the finish.

Shivering and soaked, I rolled into Bourg a near-hypothermic wreck, my extremities a haberdashery of pins and needles. I procured my hotel key, headed straight up to the room, turned the heating on full blast, stuffed my shoes with newspaper, peeled off my kit and wrung out the sweaty brownness into the sink while running a hot bath, in which I wallowed until the grimy water had slumped to a temperature lower than my morale.

It was shortly after 1 p.m. when I threw on some dry clothes, rolled up in a ball of anguish and nodded off, only to be woken minutes later by a medley of groans and other human sounds associated with hardship and vexation, as Terry squelched up the stairs.

There was no way I was going to even attempt one ascent – let alone two – of cycling's most celebrated climb, sandwiched by a perilous up-and-over whose maiden inclusion in the Tour months earlier was described as 'irresponsible' by a three-time world champion. No, siree.

# ALPE D'HUEZ

ALPE D'HUEZ

Perhaps it was my sense of duty, or the melted reblochon and charcuterie baguette I scoffed for lunch, or even the thought that fifty years of Melbourne John might succeed where I had failed. Perhaps it was, quite simply, my belated yet admirable adherence to rule #5 of the Velominati, that hallowed Bible for the discerning cyclist: to 'harden the fuck up'. But here I am, in clean, dry kit, perched by a roaring fire in the hotel foyer as I slip my double-socked feet into a pair of soggy cycling shoes, from which pulpy pages of the local rag have just been extricated by fingers still crinkly from half a day's submersion in water (both cold rain and hot bath).

Bathing and sleeping midway through a stage, while not without precedent, are hardly recipes for success. When Frenchman Manuel Busto led compatriot Guy Ignolin over the Mont Cenis pass in stage 10 of the 1961 Tour, their lead was so cosy that Busto convinced Ignolin to wait for him while he took a dip in the lake ahead of the long descent into Italy; an hour later, Busto returned the favour by allowing Ignolin to beat him in the sprint finish in Turin. No baths for cigarette-smoking, wine-slugging chimney sweep Maurice Garin, but the winner of the first Tour in 1903 did secure his second stage of the race when his closest rival on the day, Léon Georget, abandoned after falling asleep during a cheeky road-side siesta.

Melbourne John and I are the only two of our group prepared to disregard the horrific conditions and give our assent to an ascent. While he needs to snare Alpe d'Huez for his European bucket list of climbs, John clearly has no qualms about flouting rule #5 with his yellow-bellied plan to hitch a lift down from the summit to avoid descending the twenty-one bends in the rain. My own goal of scaling the Alpe twice in succession may be hanging in the balance, but at least I intend to do the full out-and-back shebang on two wheels.

We set off around half past three just as the drizzle sets back in. It's grey, cloudy and cold. Crossing the Romanche river heralds the outskirts of town. From here you can usually look up at the first five or six switchbacks but today the side of the mountain disappears into oblivion.

The French call hairpin bends *lacets* – or shoelaces – making Alpe d'Huez a full-on leather knee-high boot of a climb. A stilettoed boot at that – for there's certainly no easing into it. Pretty much immediately after the road hooks to the left at the start of the climb the gradient ramps up to double digits. Clicking instantly into the inner ring, I feel like showing the weather gods some double digits of my own. First Ventoux and now Alpe d'Huez: in the space of four days John and I have tackled two legends of the Tour; and on both occasions we have ridden through rain, our scope of vision limited to less than 100 metres. It appears our lunchtime prayers for better weather have fallen on deaf ears.

**21** The first bend on Alpe d'Huez is a double-sided slap of abruptness and choking constraint. Your first reaction on spotting the sign marked with a number 21 (alt. 806m) on the side of the road is to curse. Bloody hell, twenty more switchbacks and 1,054 metres of vertical climbing to go.

The hairpins are numbered in reverse order from bottom to top. They are also named after previous winners of stages atop the Alpe – starting with Fausto Coppi, who won on the Tour's maiden visit to the ski resort in 1952. On the first occasion the Tour was broadcast live on television, the Italian maestro easily beat France's Jean Robic – nicknamed 'Tête de Cuir' because of the ubiquitous leather crash helmet he wore as a precaution after fracturing his skull in 1944. The Tour's inaugural mountain-top finish apparently 'offered no reason to lobby for more stage finishes at altitude', according to race director Jacques Goddet. Alpe d'Huez was not revisited by the Tour for twenty-four years – although since 1976 it has become part of the Tour furniture, featuring in 2013 for the twenty-eighth and twenty-ninth time.

I look over my shoulder at John, who is struggling to keep up with my pace. 'Go ahead,' he says. 'I'll ride my own rhythm.' Off I zip with a nod.

It was hardly up there with the infamous 'look' that preceded Lance Armstrong's devastating attack in 2001 when, just 800 metres into the final ascent, the Texan peered over his shoulder and appeared to goad his rival Jan Ullrich before dancing clear on the pedals. Earlier in that stage, Armstrong had lulled Ullrich into a false sense of security after bluffing tiredness and cramps. When Armstrong completed his perfect game of poker by playing an ace on the Alpe, the German juggernaut didn't have a strong enough hand to reply. Ullrich finished the stage in second place but two minutes behind Armstrong, who seized the yellow jersey and wore it all the way to Paris.

Armstrong's name appears underneath Coppi's on the mountain's opening bend – although for how long remains to be seen: local officials were clearly not too enamoured by those tearful confessions to Oprah and are hellbent on erasing all memory of the American's exploits. Given that a modest Prix Pantani is awarded to stage winners on Alpe d'Huez – in memory of the controversial climber who currently holds the mountain's record time – this would surely open a rather large can of worms.

**20** A rambler stationed just ahead of the next bend spots me riding through the rain and he whips out his camera to record my suffering for his later amusement. If he composed the picture right he should have caught the distant, blurred figure of Melbourne John in the background. Looking to my left as I round the bend (dedicated to Dutchman Joop Zoetemelk, winner in 1976, and our old Ventoux-bossing bank condiment Iban Mayo, from 2003), I see my 'team-mate' already quite far back. It will be the last time I catch sight of his GreenEdge jersey today.

I'm just two bends into the 13.8 kilometre ascent but already my legs are rather fiery. That I had even considered doing this climb twice in one afternoon seems laughable now. If the opening few kilometres of the ascent throw the steepest gradient at you, they are also the most psychologically damaging for awestruck riders like me who find it impossible to resist counting down the bends.

The problem – or joy, depending on how you look at it – of climbing Alpe d'Huez for the first time is that it all feels so familiar. Since my interest in the Tour was kindled in the late 1980s the race has come here at least every other year. I know the mountain's twists, turns and gradients like the back of my hand – and with the completion of each corner it feels like that same hand is reaching out to slap me around the face. You're braced for the hit to the point of actively encouraging it. An odd mix of expectation, excitement and fear accompanies my pedal strokes, yet my limbs obviously still think they're asleep back in the hotel, dreaming about that bath.

**19** Another Armstrong bend, this time in commemoration of his time trial victory in 2004. I was here for that memorable victory, camping out on the grassy knoll of a roundabout in the centre of town with my brother. I remember arriving two days before the stage. Already most green spaces within a bidon's squirt of the summit formed part of a patchwork quilt of multi-coloured tents. It was as if the Glastonbury festival had transported itself 1,860 metres above sea level and replaced a roster of long-haired and bearded bands with a constant stream of smooth-legged men on bikes, riding up the hill at two-minute inter- vals. The currency of the place was beers and barbecues, while instead of T-shirts that revealed which side of the Britpop fence they sat upon, fans from all over the globe were decked out in a blur of replica cycling jerseys. This first proper taste of the Tour carnival was an experience like no other. And not being a rider back then, I only half got it.

The other name on bend nineteen is that of Hennie Kuiper, winner in 1977 for the second of eight Dutch victories in the race's first fourteen visits. The uncanny phenomenon of a Lowlander habitually starring on one of the Tour's loftiest peaks earned Alpe d'Huez the nickname 'Dutch Mountain'. Even though no Dutchman has won here for a quarter of a century, the Alpe on race day still attracts more Dutch fans than the country's annual clog-dancing festival in Valkenswaard.

Unlike Mont Ventoux, there seem to be no other riders tackling the climb other than myself and Melbourne John. Primarily, this must be because it's not the weekend. But also, unless you're a stubborn soul passing through the area with just one small window to leave your mark, the foul weather engulfing the Romanche valley is hardly an incentive to reach for the chamois cream.

**18** Hot and flustered despite the drizzle, I slow at the next bend to disrobe. Whipping off my jacket means I can now boast my vintage PDM Chrome Cassettes jersey, paying homage to the old Dutch team of the late 1980s and early '90s. It was PDM climber Gert-Jan Theunisse who was the last Dutch winner on the Alpe – the only man to have won here while wearing the polka-dot jersey. This was back in 1989 when my second brother took immense pleasure in terrifying both me and my little sister by wearing a ghoulish rubber mask better suited for somewhere like the London Dungeon. Theunisse was the human embodiment of this mask. Watching him grimace on a climb was a horrifying experience. Most children my age jumped behind the sofa because of the Daleks. For me, a breakaway by Theunisse during the evening's Tour highlights programme was enough to have me reaching for the cushion. His flowing locks and exaggerated features led to some fans calling him the Chewbacca of cycling. As a child, I certainly found Theunisse's pain-face so simian that his grizzly mountain exploits – aided by his own Doctor Who, no doubt – could well have been accompanied by a David Attenborough voice-over.

Two years after Theunisse's victory on the Alpe none of the PDM team even made it to the foot of the climb after a bizarre episode which saw all nine riders withdrawn from the Tour because of 'food poisoning'. It later emerged that the infection came from a contaminated batch of 'nutritional aid' that the team doctor, Wim Sanders, had injected into the riders. If, as he claimed, the substance was intralipid, a legal soya bean extract, that didn't make PDM seraphic practitioners of herbalism. Good golly, no. Sanders had made PDM into one of the most competitive doping teams in the business thanks to a dedicated programme of anabolic steroids and EPO, to which he later confessed during a trial for tax avoidance. There was more testosterone in the PDM camp than at one of Hugh Hefner's Christmas parties, and by wearing one of their jerseys, I was hoping some of it would rub off on me. Theunisse himself twice tested positive for the stuff – back in the day when such an infraction earned riders a mere 10-minute penalty (making today's two-year bans exactly 105,120 times worse).While vehemently denying testosterone abuse, Theunisse did later admit to using 'a great deal' of corticosteroids during his career.

This corner belongs both to Kuiper, for his 1978 win, and Frank Schleck of Luxembourg, who soloed to victory here in 2006. Poor Schleck: there was no Alpe d'Huez for him in 2013 thanks to a twelve-month ban following a positive test for the diuretic xipamide. Some said Schleck got off lightly considering he was never held accountable for making a mysterious €7,000 payment to the infamous Spanish doping doctor Eufemiano 'Operación Puerto' Fuentes back in 2005.

You see what I mean about the erasing of Armstrong's name potentially opening Pandora's box?

**16** I'm starting to get in a groove. The proof? I've ceased the futile exercise in demoralization that is hairpin counting. On this Escher sketch of a climb, it's just not worth it. With me counting up and the signs counting down, it's also mathematically beyond me in my current state. So I've stopped trying to tie up the laces. Now, as I exit the trees and approach the town of La Garde en Oisans, I try to think back over the past few kilometres and gauge where I'm at. But it's no good. I have no idea. But this is a bonus: it liberates me.

The gradient relents to a more manageable 7 per cent and a road sign indicates that the summit is 10.9 kilometres away. It was here that Tejay van Garderen and Christophe Riblon extricated themselves from the nine-man group that held a seven-minute advantage over the peloton when it started the first of two ascents of the Alpe a couple of months ago.

*You're joining us at the business end of stage 18 of the Tour de France, with two men leading the race on the first of two ascents of Alpe d'Huez. American Tejay van Garderen looks the strongest but this is still the first half of a game that will go on for another 90 minutes – plus extra time, perhaps even penalties.*

**14** The rain has stopped but the low cloud means my view is still pretty restricted. The trees have cleared a little but there's not much beyond the green banks than a misty gloom. Alpe d'Huez itself is not the prettiest of climbs, its mystique relying heavily upon the view back over the Romanche valley or down into the gorge cut out by the Sarenne river. I can see neither. Nor can I make out much of the series of approaching switchbacks other than a faint dash disappearing into nothingness.

Seeing that the end of the road is a purpose-built ski resort it's no surprise that the climb has a sense of functionality about it, especially with the constant presence of crash barriers, street furniture and lighting. This is less rural mountain pass, more semi-suburban access road. It's a dizzy multi-storey car park of a climb. It lacks – certainly in this weather – the ethereal beauty of many classic Alpine ascents and Pyrenean peaks. But if the lack of a view plays games with your sense of location, then each recognizable bend and the road itself ensures a constant sense of familiarity. For accompanying me on the whole journey are countless painted names, flags, logos and slogans that déjà-vu their way to the back of my mind.

*Now van Garderen edges clear of Riblon to assume control. Back in the peloton, his BMC team-mate Cadel Evans, winner of the 2011 Tour, has already been dropped. Sweat pours from the Australian's brow and runs through his cleft chin like a mountain stream flows down a ravine. Team Sky set the pace for their man Chris Froome, more than eight minutes behind van Garderen. We have two races going on today: for the stage and for the yellow jersey.*

**12** I'm on to the tough mid-section of the climb that cuts through woodland and features the highest volume of successive switch-backs, cut out on the side of the mountain as if from the sword of an overzealous Zorro. It's very bright all of a sudden because the sun's rays, fighting their way through the low-lying cloud, are being simultaneously refracted by the dense mist and reflected from the damp road. Corner number twelve is named after pocket-rocket mountain goat Luis Herrera, the first Colombian to win a stage on the Tour here in 1984. Nicknamed 'El Jardinerito' (the Little Gardener) from a childhood hobby of picking flowers, 'Lucho' was no pansy on the bike: in his debut Tour, the 23-year-old amateur rose above the professionals, dropping both Bernard Hinault and Laurent Fignon on Alpe d'Huez to enter a shrubbery of climbing greats still dominated by the sweet-smelling bouquet of Dutch tulips.

**10** While it's getting much brighter, the visibility remains pretty poor as I make yet another tight right-hander. I'm right in the heart of a cloud because I can feel moisture in the air and it's noticeably cooler, despite the perceptible warmth coming from the sun's hazy rays on the back of my neck. Wouldn't it be something if it clears up? I can see Irish flags painted on the road alongside the names of the two Irish riders who rode in the Tour – cousins Dan Martin and Nicolas Roche.

Martin won a hilly stage prior to the Alps, while Roche tried to break clear with a team-mate before the peloton reached Alpe d'Huez. No Irish cyclist had ever managed a top-ten finish on the Alpe and that record still stands.

**7** *Van Garderen enters a tunnel of orange as he sweeps around one of the climb's gentler yet more animated bends on the approach to Huez village. The American has a twenty-second lead over Riblon. The fans are going absolutely crazy. After all, van Garderen has a Dutch father and this is corner number seven . . .*

If Alpe d'Huez represents a cycling Mecca for the Netherlands, then Dutch Corner is their fans' Kaaba. Every time the race comes to the Alpe, thousands of Dutch revellers congregate about two-thirds up the climb on the seventh hairpin. More orange than the cast of *The Only Way Is Essex* and as inebriated as your grandfather at Christmas, they congregate around the Église Saint-Ferréol, pitching their tents on any vacant strip of grass or hand-braking their camper vans on the edge of the road well in advance of the race, ready to embark on a week-long bender of booze and blaring Euro-trance. Some of them don't even like cycling – they're just there for the party. Celebrations are so advanced nowadays that Heineken have opened a bar and big-name DJs are flown in. Bunting flutters from the spire of the church, Dutch flags are hung from the trees. One guy this year even surfed the corner on top of a team van before being yanked off by a policeman. As one journalist said, it's 'like a riot at a clown convention'.

I know I'm approaching Dutch Corner because the vowel–consonant combinations scrawled across the asphalt get a lot more complicated. But it's the comparatively easy-flowing names of Bauke Mollema and Laurens ten Dam that are particularly prominent. The Belkin duo were both in the top five when most of these slogans were painted, days ahead of the stage. Dutch fans harboured real hope for their first 'home' win in a quarter of a century.

Tom Veelers is there too. He was indirectly responsible for Mark Cavendish being doused in urine during the Tour. It wasn't his piss that a fan tossed at Cav during the time trial to Mont Saint Michel. But a day earlier, Cav had nudged Veelers during the sprint finale, causing the young Dutchman to chomp concrete at high speed. Hence the urinal retribution bestowed upon the Manxman. Such a reaction from fans was 'really disappointing', according to Cav's former team-mate Chris Froome. 'It leaves a bad taste in the mouth,' he added, perhaps unnecessarily. A week later, a bruised Veelers was the last man to finish on Alpe d'Huez. With the broom wagon looming, he got so many pushes from fans that he almost made it back to the gruppetto.

The Dutch flavour of Alpe d'Huez actually preceded the nation's run of eight stage victories in fourteen years. Father Jaap Reuten, a Dutch priest, was on a skiing holiday here in 1964 and was alarmed to see that the expanding ski village had no place of worship. He commissioned a French architect to come up with something suitably striking. The result was Notre Dame des Neiges, an eye-catching fusion of wood and concrete (from one angle, the church resembles a space shuttle about to take off). It was opened in 1969 and part-funded by the profits Reuten made flogging Dutch beer around the region. When Joop Zoetemelk netted his – and the Netherlands' – first victory on Alpe d'Huez in 1976, an excited Father Jaap rang the church bells in celebration. The media lapped it up and this became a bit of a habit over the years as Dutch riders returned for victory after victory. The church also assumed the mantle of Tour press room when the race came to town, with ashtrays in the nave and a bar in the vestry.

But it's not the futuristic Notre Dame des Neiges near the finish line that has become the main ecclesiastic focal point for Dutch fans in recent history, rather the more traditional Église Saint-Ferréol here on corner seven. It marks the gateway to the final slog up to the summit. And it's here that my epiphany happens. Something has changed. The air is clearing. Everything is visible. Not just the orange paint spattered across the kerb, the green lawn in front of the graveyard walls and the tops of tombstones. But the church walls too and, beyond the tower and through the parting mist, the top of the mountain has revealed itself, framed by blue sky. I've ridden through the rain cloud that still engulfs the entire valley below and my surroundings have taken on a game-changing dynamic.

No longer can I shelve my double ascent on meteorological grounds. Seeing that my knees are OK, nor can I play the health card. In fact, there are only two things stopping me from reverting to the original plan: time and willpower.

**6** Knowing that I will return for a second helping later this afternoon means I've taken my foot off the gas. Besides, I'm not going to beat Marco Pantani's record ascent of 37 minutes 35 seconds from 1997. I'm not even going to beat Sam's alleged 60-minute offering from last year. (I'm thinking there must have been a serious tailwind for that one.) My immediate future has shifted from a 5-kilometre uphill ride and 15-kilometre drop back to the hotel to an additional 65-kilometre round trip that will bring me back up this very same road – even though it's now well past 4 p.m.

*Riblon thumps a topless man who is running along way too close for comfort. Such confrontations are common in cycling. Back on the Alpe in 2011, Alberto Contador swung a punch at a man in a surgeon's outfit taunting him with a large cardboard cut-out of a syringe.*

*As van Garderen rides above Huez village, a spectator wearing fluorescent yellow leggings, a pink vest and a green headband runs in his wake. The gimpy-looking superhero is brought crashing to earth by a deliciously timed trip from a fan on the side of the road, almost falling into the back of van Garderen's bike. Seething with rage, the runner gets up and turns on the man responsible for putting the boot into his moment of glory. They square up. The tripper's girlfriend enters the ring. Punches are thrown. A gendarme intervenes. This is all part and parcel of the Tour. With so much alcohol doing the rounds, it's a surprise we don't see men in green mankinis and morphsuits coming to blows more often. It makes you think: if doping is banned for riders, should the same be said for spectators consuming alcohol?*

**3** After a slight dip below 7 per cent the gradient ramps up again on the long straight out of the village. This stretch of road is really open and can be seen from multiple vantage points above, making it something of a natural amphitheatre. I remember distinctly the bellowing cries of 'Ulle! Ulle! Ulle!' that accompanied Jan Ullrich on his ride during the individual time trial in 2004, reverberating up the mountain like the sound of a fierce Germanic army preparing itself for war. (You can imagine the fear Hannibal's soldiers must have felt when facing some of those rowdy Celtic tribes with their warmongering cries.)

This part of the climb is bittersweet: the end is in sight and yet there are still three more corners to negotiate, plus the winding road through the town itself. I hear a toot and the sound of a down-shifting of gears. I look over my shoulder to see James driving the van. He asks me how I'm doing and I put my thumb up. 'See you at the finish,' he says.

*Riblon has now been joined by the young Italian Moreno Moser of the Cannondale team. They have van Garderen in their sights and should catch him before the summit.*

**2** The penultimate corner – and the one before – belongs to Marco Pantani, who won in 1995 before following it up two years later with his record-breaking time. If you take Armstrong out of the equation, the Italian holds the three fastest times for the climb, even though his effort during his debut Tour in 1994 came from the main group of favourites and didn't result in the stage victory. Soon after you pass corner two you are greeted with the town sign for Alpe d'Huez. It's a welcome sight, to be sure, but there's still a few more kilometres to ride until the official finish. Nowadays the crash barriers for the Tour start around here, to protect the riders from the sprawling crowds near the top. But back in the 1990s there were no barriers until well inside the last kilometre – as 1999 winner Giuseppe Guerini found out in dramatic circumstances. The Italian had just passed the kite when a foolish fan in a cap leaped out in the road to take a photo. The collision sent Guerini sprawling across the tarmac. He quickly remounted. But an overzealous push by a man in grey shorts and T-shirt almost caused him to take a second tumble, which may have cost him the 21 seconds by which he held on to beat the Russian Pavel Tonkov. Fittingly, it's Guerini's name that appears on the next, final corner.

*Back with the favourites there's a rasping attack by Thomas Voeckler, the French favourite who really should sell advertising space on the gargantuan tongue he so often lets dangle during races. Plucky Voeckler's dig paves the way for Europcar team-mate Pierre Rolland, the reigning Alpe champion. But with van Garderen's lead still at eight minutes, a second successive win is unlikely.*

**1** I remember this final corner well. This was where I came to watch the time trial in 2004 with my brother Alex. We liberated one of the Team CSC umbrellas from the Danish bar in town and set up camp above the cutting that lines the final hairpin before town. It was here where we heard the waves of noise that preceded each rider up the hill from the crest at Dutch Corner. All the *Ulle! Ulle! Ulle!* shouts that echoed off the walls of the mountain in this high altitude basin would be enough to cause an avalanche in winter. It was on this exact corner that Armstrong – still soaked in the spit from fans further down the hill (no doubt the same Germans shouting for Ullrich) – caught and passed Ivan Basso, who had rolled down the starting ramp in Bourg d'Oisans two minutes before the American. Somewhere I have a photo of the moment, with the yellow jersey edging clear of his main rival, the pair separated by a to-the-point morsel of graffiti: LANCEPOSTAL.

There's a large ramp immediately following the bend, with the gradient returning to double figures. I stagger slightly but seeing the town ahead is enough to give anyone a second wind.

*Rounding the steep final hairpin, Riblon and Moser draw level with van Garderen. It's now a three-horse race.*

Memories flood back as I pass ski chalets, bar terraces, rustic restaurants and salami shops that have all enjoyed my custom in the past, but usually when I'm decked out in salopettes. I ride through the tunnel in the centre of town and then wind my way through the resort, getting lost and having to take a pedestrian path at least once. After a couple of roundabouts that ring a few bells, I finally find myself on the finish straight at the end of which James is waiting with the van. My time of 1 hour 10 minutes would have been better had I not stopped to take the odd photo once emerging above the cloud.

After some congratulations and a bit of grandstanding for the camera (he makes me pass the finish plaque three times), James asks me if I'm going to ride back down or join John in the van. I tell him that

I'm doing neither, that I'm going to press on with the Col de Sarenne and its deadly descent before – shudder – attempting a second stab at those twenty-one hairpins and needles. He fills my water bottles and thrusts a banana in my back pocket. There's still no sign of Melbourne John as I freewheel back through town and then hang a left towards the aerodrome and Sarenne pass.

*Moser jumps out of the saddle to take the spoils over the summit. Instead of turning on to the final straight, the three leaders join a narrow slip road and head into the unknown, on an extra loop that has no history in the Tour de France. One of them will tonight enter the record books.*

From the concrete eyesores of the ski resort to the grassy slopes of the Sarenne bowl, what strikes you most once you traverse the contours of the mountain and drop into the next valley is its complete isolation. This was hugely apparent in the Tour when the frenzied crowds that swamped the twisting main drag up the Alpe were replaced by a mere scattering of supporters. It was almost as if the Tour organizers had only opened up the Sarenne to winners of an under-publicized competition. Back then, its remote slopes were green and lush; today they're browner and bleaker, mirroring the sudden dullness of the returning clouds. As the drizzle resumes I pass by the first riders I have seen today – a group of six children on mountain bikes with a guide, sensibly, it seems, on their way back to the resort.

An exposed, rickety two-man chairlift that I have had the displeasure of braving on previous snowboarding trips hangs motionless overhead. It's the lift that runs up from the bottom of what is, at 16 kilometres, the world's longest black ski run. How apt – for what I'm about to embark upon is cycling's equivalent of a mogulled *piste noire*.

Before the notoriously dicey descent there's the small matter of the

Col de Sarenne itself. It's only three kilometres long at an average gradient of 7.8 per cent but the rain is falling quite heavily again and the road is blocked by a flock of sheep and rams, who have decided to cross at the precise time I'm riding past. A mixture of browns, blacks and whites – and some with very pointy horns – these woolly creatures refuse to give me any leeway and I'm stuck until I spot a brief opening. Unlike the constantly twisting climb to Alpe d'Huez, this one is pretty much dead straight, clinging to the side of a mountain and running above a stream. The approach from the west is so gradual and nondescript that when you reach the ridge-top summit at 1,999 metres, the sudden drop and staggering change in terrain on the other side has an even larger impact, one that elicits a gasp of incredulity.

*Moser is one of Italy's most promising young riders and took victory earlier in the season in the brutal Strade Bianche race in Tuscany. The 22-year-old is the nephew of the great Italian classics specialist Francesco Moser, but he cannot keep up with his two fellow escapees and drops back. It's van Garderen who crosses the summit ahead of Riblon. The sun may be shining but a few rain drops are falling. A shower on the descent would make things rather rum.*

Tony Martin, the German time trial champion who took his third consecutive world title in 2013, told reporters that the backside of the Sarenne had left him 'negatively surprised' after the road was tested out for the first time in competitive racing during the Critérium du Dauphiné ahead of the centenary Tour. 'It's irresponsible to send us there,' he moaned before citing the lack of guardrails which could see riders plummet 30 metres off the side of the road.

Well, Tony, you should count yourself lucky that when the Tour came down the narrow, winding, gravel track the only additional obstacle was light drizzle. I have to contend with sheep and their slippery shit, fallen rocks strewn across what is a mere path peppered with potholes, pebbles and puddles, the increasingly heavy rain and the unlikely, yet not negligible, threat of oncoming traffic. I feel fairly vertiginous, and highly nervous, just looking down over the first meandering S-bend, following the road with my squinting eyes as it hugs the side of the mountain at what looks to be a fearsome gradient. In the distance, and through the gloom, I can just make out another series of meandering hairpins.

Needless to say, I take it very slowly – almost as sluggish as that opening-day descent on the Turó de l'Home in Catalonia. This is as close to a computer game as cycling can get, every ten metres an exercise in dodging various booby traps and picking the right – perhaps the only – route. If only I can get to the end of the level without GAME OVER flashing across my screen. How I manage to avoid riding off the road, colliding with a boulder or picking up a puncture, I do not know. At one point it's so steep and I'm riding so slowly that I almost pull a front wheelie.

*Exiting the first bend van Garderen starts to stutter. In trying to shift up gears twice in succession on the bumpy road his chain appears to have slipped off the cog and become stuck between the cassette and frame. As Riblon rides clear, Moser catches and passes van Garderen, who is forced to stop and wait 40 seconds for his team car before he can switch bikes.*

There's no beating about the bush: the Sarenne is beautiful and exhilarating, but it's a nerve-wracking beast too. The road is barely wide enough for one vehicle, let alone a peloton of riders, their support cars and countless media and police motorbikes. During the Dauphiné, eventual winner Chris Froome and his Spanish rival Alberto Contador carried out an informal truce on the descent, to avoid derailing their preparations for the Tour. But during the main event Contador, at that point more than four minutes in arrears in the standings and getting more desperate by the day, pulled off a kamikaze manoeuvre by over-taking the yellow jersey, Froome, and two of his Sky team-mates on the inside of the road through what appeared to be a negligible gap. Riding clear with his skeletal Saxo-Tinkoff team-mate Roman Kreuziger, Contador's bold bid to pile pressure on Froome during the 15-kilometre descent ultimately came to nothing, but the duo certainly added some spice to the Sarenne sauce.

After a gradual zigzag, things get technical again with eight steep hairpins in succession. The maximum gradient is a white-knuckled 13.5 per cent and my weight is often so far forward that I fear being thrown over the handlebars face first into this sorry excuse for a road. On two occasions my back wheel skids in sheep poo, while my brake cables are making a terrible din as they rattle against the top tube and handlebars, harmonizing with each crack and fissure. Still the rain pounds down.

It strikes me that the Sarenne would perhaps be far better employed during the Tour if climbed as opposed to taken on with the forces of gravity in your (supposed) favour. It's fairly obvious that it would be a highly challenging climb and the novelty value would be immense. In fact, the more I think about it, the more I'm in favour of writing to the Tour organizers and suggesting a stage finale that includes the Col de Sarenne before a descent from Alpe d'Huez to the finish in Bourg d'Oisans.

Such a controversial suggestion would be met with stern facial expressions and Gallic shrugs. Using the iconic Alpe d'Huez in reverse could be tantamount to casting Angelina Jolie for a Hollywood blockbuster and then forcing her to wear goggles and a burka for the entire film. Perhaps we could agree on a compromise and base the stage on Joop Zoetemelk's second Alpe d'Huez win, in 1979, when the second of two stages to finish in the ski resort also started there: the 119-kilometre loop saw the riders first descend the twenty-one hairpins before riding an undulating circuit which brought the pack back to

Bourg d'Oisans and the concluding slog back up top. To make matters even more bizarre, Zoetemelk was at the time wearing the green jersey, ostensibly reserved for the best sprinters – the kind of riders who chug home in the gruppetto half an hour in arrears.

I'm distracted from my thoughts of becoming the next Tour director by a painted triptych that reads: FREE LANCE, JAN ULLRICH and VAMOS CONTADOR. I giggle to myself at someone's wicked sense of humour and then note the sudden improvement in the quality of the road. While the local authorities clearly couldn't be arsed to resurface the road further uphill where it really mattered, they were happy to give these gentler, wider slopes a new dusting of asphalt for the Tour. I check my speed coming into the next bend, all too aware that freshly surfaced roads can be rather slippery.

*Near disaster for Christophe Riblon as the Frenchman's back wheel locks and he's forced to ride off the road and into a shallow ditch of water! The rain has made the new surface fairly greasy and he did not brake in time ahead of that bend. Superb bike-handling skills though from Riblon, who avoids a fall and is now back on course in pursuit of Moser.*

Shortly after 'Riblon corner', the dainty village of Mizoën is even prettier now that I've dropped through the rain clouds and back into a patch of sun. Having negotiated its narrow streets, whose angled walls were clad in padding during the Tour, I pull in at a layby overlooking the glistening Lac du Chambon. Not once during the Tour coverage did we see any images of this stunning reservoir. It was as if the organizers had failed to pick up the viewing rights. I'm now riding down the road that leads up to the Col du Lautaret and the Col du Galibier – a busy main drag that I have a suspicion I'll be seeing more of tomorrow.

Before dropping the 12 kilometres back to Bourg, you have to cross the top of the mighty Chambon dam, once the highest in Europe, and pass by a chapel commemorating the thirty-odd workers who lost their lives during its construction in the early 1930s. The view from the imposing structure is of expected Alpine magnificence. Emerging from the surface of a lake now bestrewn in sunshine, in a perfect arc that frames a rampaging waterfall spurting from a gully to top up the reservoir, shimmers a faint rainbow. In a world where my exploits on two wheels take centre stage, I feel that this scene of beauty has been laid on specially for me. It's a sign that I'm on the right track; a reward for my endeavours. But the shadows cast by the mountains across the water's surface also act as a stark reminder that the day is getting on – and if I want to complete my D'Huez Double then I'm going to have to get going.

A short, punchy climb precedes a fast descent back to the Romanche valley. Roadworks, tunnels and the fact that it's past 6 p.m. and lots of people appear to be driving home from work (wherever, whatever that may be in these parts) means this is a hairier prospect than my legs. Then there's an interminable flat drag along a busy main road that stretches out without even a soupçon of a kink all the way to Bourg. I time trial my way along on the drops with only one thing – in fact, twenty-one of the same things – on my mind: those hairpins.

*Riblon returns to the wheel of Moser and the two combine before being joined on the straight by van Garderen. The French commentators announce that the UCI will carry out a surprise bike check at the finish, weighing each rider's steed and checking they conform to specifications. They have also announced that the rule that forbids riders to take on food in the last 20km will be relaxed so that supplies can be sought from team cars right up until the foot of the final climb. Back with the main favourites, who still trail the leaders by five minutes, Contador and Kreuziger give up their vain attempt to break clear and are reabsorbed by the peloton. Contador then slows to a stop alongside his team car and, rather mysteriously, changes his bike.*

**21** I glance at my watch as I approach the start of the climb for a second time. It's about 6.52 p.m. By my calculation I have just over an hour's daylight left. My first ascent of Alpe d'Huez took me just over an hour. This is going to be tight. I've plugged into some music for distraction, choosing a melancholically uplifting Australian band called The Jezabels to sing me through the next painful twenty-one stanzas of my life. The first song is actually entitled 'Hurt Me' – and with the mountain as an apparent muse, it's certainly living up to its name.

If the first segment of my opening gambit was mentally tough, then the second foray is even harder for I know exactly what to expect. Sure, there's less pressure: I've already conquered this climb. I can turn around and give up at any time, with my head held high. But the challenge is to mirror the pros – and today it's just not good enough to be William Bonnet or Alexey Lutsenko, the only riders who failed to complete stage 18 back in July.

*Moser is first to crack on the climb, dropped on the hellish opening ramp before the first corner. It looks like Riblon and van Garderen will battle it out for the prestigious stage win. It's an honorary Dutchman versus the man who can save France's blushes. It's worth adding that Riblon finished runner-up two days ago in Gap, 42 seconds behind stage winner Rui Costa. It's also three years ago to the day that the 32-year-old netted his first Tour scalp, in the Pyrenean ski resort of Ax-3 Domaines. Seven years Riblon's junior, van Garderen has never won a stage on the Tour. But he did become a father to a baby daughter in April.*

**20** Blimey. It's a word I seem to be saying pretty much every hour in every day during this adventure. I'm sure I don't utter it much when I'm in the UK. It's as if I'm hamming up some kind of Dick Van Dyke role for my Australian and American companions. Anyway, it's the right word in this context because, blimey, I forgot how tough the start of this climb was. Having already done it – and the extra 35 kilometre loop – I embarked on this final slog thinking I was on the closing straight. But there's nothing closing or straight about what lies ahead. And seeing that I have to come back down again, every pedal stroke is actually taking me further away from my destination; further away from food, a bath, bed.

*Chris Froome and Richie Porte lead the group of main favourites and seem to have everything under control. So relaxed is the spindly race leader that Froome actually has his arm around his team-mate's shoulder and is whispering something in his ear. Can you imagine Bradley Wiggins doing the same to Froome one year earlier? I thought not. Porte says something back and smiles before increasing the tempo. It would appear to any neutral onlooker that the Sky duo are completely taking the mickey out of everyone: their rivals, race organizers, the fans – even Wiggo, sat at home and watching with his feet up. They're making this second ascent look like a training ride.*

**15** The first phase is done and I'm now edging out of La Garde. I've turned on the flashing red light on my seat post because the road is still fairly busy with traffic and there's more twilight on the Alpe than on the bookshelf of an American teenager. I'm weighing up my options. It would be defeatist to turn round now. I could call up James and ask him to meet me on the summit in the van but Sam's had to take the vehicle back to Mens to catch up on some tour logistics with Dylan. There doesn't appear to be a bus service. I could take a taxi, although it could prove costly with my bike. No, my only real option is to keep on pedalling and see what happens.

*Van Garderen makes his move around 3 kilometres into the climb. Either his or Riblon's name will soon be etched underneath that of Dutchman Peter Winnen (who lived up to his name in 1981) on corner 15. The Frenchman will have taken inspiration from the name of compatriot Pierre Rolland on the previous corner beneath that of Zoetemelk. Rolland has become something of a comedy figure in this year's race, primarily because of his perplexing penchant to match his polka-dot jersey with spotted shorts, socks, gloves and bike. Thankfully, he's no longer leading the king of the mountains competition and so viewers have a temporary respite from his sartorial inelegance. Two years ago Rolland saved France's Tour by winning stage 19 here on Alpe d'Huez to secure the host nation's first win just two days before the race finale in Paris. This year the Tour visits the Alpe one day earlier but France are still searching for an elusive victory. Can Riblon emulate Rolland and end the drought?*

*Leaving La Garde, Froome, all pointy elbows and spindly legs, puts in one of his ridiculous high-cadence, in-the-saddle attacks, looking more and more like a praying mantis taking a dump on a coat hanger. Contador and Kreuziger crack. By the time the race enters Paris, neither of the Saxo-Tinkoff pair will remain on the podium. Colombian Nairo Quintana – wearing the white jersey as best young rider despite looking a decade older than most of the peloton – manages to close the gap. Quintana used to ride a bike to school every day from his family home in the mountains. He owes his climbing pedigree to the gruelling 10-kilometre ascent he'd have to carry out to get back home for dinner. Spaniards Joaquim Rodríguez and Alejandro Valverde lead the chase, with Porte sucking their wheels.*

**14** As well as giving the Ventoux a miss, Hannibal never climbed up Alpe d'Huez during his crossing into Italy. Supposing he did, there's absolutely no way he'd have led his pachyderm peloton down the other side and then promptly told them to do it all over again. Because that would have been sheer stupidity. Sensible man, Hannibal.

But I have no regrets. This second ascent of the Alpe has a completely new feel to it, primarily because the cloud, mist and rain have disappeared and I can actually appreciate my surroundings. Up ahead I can see seven switchbacks queuing up the side of the mountain like Frenchmen waiting for the *boulangerie* to open. It's quite a sight, something of a sucker punch for morale because it only accentuates the challenge in hand. Yet the bends come thick and fast; before I know it, I'll be at Dutch Corner and two-thirds to the good.

*Perhaps Froome went too early? Rodríguez has now fought back. A sluggish Froome slows to have a word with Quintana just as a little boy runs out and almost causes a collision. Froome looks astonished. He shakes his head and thanks his lucky stars. Meanwhile, 'Purito' Rodríguez takes advantage of the confusion and edges ahead.*

**11** Needing a pee, I pull in on a corner and take a leak against the back wall. You can imagine my pleasure when I look up and see a plaque bearing the name of Bernard Hinault, winner on the Alpe in 1986. I can't help but think of Greg LeMond emptying his bowels on a box full of postcards featuring the smiling face of his team-mate and rival. Pissing at the foot of Hinault's plaque is my watered-down, amateur version of this cycling sacrilege.

Hinault's name is on the eleventh corner but it could just as easily have been the American's. The two rode the whole climb shoulder to shoulder, obliterating their nearest rival by more than five minutes. Approaching the finish line, LeMond, in yellow, reached over and put his arm on Hinault's back. The Badger turned and raised his own arm. For a split second it looked like he was going to lash out. But instead, the pair hold hands and punch the air – not each other – in celebration. LeMond then slowed before giving Hinault the kind of push over the finish line that Marco Pantani would have found so disrespectful.

Seeing Hinault thump LeMond would have been no surprise. Rumour has it that the pair had a blazing row the night before and had to be separated by their La Vie Claire team owner Bernard Tapie. LeMond felt that Hinault had reneged on their deal that he would ride the '86 Tour to support him after he had put aside his own chances of glory the year previously to help Hinault secure his record-equalling fifth victory. The French veteran had a funny way of showing his support, attacking relentlessly in the opening fortnight of the race to build up a five-minute lead over his precocious team-mate after the first stage in the Pyrenees. LeMond managed to cut the deficit to 40 seconds, before moving into the yellow jersey at the Alpine resort of Serre Chevalier. After almost coming to blows that night, a truce was declared the next day as both riders put on a show of solidarity on the Alpe.

Days before I had met LeMond earlier in the summer, he had been back here on the Alpe riding alongside Hinault as the pair recreated their arm-in-arm finish for the centenary Tour celebrations. 'After the photo shoot we had a little interview and it was funny,' said LeMond, fuller in the face, greyer in the hair, but boasting the same mischievous grin. 'Bernard was telling his version of how things happened that year and was like, "Hey, yeah, the attacking was spontaneous but we were always racing together. I gave Greg my word I'd help him win." And I was like [laughs], it's OK if he thinks that, but it's not the case. You know,' he said, 'Hinault was actually a very good team-mate.' Small pause. 'Until that last year.'

For his part, Hinault clearly believed he had what it took to beat LeMond in what is thought to have been the greatest Tour in the modern era, claiming in his autobiography, with more than a hint of Merckxian cannibalism: 'I could have had the American's skin on the Alpe.'

**7** Approaching the church of Saint-Ferréol I stop to take a picture of the view back down the mountain. This second time I can actually appreciate the scale of the ascent, with the road looking like one of those aerial shots of the Amazon meandering through the jungle. There's a pink tinge to the tarmac too – a reflection of the sky now that the sun has long vanished beyond the distant peaks. I can't stop for long, mind. There's still a fair whack to go.

*For the second time in one afternoon, van Garderen passes through Dutch Corner to a raucous reception on the front of the race. He's leading Riblon by almost a minute but he's still far away from giving the Dutch fans a de facto win. When Adam Hansen, the Australian riding an astonishing sixth consecutive Grand Tour, cuts through the sea of orange later in the gruppetto he'll grab a beer from one of the spectators and take a swig. But van Garderen can't raise a glass just yet. Nor Froome, supported once again by team-mate Porte. The pair are concerned about something and seem to be spending about as much effort shouting into their respective earpieces as they are pedalling up the hill.*

**5** I reach round to my jersey pocket and whip out an energy gel. The trick with gels is to squeeze them with such force that they shoot down your throat with the alacrity of an oyster. But these blackcurrant ones are quite tasty and so I savour it in two gulps and a lingering suck. There's a reason why I'm topping up my energy levels now – and it's not just a final pick-me-up ahead of the long descent home. For it's around here, just above Huez village, that Froome – suffering what the French call *la fringale*, or hunger-knock – took on the illicit gel that earned him a 20-second penalty. I drew a line at riding off the road and putting my already sodden foot in Riblon's ditch on the Sarenne – but this is one piece of Tour retrospective mirroring I can manage.

*The yellow jersey raises his hand to signal his team car. He clearly has a problem. The commentator thinks it may be a mechanical issue – and the camera duly zooms into his back wheel, as if looking for a puncture. And where's Porte? Froome's wing-man has disappeared and now the yellow jersey is isolated with four more kilometres left to the finish. After a brief hesitation, Quintana and Rodríguez ride on. Porte then suddenly returns into the picture. He taps Froome on the shoulder then hands something over. Froome raises this something to his mouth and sucks. Ah, the problem is not 'mécanique' but 'humain', says the French commentator. And that is a flagrant flouting of the rules by Sky.*

*Karma takes care of itself almost instantaneously: while handing his bonking buddy some of his sticky juice, Porte catches his handlebars on a fan's Japanese flag and almost loses his balance. A policeman then bounds across the road in pursuit of a Marouane Fellaini lookalike wearing a pair of black briefs. It's all happening on the Alpe.*

**3** A rethink is in order. If I want to make it to the official finish then I won't be able to ride down. Dusk is calling last orders on my adventure and I need to make it back down to the valley before closing time. How about a compromise? I'll ride to the town sign before ringing the bell and calling it a day.

*Van Garderen had the win within his grasp but he's shot his bolt. Riblon has cut the lead to just 30 seconds and is very much in the ascendency. As for Froome, it's a question of damage limitation now. His main rival, Contador, is further back, while Quintana trails him by seven minutes in the overall standings. That energy gel won't win him the Tour – but it may have ensured he doesn't lose it. Almost 25 minutes later, in this exact same spot, Slovakian showman Peter Sagan – the green jersey with a penchant for pinching the pert posteriors of podium girls – will further endear himself to the crowd with a look-mum-no-hands wheelie that outdoes his hands-on-the-bars one-wheeled effort a few days ago on Mont Ventoux.*

**2** After the penultimate hairpin I stop at the Alpe d'Huez sign to pose for some blurred yet smug selfies as I pull off a Churchillian V-for-victory – one finger for each ascent. But I can't stop here, surely? I need to ride at least beyond the first hairpin.

*Riblon passes under the 3km-to-go banner after Pantani's second corner. He has cut the deficit to 20 seconds. Now that the crowds are held back by the barriers France's saviour can see his prey ahead.*

**1** As much as I'd like to continue to the official summit I really have to turn round now. Look, it's OK, I made it to the town, and fittingly, this is the corner responsible for my first ever Alpe d'Huez experience back in 2004. As I gaze up towards the town there's a linear flicker as the street lights come on. Ah, it's like those grim moments from my youth when the lights would come on in dirty nightclubs, revealing quite how rough everyone looks, including the girl you've been dancing with. If ever there was a time to do a runner, this was it. I toy with the idea of sending James a text to tell him to hold off calling the police because I'm on my way. But this will take time and cost a notoriously tight half-Scot 50p to send. Let's get this dark descent started.

*Riblon rounds the final hairpin and dances up the steep ramp with van Garderen in touching distance. Following in the Ag2R team car, his directeur sportif shouts encouragement from behind the wheel. France are on their way to successive victories on the most famous mountain-top finish in the biggest bike race in the world. Just under the 2km-to-go banner, Riblon catches his American counterpart, who betrays his Dutch roots by pedalling in an invisible pair of clogs.*

I've barely negotiated two downward bends when I round a kink in the road and skid to a halt in front of a truly startling sight. Beyond the snug hairpin of corner four, between the opposing jagged sides of the Sarenne gorge, a full moon shines bright after a theatrical parting of the clouds reminiscent of the very best of Hollywood werewolf films. The brightness of the moon illuminates the road to reveal slogans dedicated to Bjarne Riis's Saxo-Tinkoff team and the Danish riders Lars Bak and Jakob Fuglsang. Now I really can tell the world that I descended Alpe d'Huez by moonlight.

Not that my guiding light lasts for long. All of 20 vertical metres later and the moon's glow is obscured by the mountain. Riding through near darkness can be chalked down as another nod to Tours of times past. In the early days, stages averaged over 400 kilometres in length and most would start well before dawn. The final stage of the inaugural Tour – a ridiculous 471 kilometres from Nantes to Paris – actually started at 9 p.m., forcing the peloton to ride through the night to ensure a prime-time finish in front of 20,000 spectators.

One of Jacques 'To prepare for a race there is nothing better than a good pheasant, some champagne, and a woman' Anquetil's most memorable exploits came with his back-to-back victories in the Dauphiné and the 557-kilometre classic Bordeaux–Paris. Just hours after winning the stage race in the Alps, Anquetil flew to Bordeaux and demolished a midnight meal before taking to the start of the marathon night-time race. Understandably, he wasn't feeling very perky during those early hours of the day. He had stomach cramps and was on the verge of retiring when his team manager swore at him and called him 'a massive poof'. This spurred on Anquetil, a man who thrived in his red-blooded heterosexuality. He responded to a series of attacks from Tom 'To prepare for a race there's clearly nothing worse than amphetamines and a shot of Pernod' Simpson before taking the win. He then had to make the long journey to Maubeuge in north-east France because he was due to take part in a criterium the next day.

Looking back at this exploit, five-time Tour-winning thoroughbred Anquetil – who was unashamedly open about his pharmaceutical help – allegedly once told the French minister for sport: 'You can't win the Dauphiné and Bordeaux–Paris on a sugar cube.' For his part, Fausto Coppi – a great believer in moderation – famously admitted to doping only when he needed to. 'Which is almost all the time,' he added.

My own night ride is admittedly shorter than Anquetil's nocturnal schlep to Paris and I clearly have less need for 'La Bomba' to keep me going. But every little helps – and the street lights of Huez are very welcome for someone not benefitting from any medicinal 'glow-time'. Leaving the village my path darkens yet again – although there appears to be a fantastical glimmer shining through the fog from beyond the next ridge. My instinct tells me it's a fire but that seems highly unlikely. Up here, alone, in the middle of nowhere and on a bike, I'm feeling marginally scared. I try not to think of Gert-Jan Theunisse, the horror mask or even – given that it's a full moon tonight – hairy teen-wolf Michael J. Fox on the rampage with a basketball.

Nothing prepares me for the sight I'm treated to when making the left-hand bend (not acute enough to warrant hairpin status) before Dutch Corner. For the Église Saint-Ferréol is floodlit, with orange beacons illuminating the walls of the church and tower, as well as emanating from the belfry below the spire. It's an astonishing vision, chiefly because of its total unexpectedness. It's a sight I shouldn't be seeing because, frankly, I shouldn't be here. No one cycles up or down the Alpe in the dark, making me privy to something I reckon none of my friends, followers or colleagues in the cycling world have seen. This corner is arguably the most famous corner in cycling – and yet this is a side to it that has been revealed to me, and me alone. If that's not something to simultaneously smile and shed a tear at, then I might as well be made of stone. So smile and shed a tear I do.

Feeling blessed yet somewhat perturbed by the prospect of having to descend another 650 vertical metres in the dark, I press on, wishing I had eaten more carrots as a youngster. Seeing the lights of Bourg d'Oisans below is yet another glorious visual gift for the memory bank but it's not helping the immediate task in hand. Nor is the wooded section of road between here and La Garde. Every now and then cars pass by in the opposite direction, their lights dazzling yet useful. Some of the drivers, quite rightly, give me a honk. None of them, thankfully, wind down their windows and call me 'a great poof'.

It's so dark that I fail to see if the local council have put up Christophe Riblon's name on corner 15 (for it was the Frenchman who did indeed beat Tejay van Garderen last July – by 59 seconds in the end). There's some respite in La Garde because of the return of glowing street lights, but the final five bends are rather chancy and what I am doing is undeniably dangerous – right up there with a game of Russian roulette. Cars and cliff edges aside, I can barely see the road ahead and so it's all pot luck as to whether or not I snag a rock or hole. On the penultimate straight ahead of corner 21 I narrowly miss a boulder the size of a child's head which only comes into view as I pass – funnily enough just as I'm hitting my peak nocturnal downhill speed of 42 kmph. I clearly have good old Saint Ferréol on my side.

His mobile held to his ear, James looks flustered on the outside stairs of the hotel as I roll home at 8.30 p.m. 'Ah, forget that, Sam,' he says. 'Crisis over: he's just got back.'

The restaurant has stopped serving but James – a man after my own heart – put in an earlier order for me. Sharing my soft spot for good, honest mountain food, he's got me the closest thing to a *tartiflette* on the menu: a baked pasta and potato dish with melted cheese, onions and sausage. I wolf it down with a huge side salad before joining Roddy and Melbourne John in demolishing a round of warm chocolate fondants. I eat with the prurience of palate that you'd expect from someone who has shed the best part of 6,000 calories while riding a largely sodden 126 kilometres – including 3,200 vertical metres – for a total saddle time of 7 hours and 23 minutes. I eat with a clear conscience, unlike Chris Froome, whose illegal, legal pick-me-up earned him a 20-second penalty – considerably less time than he would have lost had his bonk gone unanswered. Quite ridiculously, the race leader complained to the commissaires, claiming it was Porte who actually broke the rules by taking gels from the team car, and so the Tasmanian should have been sanctioned.

As far as defences go, it was right up there in the Alberto Contador school of excuses. Talking of the Spaniard, Froome did at least resist the temptation to divert attention by questioning his rival's timely bike swap . . . Ho hum.

# BOURG D'OISANS TO COL AGNEL

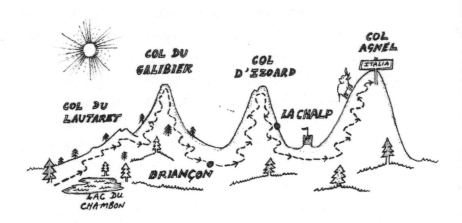

MY PENALTY FOR BEING EVEN MORE sluggish to rise than usual was to miss out on all the freshly baked croissants and pains au chocolat at breakfast. The thought – entirely reasonable in my books – that this double conqueror of Alpe d'Huez would appreciate something crispy, fluffy, warm and buttery to dip into his (criminally instant) coffee clearly did not cross the minds of my companions, well rested after their respective half days. 'Oh, sorry – I had three,' said Terry, sticking the butter knife in.

A lacklustre breakfast followed, of individually wrapped brioche buns, tinned fruit, syrupy orange juice and chocolate cardboard chunks doused in tepid long-life milk. A disappointing showing from a gastronomic titan of a country responsible for bringing to the world the combined delights of foie gras, strangled duck and a type of bread called *batard* ('bastard' to you or me). In a land where cows roam free and are even immortalized in three-ton stone busts, it's quite perplexing that UHT milk should be the norm, while the accumulation of processed juice and flavourless coffee-themed hot beverages made a mockery of all those French role plays we used to do at school, asking the *garçon* for the universally feted *orange pressée* along with a *café au lait, s'il vous plaît.* You'd expect French milk to be so unpasteurized that your morning cereal could feasibly count as an extension to the previous night's cheese course. Meanwhile, for every warm, doughy baguette there would instead be a pre-packed crispy couplet that someone had the audacity to call 'toast', both slices of which would crumble into pieces when introduced, with a knife, to a rock-hard rectangle of counterfeit butter, not to mention a sorry excuse for apricot jam that put the 'con' into *confiture*.

Not that I let the occasional slipping in culinary standards get to me. Hardly a Henry VIII on wheels, I was prepared to lower my expectations when necessary – even accept quantity over quality if required. Although the daily riding of triple-digit kilometres did make me highly adept at being prepared to shovel whatever I could down my trap, uncanny cravings become commonplace – pots of processed apple compote, for instance, or triangles of the Laughing Cow 'cheese'. And if the ongoing bemoaning of sub-par baristas in France was as consistent as, say, the welcome appearance of duck on most evening menus, then the thought of Italy's superior caffè culture filliped our progression as we edged nearer and nearer to the final frontier of our journey.

Besides, that day I was late. Even later than Pedro Delgado was to the opening prologue of the 1989 Tour. Rumours flew thick and fast. The Spanish defending champion had fallen asleep in his hotel room; he had been drinking coffee with friends; the car transporting him to the start in Luxembourg was stopped by police. Delgado himself downplayed the episode, saying he'd merely been out training and then lost track of time while quizzing prologue specialist Thierry Marie about the course. This wasn't the most flattering way to describe his Anquetilian tryst with a seductress allegedly hired by Laurent Fignon to ensure his rival started the race in a preoccupied state (one of the saucier and more outlandish rumours to fly around the peloton). In what was a blow to his Tour chances (not to mention an indirect slur on his sexual stamina), Delgado eventually rolled down the ramp 2 minutes 40 seconds behind schedule – far more impressive than the combination of Boris Becker and a cupboard, but hardly enough to ruffle Sting's feathers.

Delgado became the only defending champion in history to start the first road stage of the Tour in last place – having already adhered to the old cliché of 'peaking too soon'. The next day, he bonked spectacularly in the team time trial, slipping more than seven minutes in arrears. As far as starts go, this was like Barcelona conceding three goals in the first five minutes of the opening game of the Spanish season – and having their goalkeeper sent off. Miraculously, Delgado would still finish on the podium in Paris, three and a half minutes down on Greg LeMond, who pipped Fignon by those slender 8 seconds. If only the ponytailed 'Professor' had sent 'Madame Prologue' to knock on the American's door instead . . .

Of course, some might say that starting the defence of your crown with a three-minute handicap was seven minutes more favourable than the penalty Delgado *should* have received for testing positive for a controversial masking agent the year before when in yellow. The kidney-cleaning drug in question, probenecid, was just one month away from making the UCI list of banned substances and so, technically, Delgado had broken no law. That the race leader escaped sanction caused an almighty kerfuffle – especially in the light of Delgado's main rival, that man Gert-Jan Theunisse, having himself been dealt the regulation ten-minute penalty for his own misdemeanour during the same race. One year on, and an injection of the *Kama Sutra* had supposedly supplied some suitable karma.

The next two days would take us over four mammoth peaks – including Europe's highest border crossing – as we bade farewell to France and rolled down into the Po valley to gorge ourselves silly on pasta. Stage 13 warmed up with the lengthy but not too fiendish ascent of the Col del Lautaret ahead of an optional schlep up the mythical Col du Galibier, a zippy descent down to Briançon and then an exacting slog up the Col d'Izoard before dropping through the eerie Mars-like *Casse Déserte*.

I tackled the Lautaret with precisely the kind of languor you might associate with a croissant-less teenager in an Amsterdam tea house. Starting off at the back with my knees justifiably waving the white flag after yesterday's punishing schedule, I grimaced my way back up the busy road to the Lac du Chambon, retracing in reverse my movements from the foot of the Col de Sarenne. There was no rainbow this time but the view was just as impressive: the rising sun breaking through low cloud and reflecting off the shimmering surface of the water.

The Lautaret has been used countless times in the Tour but usually as a warm-up to the more gruesome Galibier, the south side of which is accessed from the summit of what is usually a second-category climb during major races. Its lowly status is misleading: the western ascent pretty much starts as soon as you leave Bourg d'Oisans – and lasts for the best part of 40 kilometres, with an average gradient of 6 per cent. Rather than an hors d'oeuvre to the Galibier's main course, think of it more as a swanky drinks reception during which you guzzle a tray of canapés, often get caught up with bad company, and need quite a few top-ups to get yourself through.

More often than not, the wind – and not the gradient – is the worst enemy. We were lucky: although chilly in the shade it was a calm and pleasant day. Certainly one for the leg warmers, but once in a while, the sleeves could be detached and the somewhat neglected tan worked upon. After negotiating numerous tunnels – including one as long as 700 metres, where deafening cars roared up behind you like dragons closing in on their prey – we stopped in the pretty ski village of La Grave for a coffee opposite the towering peak of La Meije and the nacreous, grooved glacier of the Écrins Massif. James was in the van, giving Sam a chance to test ride one of the three twisted titanium steeds that he and Dylan were given in that sponsorship deal with the US bike manufacturer Lynskey (Javier, the Ecuadorian jack-of-all-trades, had driven the bikes all the way from Barcelona overnight).

It had been two days since we passed through the alleged site of Hannibal's ambush in the Gorges des Gats and Sam was aware that there were some gaps to fill; he was equally aware that he couldn't really fill them.

'Tomorrow we'll talk more about Hannibal's actual crossing into Italy but all I can say for certainty now is that his army could well have come up this same valley,' he said, before admitting that Hannibal could just have well come up the next valley, the Maurienne. The problem for those trying to crack the Hannibal conundrum is that neither Polybius nor Livy actually mention any place names in their accounts of the Alpine crossing, while no archaeological findings, such as Carthaginian coins or elephant skeletons, have been discovered.

One reason for the lack of bones to pick with the pachyderms is the simple fact that none of Hannibal's thirty-seven treasured war elephants perished in the mountains – quite impressive if you consider the warmer conditions these animals were used to. The poet John Donne might have described the elephant as 'the only harmless great thing' but try telling that to one of Carthage's enemies or the countless Celtic tribes whose territory Hannibal traversed en route from Catalonia. The Roman historian Lucretius writes of humongous beasts with towers attached to their backs and a 'serpent-shaped hand . . . throwing martial battalions into confusion'. It's no surprise that the parts of Hannibal's train that never came under severe attack were those bolstered by elephants, the enemies being terrified by both the strangeness and enormity of their appearance.

The shock and awe factor of three tonnes of bulbous trumpeting flesh – atop tree-trunk legs and beneath ears that opened up like sails – cannot be underestimated. Long before their rise to Barcid totemic animal status, elephants had become 'must have' accessories for aspiring warmongers. One of the oldest known stories of elephants in combat dates back to around 800 BC when an Assyrian queen decided to invade India to plunder its wealth. Vexed by news that the Indians were training an army of elephants, the queen ordered the slaughter of 300,000 oxen, whose black hides were bound, stuffed and draped over thousands of unsuspecting camels to give the impression that the Assyrians had their own elephant troupe.

The plan initially worked. According to one dusty history book in the British Library, 'The Indian scouts, mistaking them for real, gave a dreadful account of their multitudes, and struck terror into their countrymen, who could not conceive whence the Assyrians should have furnished themselves with these tremendous animals.' But once some spoilsport deserters revealed the truth about the pachyderm puppets, all hell broke loose – largely thanks to the real Indian elephants. Diodorus wrote of 'these monsters [. . .] of incredible ferocity' and 'a prodigious killing' that took place in many guises: 'Some fell beneath their feet and others were torn apart by their tusks, while yet others were tossed about by their trunks. Multitudes of corpses soon lay about in heaps.'

It was perhaps these tales of ferocious Indian elephants which made King Darius of Persia so wary. In a battle in 520 BC, he ordered his men to load herds of camels with containers of flammables before lighting them up and driving the flaming animals towards the enemy elephants. Both these stories are, admittedly, just as much an example of the chronic savagery of man on the humble camel as they are elephant on man, but they do at least show how these supposedly harmless creatures had become the weapons of mass destruction of their time. Indeed, a terracotta statue from Asia Minor, dated around 275 BC, shows a war elephant complete with driver (mahout) and tower (howdah) on its back, simultaneously throttling a pained barbarian warrior with its trunk while impaling him with its mammoth tusks and trampling him underfoot. Such a multitaskingly macabre way to go makes the Carthaginian tradition of plain crucifixion seem like a mere massage in comparison.

Carthage first came across elephants when fighting the Greek general Pyrrhus – he of costly victories – in Sicily before the First Punic War with Rome. Soon elephants replaced chariots as their main striking power. You could say elephants were the tanks of their time. Given their life expectancy of sixty years, they certainly had a good mileage. Although they were fuel guzzlers: needing 300 pounds of food a day made each beast hungrier than twenty horses. That said, their powerful diesel engine – which saw Hannibal's elephants peak at 30 kilometres a day – was of an economical hybrid variety: the self-sufficient heffalumps were instinctive foragers who would only rely on a few extra treats from their friendly mahouts.

Elephant driving licences were hard to come by. Mahouts were the Formula 1 pilots of their age – highly trained men who were not easily replaceable. If, for instance, several mahouts had drowned during the crossing of the Rhône, problems would have ensued, for elephants are known to grow emotionally attached to their trainers. Which is odd considering the Carthaginians equipped all their mahouts with a rather primitive prototype of a handbrake: a metal spike which they were expected to hammer into the soft nape of their elephant's neck should control be lost.

This was a common problem with elephants. Weapons of mass destruction they were – but it wasn't necessarily the enemies who were in the firing line. Early attempts to incorporate elephants into combat during the First Punic War were mixed. In the Battle of Agrigentum in 262 BC, sixty Carthaginian elephants fled, trampling their own soldiers underfoot. Seven years later, however, Carthage beat Rome in Sparta with the elephants putting in a stand-out performance. Judging by the staying power of Hannibal's elephants, it seems like the Barcid dynasty had finally perfected the use and handling of the creatures.

It's worth adding that Hannibal's elephants were not of the larger African bush or Asian variety, but a smaller forest species from the Moroccan Atlas mountains, now extinct. Measuring 2.5 metres high at the shoulder, they boasted ears with enormous flaps and rounded lobes; their backs were domed, their tusks long and their trunks ringed and not smooth. But despite their relative diminutiveness, they were still physically intimidating creatures – certainly more so than a camel in fancy dress.

One thing's for certain: in war, you'd prefer lining up with the elephants on your side. Much like that moment when you scoured the opposition before kick-off at school rugby games, when the sight of some gigantic post-pubescent prop-forward waiting to pummel you into a pulp was a potential pant-wetter.

The protracted trudge up the otherworldly Col du Lautaret gave me ample time to muse over Hannibal's Pantani-style army of stunted elephants. I even had the luxury of dictating the introduction of my latest blog post into my phone, which, when played back, included much huffing and puffing, as well as the drone of numerous passing cars and trucks. This was, after all, the Route Nationale 91 – the busy highway or, ahem, trunk road, between Grenoble and Briançon.

Bob, Sam and myself were the only three riders keen to test our legs with the optional 8.5-kilometre detour up the Galibier and so had curtailed our coffee break to make some headway on the others. As Bob and Sam rode clear, I eased off to clear my thoughts and keep my legs fresh for the main attraction.

When the Galibier was first introduced to the Tour de France back in 1911, only three riders made it to the summit without dismounting. Despite being hit by a car and sent tumbling into a ravine earlier in the race, Émile Georget was first, followed by fierce rivals Paul Duboc and Gustave Garrigou. One of the seventy-odd riders who did resort to walking was Julien Gabory, who lost his shoes in the mud and had to finish barefoot (serves him right for cheating in the 1906 Tour by taking a train with three of his colleagues). Later in the race, when Duboc was taken ill in the Pyrenees because of food poisoning from a suspected spiked drink, Garrigou was accused of foul play. The eventual winner received so many death threats that, when passing through Duboc's home town of Rouen, Garrigou not only needed a bodyguard, he was also heavily disguised. (Hannibal, too, was in the habit of wearing wigs and other disguises when passing through the Alps – primarily because of his distrust of the Celtic tribes with whom he had made flimsy alliances.) Once in Paris, it was Duboc the people cheered as overall winner rather than his compatriot Garrigou, who claimed innocence in the spat until the day he died.

To celebrate the centenary of the maiden ascent of the most visited climb in the Alps, the 2011 Tour included a first ever summit finish on the Galibier – the highest in the race's history. The winner that day was softly spoken mountain whippet Andy Schleck, a true Luxembourgeois *gentilhomme* if ever there was one, who seized the yellow jersey from the shoulders of spirited Frenchman Thomas Voeckler (who, at school, surely never received lower than an A for effort) after a 60-kilometre solo break. Ahead of the rather subdued one-man Galibier showdown, stage 18 of the race included ascents of both the Col Agnel (from the Italian side) and the Col d'Izoard – pretty much our exact itinerary in reverse (except we had a night off scheduled before tackling the Agnel). Second that day was Schleck's older brother and team-mate Frank, often mistaken during the off-season for the lead singer of the glam rock outfit Muse.

The painted names of both Schleck siblings were still visible on the road two years later as I toiled up the magnificent route in the most merciful gear available. To make myself feel better about my listless legs, I remembered those early pre-war cycling trailblazers who had but two gears at their disposal, the most lenient of which was accessible only by physically stopping, removing the rear wheel and turning it around – a far cry from today's professionals, many of whom have cushy electric gearing systems at the push of a button.

The summit of the Galibier is accessed via a small road that leaves the busy N91 at the top of the Lautaret, shortly after the turn-off to what must be the loftiest botanical garden in the world. Snowfall closes the road between late October and May most years – although the harsh spring in 2013 meant the Giro's first ever foray up the Galibier in June was forced to stop 4 kilometres from the summit on the north side, next to the memorial to Marco Pantani, who sowed the seeds of his 1998 Tour triumph with a solo attack up this mystical peak.

As I passed by the car park at the foot of the climb, I spotted two men with bikes preparing themselves for an ascent. I waved, knowing that our paths would no doubt soon cross. The initial slopes of the climb were a pleasant surprise. The road sweeps round a grassy bowl at a gentle 6 per cent for a kilometre or so, easing you into the challenge ahead. With the sun shining bright in a blue sky across which strokes of slowly disappearing white puffs had been daubed by aeroplane contrails, this was gratefully inconsistent with my experiences on previous legends of the Tour.

Where my ascents of Ventoux and Alpe d'Huez were hampered by foul weather, the third scene in this operatic small ring cycle couldn't have been more perfect. The climbs differ too. Where both Ventoux and the Alpe have distinct forested areas and are played out on busy roads, the Galibier is beautifully desolate, a calming experience in acute contrast with the physical demands it exerts on those willingly drawn into its web. Head to the Alpe if you want a disco or Ventoux for the full theme park experience. But the inspiring Galibier purifies the soul and takes you on a farther-reaching journey amid its awesome arena. The road here actually feels like part of the mountain – not a modern-day infliction.

After a couple of kilometres during which I was met by the odd cyclist careering down the mountain, the road swept round to open up views along the Guisane valley beyond the jumble of twisting roads converging at the now-distant Lautaret crossroads. Two cyclists – probably the chaps from the car park – were riding side by side at a steady pace in pursuit. The only trees visible were those of the lush Jardin Alpin, which boasts 2,100 species of alpine plants, one for every metre the site stands above sea level. Over my shoulder I could see the towering Pointe Piaget and Pic Gaspard, the gullies of their jagged peaks packed with ice and snow, contrasting dramatically with the greenery of the nearer slopes, the grey matter of the rocks and road, and the deep blue of the sky. Stretching out ahead of me, the road reached for the heavens, its white, ordered markings colliding on the horizon and seemingly taking flight to merge with those plane contrails.

A brown sign on the right of the road states that I'm on the Route des Grandes Alpes, a tourist trail that runs from Lake Geneva to the French Riviera, taking in the highest passes of the Alps. It strikes me that this is not the first time this year that I've ridden past such a sign. Indeed, the Col des Saisies, Col de l'Iseran and Col de Vars, which I scaled in those training sportives, are all on the same route, as are the upcoming Izoard and Agnel. The parents of a close friend drove down the entire route in a vintage MG earlier in the summer and they're following my progress via my blog with piqued interest. It's not so much classic cars as revving motorbikes tackling the route today – their noisy motors momentarily piercing the blissful silence.

Our chosen forms of two-wheeled transport couldn't be more different. Although if you believe one controversial rider, the line between cyclist and biker is somewhat blurred. Not long after receiving a lifetime ban for a third doping offence in the wake of the 2013 Giro, debonair Italian veteran Danilo Di Luca made an audacious claim that many riders had 150-watt motors hidden inside their top tubes. It wasn't the first time such allegations had been made, with Fabian Cancellara's Tour of Flanders and Paris–Roubaix double in 2010 linked (wrongly) to alleged motorized assistance. In the same interview, Di Luca also claimed that '90 per cent of the peloton were on drugs during the Giro' and that the remaining 10 per cent were merely using the race as training. It's worth adding that the interview was with one of Italy's popular satirical television shows so there is a slim chance that Di Luca was merely playing a parody of himself – although that would have required an ounce of intelligence and ingenuity.

Still, the UCI clearly gave Di Luca's claims some credence: a number of bikes were checked at the 2014 cyclocross world championships for evidence of mechanical doping. No motors were found. Personally, I could do with an engine right now – although deep down I'm clear in my view that the dress code for places like the Galibier should be Lycra, not leather.

A tight bend crosses a gurgling stream at the most westerly part of the climb. Doubling back, I can see those two cyclists closing in. The competitive side of me is stirred – I must hold them off until the summit – but the sentimental side is won over by the aura of the mountain. I slow to take some photos, including one of a road ode to the 'SAXO BOYS' – the Danish contingent of Alberto Contador's Saxo-Tinkoff team. The faint noise of cowbells drifts up the slope and makes me smile, reminding me of my childhood and Milka chocolate.

Ahead, a bus is parked on the side of the road beside the cliff face. Thinking this could well herald the summit, I up my tempo, content to have staved off the threat from my two pursuers. But no. The bus belongs to a group of students on a school field trip, gathered in a large bunch on the side of the road with clipboards in hand. They cheer me rather half-heartedly as I swing round the corner and discover, rather alarmingly, that there's still the best part of 3 kilometres to go until the top.

A series of sweeping bends leads to the tunnel alongside the monument to Henri Desgrange, the founder of the Tour who rated the Galibier as far more superior to the 'pale and vulgar concoctions' of the Pyrenees first used one year earlier in the race. 'Before this giant we can but doff our cap and take a bow,' he said of the Galibier on the Alps's introduction to the Tour in 1911. Not that the riders shared his opinion: 'You are bandits,' cursed Garrigou when crossing the finish line in Grenoble. To this day, the 'Souvenir Henri Desgrange' is awarded to the first rider over the highest peak of each Tour. With recent winners including Michael Rasmussen, Stefan Schumacher, Alexandre Vinokourov, Tony Rominger and Franco Pellizotti, the ghost of Desgrange would arguably be within his rights to retort that banditry was not entirely absent from the peloton either.

The tunnel was used by the Tour until 1976 when it was closed for repair. Following the closure, the higher road was improved on both sides to add roughly another kilometre on to the climb and take riders up to 2,642 metres. The extra road is a tight coil of bends where the gradient ramps up to a knee-jarring, lung-testing 9.2 per cent. It's here that two things happen: first I'm joined by my pursuers, who turn out to be a pair of Spaniards in matching blue and white kit; Bob then passes in the opposite direction, congratulates me (on coming to a near standstill on the inside of the first bend) before edging off with caution towards his lunch.

At first I feel the game's up. But then I find myself riding back on to the wheels of the Spanish duo. I'm caught in the crossfire, feeling every bit the Galibier gooseberry as the two of them chatter away to each other. Sam approaches on his way down. I slow to wave and confirm a Briançon luncheon rendezvous. And then – a final deterrent for the weak of will and a slap-in-the-face to all others – the gradient picks up to a beastly 13 per cent. The longer-haired Spaniard is on the ropes and I spot my chance. Performing my own out-of-the-saddle fandango, I dance up the slope and pip him over the line. It's a *bocadillo* of a podium, with me the lean and gristly meat filling separating first from third.

Being such a beanpole, I'm used to lofty vantage points. But the view from the fourth highest mountain pass in France was just sensational – to the point that doffing my cap and taking a bow felt wholly inadequate. I would have performed some kind of jig while serenading my surroundings were it not for the presence of a gang of brutish-looking German bikers with crewcuts and earrings and massive black boots, the soles of which I did not fancy becoming acquainted with – the very same bikers in whose general direction I had gesticulated with opened fingers as they whipped past me earlier, clearly not anticipating their prolonged get-together on the summit.

In a show of solidarity I cosied up to Tony and Pablo, my Spanish allies, and offered to take a photo of them both beside the large signs indicating the border between the departments of Savoie and Hautes Alpes. Emphasizing the levels of provincial pride in these parts, someone has painted a line across the road with 'SAVOIE' on one side and 'FRANCE' on the other. We chatted in French because their English and my Spanish spawned scenes worse than the now-defunct soap opera *Eldorado*. I asked them what they thought of Chris Horner's recent win in their back garden.

'It was a wonderful victory. The Vuelta was won by the best man,' said Tony (or Pablo). The Spanish not being renowned for their sarcasm, I had to assume the answer was said with complete sincerity.

'But you weren't suspicious of a 41-year-old riding so much better than everyone else?' I asked, trying to strike a nerve. They shook their heads as if I were crazy.

'We're the same age as Horner and we don't need drugs.'

'But I managed to keep up with you – just – and I certainly couldn't win the Vuelta.'

'You must look at the race in the context of the season. Horner was fresh and had only raced for fifteen days all year before the Vuelta. His rivals were all very tired after the Giro and the Tour. It's normal for Horner to win in these circumstances.' They certainly made my inherently sceptical mind accept that there was another side to the Horner debate – even if I still considered it far from normal that a rider in his fifth decade could cross-train away from his much younger opponents.

On that defiant note, Tony and Pablo braced themselves for their swift descent back to the Lautaret car park. Their plan was to drive on to Bourg d'Oisans and scale Alpe d'Huez in the afternoon. '*Petits joueurs*,' I said. 'I did it twice yesterday afternoon and then rode up here this morning.' After lapping up a round of laudatory *Oi, oi, ois* (the Spanish equivalent of the French *Oo la la* but without the steamy undertones), I couldn't resist throwing in the names of my ultimate destination and our original starting point two weeks previously. This swiftly prompted the kind of reverence old Desgrange held for the mighty Galibier.

'Barcelona to Rome? Wow. Maybe you *should* do the Vuelta next year after all,' said Pablo (or Tony).

After a few minutes of self-reflection I myself followed the sign marked 'Briançon 35km'. Despite being well aware of the distance which separated my now-famished self from lunch, I was not going to risk all on the Galibier descent. The view is just too special to overlook in favour of downhill speeding; also, those drops off the side of the road are frightfully steep and I didn't fancy testing the robustness of my skull on the taunting rocks below. This descent is partly responsible for the Tour's first ever fatality back in 1935. Basque journeyman Francesco Cepeda was riding his fourth Tour and hoped to improve on his record of two successive withdrawals. At the end of a tricky first week, he sent a postcard to his local cafe in Bilbao, sending his regards to friends and family ahead of the seventh stage.

'A warm welcome to you all from Aix-les-Bains in the Tour de France,' the 29-year-old, then seventy-second in the standings, wrote. 'I imagine that you're up to date with the news from the first stages of the race, which were ridden at a tremendous pace. That's to blame for our low position and for the unjustified withdrawals of some of my team-mates. But I will continue to fight as hard as I can and make it to Paris – just as long as nothing serious comes my way. Hello to everybody and see you on my return.' But young Cepeda never did return.

The basic version of events has been simplified over the years, and goes something like this: Cepeda crashed down a ravine on the Lautaret side of the Galibier and died from his injuries three days later. What actually happened is less clearcut. It was a fiercely hot day and numerous riders in the peloton suffered punctures and accidents. Cepeda himself left the road at Saint-Jean-de-Maurienne ahead of the Col du Télégraphe. He is also known to have crashed outside the town of Vizille, near the stage finish at Grenoble. A series of photos published in a sports magazine at the time include an image of Cepeda being helped back on his bike. The caption reads: 'Finally, standing upright for the last time, after his fatal crash on the outskirts of Vizille. Almost unconscious, he is ready, encouraged by the spectators, to get back on his bike . . . Unfortunately, he has a fractured skull and will die in hospital without regaining consciousness.'

It transpires that Cepeda also experienced a third fall that day, perhaps into the back of a parked or moving car, on the descent of the Galibier. It was this crash, the second of the three, that is thought to have done the damage – meaning the poor numbskull rode the best part of 80 kilometres with a ticking time bomb in his head that finally exploded in Vizille. To add another layer of controversy, blame was apportioned to the overheating of Cepeda's newly designed aluminium rims, which caused the tyres to peel off at top speed.

If you discount the unfortunate case of Adolphe Hélière (who suffered a stroke while swimming on the French Riviera on the rest day of the 1910 Tour), Cepeda was the first of only three rider fatalities in Tour history, the second being Tom Simpson in 1967 and the third Fabio Casartelli, the reigning Olympic champion who crashed fatally on a Pyrenean descent in 1995. The perils of cycling at speed downhill were only too apparent when I rejoined the N91 at the Lautaret crossroads and was caught off-guard by a wild gust of wind roistering up the valley. Lurching across the road and frantically trying to regain control of my quivering handlebars, I just managed to maintain balance and get back in lane. Shaken, rattled but fortunately not rolled, I recovered my composure, thanking my lucky stars for the second time in a week that there had been no oncoming traffic during my momentary flirtation with fatality.

If my mindset while riding up dastardly gradients is constantly tempered by feelings of fatigue, then my elation levels going down are haunted by the phantom of good, old-fashioned fear. I just don't do fast descents. Ever since that hip-ripping crash as a teenager, I've been petrified of hitting potholes at a velocity better suited to those wearing seatbelts and protected by an airbag. Watching countless peloton pile-ups on TV hasn't helped and I have winced at quite enough road-rashed limbs and broken collarbones to fill my veins with pathological anxiety. Which brings me to Wouter Weylandt. The promising Belgian rider was only 26 years old when, looking over his shoulder, he clipped a concrete bollard at 80 kmph in stage three of the 2011 Giro. He was catapulted face first across the road and into the cliff edge on the narrow descent of the Passo del Bocco around 17 kilometres from the finish. Exactly twelve months earlier, Weylandt had won stage three of the 2010 Giro; the corresponding stage at the following year's race had now killed him.

Those horrific images still haunt me. Whoever was directing the host feed sensed the gravity of the situation and the coverage cut to another camera almost instantly, but the few seconds of hazy live footage of the immediate aftermath of the crash – images that will probably never be shown on television again – were enough for me to deduce that the rider lying motionless on the road was dead.

Jonathan Vaughters, manager of the Garmin team, later likened the crash to jumping out of a fast-moving car wearing only your underwear. 'Quite frankly, on the level of athletes putting their safety on the line for a sport, the American macho sports like football and other typical "guy sports" are a joke,' Vaughters told the *New York Times*. 'Bicycle racing is an unbelievably brutal and dangerous sport with no margin for error.' Covering the event for a live internet audience, I had to maintain my objectivity and decorum. But I told my colleagues in the office that someone had just died. Although yet to be confirmed, it was that obvious. The race doctor later said that he was on the scene within twenty seconds of the crash but that Weylandt had been killed on impact.

His girlfriend was five months pregnant with the couple's first child.

It makes you well up just thinking about it. And think about it I do on similarly narrow, steep and technical descents, where I'm fully aware that a moment's indecision, recklessness or – as was the case with poor Weylandt – simply bad luck, could end it all.

But the descent to Briançon was not in this category. A wide, straight road, recently surfaced, with few kinks or bumps, a favourable tailwind, a consistent slight downhill gradient and the light traffic of a Thursday lunchtime all conspired to rouse the daredevil inside me. It was incredibly inviting and without knowing it I was suddenly pushing 90 kmph. Such a speed seems reckless and inconceivable to me now – blimey, it seemed reckless as I mused over it at the dinner table six hours later. But it was not even the fastest I would travel that day – for on the final drop off the back of the Col d'Izoard and towards our chalet accommodation I peaked out at a terrifying 93.2 kmph. This speed haunted me in my nightmares for weeks to come. It was a speed which, when referred to in my blog, prompted a series of text messages from my oldest brother, his perspectives now changed by fatherhood.

'Take it careful . . . one tyre blowing and u in a world of pain . . .'

'Seriously . . . be careful, it's not closed roads.'

'Cars one thing . . . animals from trees . . . oil on road . . . tyre problem . . . that's way too fast.'

My father emailed me the next day to remind me that there would be 'trouble if you come off at such a speed'. I heard them both loud and clear; my highest speed over the course of the remainder of the whole ride to Rome was a whole 20 kmph slower. I'd much prefer to spend more time on two wheels one behind the other than two wheels side by side, separated by a chair – or worse.

The ski resort of Serre Chevalier ushered in some familiar surroundings. It was here that the first of my two stages on the Haute Route

finished exactly a month earlier. I had ridden 160 kilometres from
the ski resort of Val d'Isère, crossing the Col de l'Iseran, Col du Mont
Cenis and Col de l'Échelle, only to then have to turn round and ride
5 kilometres back to my Briançon hostel for the night, the aptly named
Auberge de l'Impossible. I passed by that old haunt before negotiating
the tricky one-way system into town, spotting John and Kay looking
bewildered on the side of the road, but unable to stop because of a
caravan driving right on my back wheel. It has been said that the Tour
is won at Briançon before it's won in Paris – primarily because of the
town's proximity to both the Galibier and our next challenge, the Col
d'Izoard. But before my second date with the Izoard – the first of three
climbs on my second stage at the Haute Route – there was a much-
needed lunch to be savoured.

The remainder of the group were at varying stages of replenishment
when I pitched up at a cafe in the town's main square. My fellow Galibier
conquerors Bob and Sam's lunch had just arrived and the burgers did
look rather tempting. A glance over the menu and I really couldn't
resist: fifteen minutes later my rare patty with melted reblochon cheese
and bacon arrived, as well as a healthy side of thrice-cooked chips.
The soft brioche bun was soggy with combined meat and cheese
juices. Haute cuisine it was not, but my 'Serre Che' burger hit the spot
beautifully.

As much as the burger filled a Galibier-shaped hole in my growling
stomach, it certainly hampered my performance on the Izoard. While
five-time Tour winner Jacques 'I tried to drink water once; it made
me sick' Anquetil was famous for filling his bidons with Pernod and
Champagne, even this notorious gourmand – whose favourite platters
included peppered steak tartare, sweetbreads in a cream sauce with
creamed spinach, and langoustine with slathers of mayonnaise – stopped
short of eating goose liver pâté on race days (although he was known to
provoke journalists by smoking before stages – and must have been the

only rider whose myriad victories could be attributed more to mussels than muscles).

When I tackled the intimidating Izoard one month earlier it was the opening test in a 110-kilometre stage of diminishing difficulty, which culminated in the ski resort of Pra Loup after a midway schlep over the Col de Vars. The sun had barely risen when we set off from freezing Briançon for a crowded ride up and out of town. Once the pack began to thin out, I rather shamefully popped my first energy gel.

'Bit early for one of those?' said a fellow straggler. I felt so chastened that I had seriously considered lying through gritted teeth, claiming that these were special pure fruit gels for Type 2 diabetics like me who should really be at home on the sofa as opposed to overtaking healthy men, like him, in the saddle. But I'm glad I bit my tongue because of the next rider I passed: a one-legged man making light work of the 6 per cent gradient ahead of the village of Cervières.

This was Haute Route legend Christian Haettich, who took up cycling twenty years after, aged 15, a road accident resulted in the amputation of his left leg and hand. While I was out as a two-day training tourist, Christian was doing the whole week-long race, and then taking on the Haute Route Pyrenees for a double known as the 'Iron Challenge'. Next year, he's doing the triple when the Haute Route adds on a third leg in the Dolomites. His story is one of true inspiration, and helped me through many a painful day when my comparatively minor knee and lower-back quibbles were getting me down.

A month on and it's not a gel I need but some water. I forgot to refill my bidons down in Briançon and those chips at lunch were saltier than my armpits. Sam and I were last to leave after I faffed around buying sweets and painkillers. We passed John and Kay on the initial rise out of town before burger-burping our way along the pleasant plateau that runs alongside the gorge at the foot of the mountain, chewing the fat and generally taking things easy in a partial post-prandial stupor.

At Cervières, Sam spots Melbourne John leaving the road to visit a cafe and stops himself to check he's OK. I should really stop also because it's hot and my water situation is getting desperate. But I'm getting into a rhythm and both Sharon and Terry are dangling ahead like Mexican piñatas ready to be smashed to smithereens. I pass them at exactly the same spot as I guiltily rode clear of mono-limbed marvel Christian, around 8 kilometres into the onerous 19-kilometre climb and just before things get serious. My passive-aggressive laments of being out of water fall on deaf ears; neither of my companions feel the urge to share a drop. I'm relying on James coming to the rescue in the support van – but that's been the tactic for the past 10 kilometres and hope is running dry.

It's a time like this when I dearly need the one thing that unified Fausto Coppi and Gino Bartali. In the wake of the Second World War, the two Italian arch-rivals played out a battle that enthralled a nation for years – even if it did divide Italian *tifosi* into *coppiani* and *bartaliani*. In one corner was the older, conservative and religious Bartali from the agricultural south; in the other was his mercurial challenger – a dashing rogue from the industrial north known as 'The Sinner' because of his adulterous affair with a married woman.

The roots of their rivalry were sown in the 1940 Giro when beginner Coppi joined the more experienced Bartali's team and won the race with a massive lead which affronted his superior. Their careers put on hold during the war – although Coppi did manage to break the Hour Record in 1942 while bombs dropped on Milan, before being thrown into a North African prisoner-of-war camp by the English – both men would win Grand Tours after peace was declared. Their rivalry came to a head in the 1948 world championships when both climbed off their bikes rather than help each other – a tactic seemingly copied by Messrs Froome and Wiggins some sixty-five years later in Florence. Such was their antagonism, they seemed to care less about winning races than beating each other – and when their falling-out resulted in Fausto skipping the '48 Tour, 'Gino the Pious' triumphed and in doing so was celebrated as the man who prevented a revolution in Italy.

One picture perfectly sums up the complex relationship of these two champions: a black-and-white image from Coppi's victorious 1952 Tour shows the riders exchanging a bottle of Perrier on the Galibier. For years, Coppi insisted he was handing the water to Bartali, while his rival always claimed the contrary. Even in rare moments of support, the pair could not find common ground.

A deserted bar saves me. I order an orange juice, which disappears in two long gulps, and ask, not without trepidation, to fill up my water bottles. The landlady obliges and I'm good to go – but not without the spectre of one of Greg LeMond's quirky anecdotes hanging overhead. It was spring time in 1986 and Greg had arrived in north Italy ahead of the Giro and decided to go on a chilly ride on the St Bernard Pass near Mont Blanc. With no money or bidons, he entered a remote bar 'full of farmers' and, parched, asked for some water. The four glasses he 'pounded down' had a rapid effect.

'I started walking towards my bike and all of a sudden I felt like –' Greg makes a gargling noise – 'yeah, and it was like –' and another noise – 'and then I was like, "ah shit!" I yanked up my jersey but it was too late. I had three layers on and full bib tights too. I was just on to my last jersey when, boom, it happened. I didn't let it go so much as it just went. It just happened like that.' He snaps his fingers. 'I had no option but to take my clothes off and get totally naked inside a cow trough to wash it all off. So,' he continues, unabashed, 'if you're riding in the area, avoid drinking out of faucets from farms. And avoid the troughs – they've probably got loads of faeces in them. In fact, just take a diaper.'

It has to be said: throughout his *annus mirabilis* of '86, Greg LeMond certainly showed consistency in his *anus terribilis*. I return to the saddle hoping that the mountain tap doesn't have a similar effect on me.

Perhaps it's because I've stuttered here before that I find the Izoard such a chore. It's a long slog and the milestones are a constant reminder of its magnitude. For the most part, it's enclosed and the surroundings are rather dull. There's really not much to look at until you break through the trees a couple of kilometres from the top to reveal the first glimpse of the jagged, barren and beautifully bleak rubble-sheathed ridges that roof this giant. By this point I've ghosted past Roddy despite his huge head start following lunch. Toiling dramatically, he was reduced to putting in short bursts interspersed with stationary breathers. I followed his lead in taking off my helmet and attaching it to my handlebars; the feeling of liberation far outdoing any safety concerns of a slow-speed uphill tumble.

'Hi, mate. How you going?' Surprised, I turn and see Sam. I must have slowed so much he had time to claw himself back. It's true that when I later compare my leisurely time on the Izoard to my more aggressive effort on the competitive Haute Route – where I was jostling for position with 400-odd opponents – it is a full fifteen minutes slower. But I did stop for water, there hasn't been a race feel to things, and today the Izoard is the last – and not the first – of three climbs.

In fact, my time for the last kilometre is 53 seconds faster than my previous effort, clearly because Sam and I find ourselves neck-and-neck for the very first time. I know that Sam – fresh, competitive and in possession of a pair of André Greipel-esque thighs – will try and sprint clear. Provocatively I pre-empt this with an early dig outside the Refuge Napoléon. Sam seems to take such effrontery as a slight. The bait is like a red rag to a bull, and he reacts by roaring clear. Gradually, I return to his wheel ahead of the final bend. But when he throws down the hammer for a second time I have no option but to be the anvil and accept the blow. He takes the king of the mountains points, but there will be ample time left between here and Rome to seize back those polka dots.

Bob, who we overtook during the death throes of our tussle, comes and joins us at the obelisk on the summit. The sun reflects off the bright veneers of his Hollywood smile as I take a snap of him and Sam posing beside the monument. Bob's beaming – and so he should be. A year ago, he had to fall on his sword and hitch a lift in the van on the Izoard. To come back and set the record straight – and do so after beasting the Galibier – is a huge personal achievement. He's so tenacious and strong that you forget he's in his eighth decade on this planet. If I'm still riding as hungrily and as elegantly when I'm Bob's age then something will have gone right. Either that or they'll have invented some EPO-based old biker's Viagra.

One day I'd love to ride *up* through the unearthly and bombastic *Casse Déserte* on the south side of the Izoard, but so far I've been pretty happy taking it in with a gravitational advantage. Much of the Izoard's reputation comes from its longer and more demanding south side – and the last 10 kilometres of the 30-kilometre ascent is thought to be up there with the hardest on any Grand Tour itinerary. Much of this is down to the dramatic backdrop of the 'Broken Desert' and its uneven slopes, vicious gradients and supernatural surroundings. Orange rock stacks twist upwards from blanched scree like something from a Salvador Dalí painting – propped up by their horizontal late-afternoon shadows that mingle with the pines that pepper the rusty ridges below. These stripped and twisting chimneys of sedimentary cargneule rocks apparently owe their appearance to being dedolomitized, which is what rocks of a certain persuasion get up to in separating their calcium carbonates from their magnesium carbonates. The exposed corniche cuts across the side of the mountain, drawing a line through what looks like a volcanic landslide of rubble. Old black-and-white photos transport the riders of yesteryear on to a bleached lunar wasteland, although the snazzy shades of today, with their red filters, must give the *Casse Déserte* more of a Martian aspect.

Two kilometres from the top I stopped at one of these pointy monolithic rocks which is now home to memorials to the two riders most readily associated with the Izoard: Louison Bobet and Fausto Coppi. Between 1949 and 1954 – when the road was just a rustic dirt track and riders had to dodge sharp flints as they toiled up the backbone, over the bare shoulders and towards the frowning brow of the mountain – both men soloed to victories with decisive attacks on the Izoard, Coppi twice and Bobet three times. In 1953, once Coppi had retired, the Italian legend stood on the same corner as the memorial today now stands and, camera in hand, cheered on his old friend alongside other Tour fans. Riding five minutes clear of his nearest rival, Bobet looked up and saw his hero, giving him a friendly nod as he passed en route to the yellow.

Part of the Izoard's mystique comes in its timeless ability to inspire legendary Tour figures in yellow to put in winning turns through the arid no-man's land of the *Casse Déserte*. So too is – or at least, was – the climb's knack of calling time on the careers of some of cycling's celebrated heroes. Just as Court No. 2 at Wimbledon has a reputation for being the graveyard of champions, so too has the Izoard hammered nails into the coffins of the seemingly immortal. Eddy Merckx was caught and passed by Bernard Thévenet in the petrified wilderness during a key stage of the 1975 Tour on 14 July, one day after Thévenet had definitively wrested the yellow from the Belgian's shoulders (a bikini-clad fan beside the road held a placard likening Merckx's fall to that of the Bastille). Another five-time winner's reign ended on the Izoard eleven years later when Bernard Hinault conceded the yellow jersey to Greg LeMond, who powered clear of his team-mate in the *Casse Déserte*. That night they had their much-publicized spat ahead of the truce which led to the arm-in-arm finale on Alpe d'Huez.

But everyone's best Izoard anecdote, by a country mile, comes from the 1946 five-day Monaco–Paris race, which was being run instead of the Tour following the fallout from the Second World War. In stage two, lone leader Apo Lazaridès, a young Frenchman of Greek descent who used his pedalling prowess to courier supplies to the French Resistance during the Occupation, inexplicably stopped near the summit and waited for his rivals to catch up. It turned out that poor Apo had never experienced anything like the ghostly remoteness and savage landscape of the *Casse Déserte*. He'd heard talk of bears inhabiting the forests of the Alps and he suffered a huge panic attack, his legs effectively turning to honey. Unwisely admitting these fears to his avuncular yet tyrannical team leader René Vietto that night, Apo was promptly slapped in the face. It wasn't the last piece of physical abuse 'Le Roi René' would inflict upon his 21-year-old insubordinate.

One year later, when Vietto contracted sepsis during the spring, the hot-headed Frenchman ordered his team doctor to cut off the offending toe. 'I'll be lighter in the mountains,' Vietto deadpanned before turning to the impressionable Apo and ordering him to join him on the operating table.

'*Mais pourquoi?* My toe is fine,' pleaded Apo with undisputed logic.

But Vietto was having none of it. He wanted his climbing domestique to feel the same pain, believing their shared experience would bind them closer together. 'Because I say so,' he replied.

Being a digit down didn't stop both men finishing in the top ten of the Tour later that summer – although who's to know what kind of feats they may have achieved with a full complement of toes. Given the iron fist with which he ruled, it's a good thing Vietto never suffered a road accident as serious as Christian Haettich, otherwise the unfortunate

Apo may have spent the rest of his life bear-dodging in the mountains with only one leg and one arm. As it is, Lazaridès probably got off lightly, merely walking with a wobble during the latter stages of his life (which saw him open up a mini-golf course on the Côte d'Azur). Legend has it that their toes are preserved in formaldehyde in a bar in Marseille. If only Damien Hirst would do something as artistic with his own fingers.

It's worth pointing out that Vietto was not always such a despot; his is that all-too-familiar case of the bullied becoming the bully. Riding his debut Tour aged 20, Vietto had already notched three wins in the opening fortnight when, in a long Alpine slog, he was forced to give his wheel to team leader Antonin Magne, in yellow since the second day of the race. A photographer caught Vietto bawling his eyes out while sitting on a wall and waiting for his team car to replace his wheel. The next day, as Vietto rode clear on a Pyrenean descent, a marshal drew alongside the youngster and informed him that Magne's bike had broken and his leader's *maillot jaune* was in jeopardy. Vietto then turned round and rode uphill so that he could hand over his bike. Thanks to his team-mate, Magne held on to the yellow all the way to Paris, while Vietto rode into Paris in fifth place, and was praised by the public as the moral winner of the Tour.

Despite Magne's constant graciousness towards his saviour, Vietto never forgave him for ruining his chances of glory in his maiden Tour. The Second World War took seven years out of Vietto's career. He wore the yellow jersey for eleven days in 1939 and fifteen days in 1947 but never managed to take an overall win. He died living as a recluse on a pig farm, which presumably contained just nine little piggies.

The rock dune nostalgia of the *Casse Déserte* now behind me, the highlight of the descent was, obviously, hitting my tour top speed on the 8 per cent straight into La Chalp, where the homely Chalet Viso welcomed us for the night. I enjoyed a shandy with Bob and Bernadette on the balcony in the late afternoon sun as the others rolled home in dribs and drabs. Going through my photos from the day I discovered a video I'd made what seemed like an eternity ago on the first climb of the day.

'Hi. *Blazin' Saddles* here, Saddleblaze, Felix Lowe,' baritones an unshaven, vaguely familiar-looking chap in a bright purple top. The picture then morphs into a kaleidoscopic blur before the angular face comes back into focus.

'Sorry, had to scratch my nose,' I say, after apparently scratching the peak now taking up centre stage.

'So, we're going up the Lautaret here. It's just opened up and it's absolutely beautiful. Absolutely beautiful. Let me show you . . . ' I do just that, giving the viewer a 360-degree panorama that includes trees, ravines, grassy plains and craggy snow-dusted summits.

'Today we're doing – I was tired this morning, bloody hell! – today we're doing the Lautaret, the Galibier, lunch in Briançon, and then the Izoard. It's going to be hell. I did the Izoard last month for the Haute Route and it was a real killer.

'Check this view . . .' The camera pans round, through the sun's glare, to reveal a straight road rising towards the mountainous horizon. 'Pretty damn good,' I summarize, with all the eloquence of Tim-Nice-But-Dim on wheels.

'I'm a bit sore, but I have to press on,' I say, getting serious.

'It's every cyclist's dream to be able to do this, so I'm very happy.' My sentimental side makes a brief appearance, before the consumer within restores the natural order: 'I'm looking forward to dinner, though. Dinner and sleep.'

I had good reason to look forward to dinner, where quiche Lorraine kicked things off, followed by a historic *lupin à la moutarde*, some stinky local cheeses and a génépi sorbet which teetotaller Bob devoured in record time. An extra helping of the dry yet flavoursome rabbit helped replenish my body's six-thousand-calorie deficit and made my stomach put in an extra shift as I toiled with the dual obstacles to sleep provided by Terry's snoring and beds so narrow they would have even ruffled the intergalactic feathers of David Bowie.

We had an injection of fresh blood at the Chalet Viso. That's not to say we unravelled some coat hangers, emptied out the mini-bar and performed a Riccardo Riccò-style home-grown autologous transfusion. For those not au fait with the consanguineous antics of the professional peloton, Italian climber Ricco almost killed himself while covertly pumping a load of his own badly refrigerated blood back into his body while his team-mates ate dinner a few floors below. Seeing that he barely survived to tell the tale (or at least his heavily doctored version of the tale – although clearly not doctored enough), the self-styled Cobra's life ban was a rather lucky escape.

No, our fresh blood came in the form of two newcomers to the Tour: fellow Brits of admirable bulk and wobble, Simon and Richard, who had signed up for a long weekend of riding. Their arrival was much later than expected after a monumental gaffe from their Italian taxi driver had seen them delivered to the wrong destination. As well as sounding a bit like an STD, La Chalp is an extremely common name for small mountain communities in the Alps whose inhabitants can't be bothered to come up with an original name – perhaps because they all believe their Chalp to be the authentic Chalp. There are almost more Chalps in the Alps as there are actual Alps without Chalps. Certainly the Chalp count is dearer than the number of Hannos in Carthage – and that's saying something.

By some Chalp catastrophe which must happen with considerable consistency, the Chalp that showed up on the driver's GPS was the Chalp by Val d'Isère, adding three Chalping hours and three hundred euros on to their journey. If only the hapless driver's blunder had taken them to the Chalp which we rode through the next day, just 20 kilometres away from our Chalp, then things would not have been so bad. But the story wouldn't have been half as funny.

Buoyed by the arrival of two extra British accents, I had started our final day in France alongside Simon and Richard at the back of our group. It's fair to say, both my new companions were carrying considerably more tummy padding than yours truly, and coupled with a desire to let rip after a much longer journey than they'd bargained for, they dropped like stones as we resumed the descent of the Izoard in conditions so crisp that Terry had once again donned his ski jacket. Having gleaned lashings of respect from them over tales of my daring D'Huez Double, I could hardly slink off the back at the first opportunity – even if memories of the previous day's blistering top speed had kept me tossing and turning during the night.

After 6 fraught kilometres, we reached the intersection opposite the river Guil.

'Lovely way to start the day,' said Simon.

'Yes, wonderful.' I tried to sound convincing. Last month, I had taken a sharp right here en route to the Col de Vars on the Haute Route. This time round, our itinerary took us in the opposite direction towards the medieval fort of Queyras, perched on a rocky outcrop above the rapids below. The road snaked its way along a ridge on a sheer cliff face, separated from the outcrop by a large abyss.

Some historians – Sam included – believe Queyras to be the location of what Polybius describes as 'a certain difficult and precipitous gorge' that Hannibal's army was crossing when they suffered another crushing ambush. It was certainly easy to comprehend how the enemy 'threw the Carthaginians into such extreme peril and confusion by rolling rocks down or by hurtling stones' from the higher ground. The chaos was such that the train was split and Hannibal was forced to spend a night with half his force on an exposed plateau before his army could regroup and pass through the defile the next day.

Our own mini army was splitting as the ascent of the Col Agnel started in earnest, with Richard – wearing the black-and-pink Lampre 'away strip' – edging clear. Either laziness or maturity prompted me to let him do just that: the former because it was very early and I had barely digested my croissants (this time fresh, plentiful and accompanied by a record six varieties of home-made jam); the latter because, well, I had seen the first milestone at the start of the climb and the 'Sommet à 22km' part hardly filled me with the desire to leap out of the saddle and up the tempo.

I'll give him his dues – Richard, a media man by trade, was a solid climber given the extra weight of his natural panniers. But I was happy to hold him on an invisible cord 100 metres up the road as we chiselled away at the others. For his part Simon, a debonair spinning instructor renowned for his themed sessions (his recent two-hour David Lynch spin was so brutal only half his class went the distance), was not as comfortable now the gradients were reversed, but like a reliable diesel engine he was able to get in the right gear and chug along contentedly.

Approaching the town of Molines en Queyras, with the gradient rising to 7 per cent after 7 kilometres of gradual uphill, I decided to nullify Richard's ambush and throw a proposal his way. Today's stage was only 90 kilometres long and so I needed to conjure up an extra 10 kilometres to keep my sequence going. A slight detour to the village of Saint-Véran should do the trick. Richard was game and soon, with much mirth, we found ourselves edging through the commune of La Chalp en route to the tiny ski station which, at a height of 2,042 metres, prides itself on being the highest inhabited village in Europe. As befits somewhere that has made the 156-strong official list of 'Les Plus Beaux Villages de France', Saint-Véran was keen to remind us of this becoming status with numerous signs stressing its place among the pantheon of France's most beautiful settlements. It need not have done so; the rickety wood and stone chalets tiled traditionally with slate and adorned with outdoor fountains, troughs, sundials, myriad farming equipment, upturned horseshoes, blooming flower pots and other such everyday heritage, was evidence enough.

What Saint-Véran didn't have was a discernible living population. Or a functioning cafe. Perhaps the cherubic eleven o'clock chimes from the numerous chapels meant all hands were on deck with bell-ringing duties. Our plans for a high-altitude coffee in the most pretty village of the Alps thwarted, we pressed on, passing the arrival of an incongruous coachload of Russian tourists whose own caffeine cravings would no doubt soon be left unanswered too. By now the road had become a mere track as it looped back on itself, crossed an exposed plain and then dipped down through a wood. We rode this at a leisurely pace, chatting about Richard's recent riding experiences in Spain where he had been on a package tour that followed the Pyrenean stages of the Vuelta, offering guests the chance to ride the key climbs ahead of the stage finishes. That explained his excellent mountain legs, then.

After our loop we rejoined the main Agnel route just 2 kilometres further upstream as Sharon was passing by. One knee bandaged from an innocuous fall on the cobbles outside the hotel in Bourg d'Oisans, Sharon had rallied against her oppressor and Terry now languished a hundred metres further back. Like Bob on the Izoard, Terry had been defeated by the Agnel last year. He knew the next hour or so was going to be tough. The sun's rays now warm, the ski jacket was tied around his waist. Further maintaining a measure of sartorial inelegance that could only be applauded, Terry had donned an old golfing visor from the 1980s which jutted out from under his helmet. It was show time.

Richard and I rode in tandem up the initial valley, the gradient as kindly as the setting was idyllic. For 3 kilometres after the final settlement of Fontgillard the road rose at just 3 per cent as it ran alongside a gently flowing stream. Pine trees covered the steeper slopes to the right while the apron of the grassy plains to the left was bright pink with the metre-long stalks of rosebay willowherb swaying in the breeze. The air was filled with weightless pollen, suspended at head height, every now and then catching the sun with a sparkle of silver, giving this secluded spot a spellbinding appearance. A sudden ramp 7 kilometres from the summit heralded the sting in the tail of what had been an otherwise wholly pleasant ascent. Richard, banana in mouth, waved me clear.

Usual service had been resumed: one man, his bike and the open road.

The Col Agnel is rarely used in Grand Tours, with just two appearances in the Tour and three in the Giro – all coming in the last twenty years. Only once has the climb been tackled from the French side, during the 2008 Tour when Basque climber Egoi Martínez crossed the summit first on the day Simon Gerrans opened up his Grand Tour account – the Australian has victories in all three races – in Prato Nevoso. Even then, the Agnel was invited to the party as an after-thought: a landslide on the nearby Col de Larche forced the organizers to alter the route.

As such, the Agnel is not steeped in cycling folklore – reflected, perhaps, by the noticeable lack of painted names on the roads. I spotted just two on the whole of the ascent: that of Dutchman Pieter Weening written in red, below a large arrow pointing uphill, and the surname of the late Marco Pantani. Both names appeared on the top tier of consecutive switchbacks, 3 and 2 kilometres from the summit respectively, at points where the incline was at its most demanding. Weening's name made little impression on me, but that neat and evocative 'PANTANI' made me feel all tingly inside.

As I pressed on to the summit, which now appeared to the right of a pyramidal peak worthy of the Dahshur necropolis, I stopped counting the cute, bushy marmots with their buck teeth that emerged from various nooks and crannies amid a cacophony of chirps and whistles (last count: five). The stamp of Pantani had got me thinking. Was there a subliminal message in the improbable encounter of that name on the Agnel of all places? After all, Pantani had been six feet under for four years when the Tour first swung by in 2008. Twice during his career Pantani had tamed the Italian side of this *hors catégorie* peak – in 1994 alongside fellow GC favourites Evgeni Berzin and Miguel Indurain, and more notably in 2000, when he took second place in Briançon in support of team-mate Stefano Garzelli, the overall winner.

No, the presence of Pantani's name on this isolated stretch of asphalt on the French side of the border couldn't have much to do with his rare performances on this mountain, solid as they may have been. His painted name was clearly the work of a maverick with his own agenda. The clue I concocted while spinning away had its roots in Pantani's nicknames. One of the few riders to do the Tour–Giro double, Pantani famously branded himself as '*Il Pirata*', the Pirate. Leaning on his seaside roots from northern Italy, the explosive climber grew a goatee and also wore bandanas and hooped earrings to perfect his landlubbing-buccaneer-on-wheels look. Pantani really pushed the boat out, creating a line of headbands, saddles and other accessories featuring a skull and crossbones motif. His team launch in 1999 even included a vast mock-up of a pirate ship.

But as pantomime villain Lance Armstrong – the former mastodon of the pro peloton – so often cruelly reminded him, Pantani was only ever a Pirate by default. The real reason why the big-eared, crooked-nosed and bald-headed star created his new look in the first place was because he so passionately hated that nickname the Italian fans first festooned him with: *Il Elefantino* the Little Elephant.

Always one to look for subliminal messages in everything, I felt I had cracked – at least, spiritually – the mystery that had thwarted historians through the ages, namely the whereabouts of the path taken by Hannibal and his thirty-seven little elephants into Italy. If a plaque commemorating Hannibal's troops some 7 kilometres from the summit is meagre enough proof of the Agnel's credentials, then this certainly swayed things for me. Pantani's name was a clear message that we were on the right track. As they say in piratical parlance: X marks the spot.

'Did you see the plaque?' Sam asked as I reached the summit, Hannibalic thoughts apparently seeping from my pores as profusely as the sweat forming a puddle around my feet. Funnily enough, I hadn't. I was aware of the plaque but it must have passed me by – perhaps while Richard and I were on our detour to Saint-Véran.

'Do you want to go back and see it?' Sam asked as Richard later rolled over the summit, his face betraying varying degrees of distress and ecstasy. 'You have to be kidding,' I replied. 'There's no way I'm riding back down and up again!' The last twisting couple of kilometres had been just as hard as the steeper sections of the Izoard and I was very much looking forward to the long ride into Italy and our lakeside lunch. 'Hop in the van,' said Sam, the consummate host. 'I've got to check up on the stragglers anyway. Roddy may need picking up.'

It was my first taste of the broom wagon since that 'pre-race' lift from Dylan back in the Montseny National Park. Seeing the trail of devastation in my wake was a real treat. While Bob, Bernadette, James, Melbourne John and Simon had exploited our thwarted coffee detour to make it to the top before Richard and me, the others were still embroiled in painful internal battles against both their minds and legs. We passed Sharon about one kilometre from the top as we drew alongside a tiny cottage on the side of the road. Its doors and windows boarded up, the mountain shack presides over the grassy plateau beneath the summit and has expansive views as far back as the snow-clad tips of the Écrins peaks in the distance. I had never seen a more isolated and unlikely building in my life. Imagine living there and running out of sugar. Knocking on your neighbour's door would have necessitated an hour-long round trip to the nearest Chalp.

Edging down the mountain in such a bulky vehicle emphasized both the narrowness and steepness of a road barely wide enough for two cars – let alone one van and a delirious Terry. His head down and shoulders hunched over the handlebars, my elderly room-mate was a man possessed, meandering all over the road in such a giddy state that there was no recognition in his eyes as they met mine while shouting encouragement out of the window. It was as if he had been struck down by dementia during the ascent with his brain retaining but one atavistic faculty – that of a mad, frenzied, corybantic foot-drumming on the pedals, his only path to salvation.

But fair play to Terry, for further down the road, on the initial cruel ramp heading into the second of two successive Z-bends, thirsty fellow sexagenarians John and Kay had resorted to pushing their bikes uphill – folly given the combined gradient, slippery nature of their cleats and lack of guardrail separating the road from its adjoining green precipice. 'We're out of water,' said John, laconically. 'It's just too steep,' added Kay, outlining the second pith of the matter. Bottles refilled, off they went in their matching club kits.

Another kilometre further down the valley a figure sat on the side of the road, his stylishly socked feet removed from his immaculate shoes and his delight of a bike propped against the grass verge. Symbolically sporting the old black-and-white colours of Fausto Coppi's Carpano team from the late 1950s, when the ageing Italian's career was in free-fall, Roddy, ill, exhausted and rather fed up, had not so much thrown in the towel as feebly fumbled the flannel. The Agnel was the final nail in his Hannibalic coffin – the ultimate concession that a training regime of sweltering early-morning Ramadan rides through the parched Arabian desert around Dubai was far from ideal preparation for a week tackling some of the most demanding climbs the Alps has to offer.

Another few kilometres downstream we found what we had set out for – the plaque commemorating Hannibal's soldiers, along with various other armies and famous figures who 'crossed in front of this rock', including Caesar's legions in 51 BC, the Chevalier de Bayard in 1515 and the son of King Philip of Spain in 1743. That's not all. The same rock bore memorials to those killed during the Second World War, to Marguerite Eyméoud – a local heroine of the Resistance – and to a feted French general called Augustin Guillaume, who, during a long career that stretched from campaigning in the Atlas mountains in the 1920s to becoming mayor of nearby Guillestre during the 1960s, somehow found time to father nineteen children. In the dawn of his long career, old Guillaume would oversee the construction of the very road I had just ridden up, which was completed in 1973 (a valid reason, indeed, for the Agnel's short Tour history). Bearing an uncanny resemblance to Inspecteur Clouseau, the much-loved Guillaume also wrote a dozen war-related books including one on Hannibal's crossing of the Alps. A busy man, indeed.

The defiant plaque may set the Col Agnel apart from many other possible routes taken by Hannibal in 218 BC but it's not the only plaque in the Alps to make such a claim – although the metal plate that acknowledges the Roman heritage of the Clapier pass some 60 kilometres north of the Agnel does only cautiously add that it is 'maybe the route used by Hannibal'. One advocate of the Col du Clapier route was a sprightly British engineer called John Hoyte who, in 1959, led a gloriously gung-ho expedition that tried to reenact aspects of Hannibal's crossing. When the madcap graduate from Cambridge wrote to the British Consuls in Lyon, Geneva and Turin for advice on how to rent an elephant for an Alpine experiment, he probably didn't have high hopes for a positive reply.

But a week later he received a letter from Turin: 'Dear Sir: Unaccustomed as I am, as Her Majesty's Consul General, to receive such requests, I am delighted to tell you I have an elephant for you.' It turned out that on the same day his request had popped through the letterbox, the local newspaper had published a story about the arrival of a frisky female Asian elephant at Turin zoo. Eleven-year-old Jumbo was circus-trained, and his owner was not only eager to offer Hoyte his elephant but prepared to cover major expenses for the entire trip.

Lloyd's of London stepped in with one of their lesser-known elephant insurance policies and *Life* magazine sent a photographer to accompany the eight-man team on what became the British Alpine Hannibal Expedition. Hoyte's target was to prove the feasibility of crossing the Clapier pass on a 2.6-ton elephant; following an extensive summer rambling over the Alps with some of his Cambridge chums with laminated copies of Polybius and Livy in his hand, he had decided on the Clapier as the most likely route of Hannibal's army.

The expedition set off in July. Jumbo – Hoyte had tried without success to rename her Hannibella (she didn't respond; can you blame her?) – was equipped with special leather boots and knee pads for the most treacherous passages of the climb. The pampered pachyderm also had a bespoke thick woolly coat to keep her warm. Her daily diet consisted of Chris Froome's optimum bodyweight (68kg) in hay, as well as an André Greipel thigh's worth of apples (23kg), 18kg of bread and 9kg of carrots. Her doping regime consisted of a solitary vitamin B supplement, ingested intravenously via the trunk. Despite a hefty food intake loyal to the 'quantity not quality' adage, Jumbo lost around 140kg (roughly the weight of Jan Ullrich in the off-season) during the first four days of the trip.

Then disaster struck: while approaching the summit of the Clapier pass on the ancient mule road – the only path vaguely navigable by elephants (not that there were any recent precursors) – the team ran into an enormous rockfall. The expedition was forced to switch routes and enter Italy via the next valley, across the resplendent Col du Mont Cenis. Further complications loomed in the form of an unsavoury legal spat involving elephant-ownership rights. Amid the extensive press coverage of the zany escapade, a disgruntled Barcelona businessman came forward claiming he had an agreement with Turin zoo to buy Jumbo for the zoo of his home town. As Hoyte crested the summit of Mont Cenis, he was notified by this man that he would seize Jumbo with a court writ as soon as the elephant set hoof in Italy.

I had ridden the Mont Cenis pass as part of my training. It was hard to imagine an elephant roaming around up there – although she would have enjoyed a dip in the lake which now covers much of the basin where Hannibal's army theoretically camped prior to their descent into Italy. A church and museum built in the shape of a pyramid now overlooks the turquoise-blue waters of this reservoir, commemorating Napoleon, who was responsible for the first road being built there between 1803 and 1810.

One of Hannibal's biggest fans, Napoleon was a firm advocate of Mont Cenis being the location of his crossing. Riding the wonderful 35-kilometre descent down the Italian side of the Moncenisio to Susa is a mind-boggling experience – one of the most enjoyable stretches of downhill riding a cyclist could imagine. Jumbo must have had her work cut out, mind. Beyond the lake and final dam, and just ahead of the border, the road zigzags down a sheer drop in a scribble of evocative hairpins; riders can then really let rip on a series of tree-lined straights with an asphalt surface worthy of any airport runway.

Jumbo was able to negotiate the lion's share of the descent, save for a testing segment that was deemed unsafe even for her own heavily protected feet. Luckily, there was no sign of the man from Barcelona and, after ten days on the road, Jumbo, having shed almost 10 per cent of her body weight (roughly three and a third Bradley Wigginses), carried a triumphant Hoyte into the town of Susa to a raucous (if a little bemused) reception. On arrival she was given a large celebratory cake to eat, as well as a magnum of Chianti – the favourite wine of another famous Hannibal, Mr Lecter.

Professor Hoyte may have been the first, but he was not the last figure to have attempted to recreate the Hannibal legend in the twentieth century. Two decades later, a right-wing American adventurer dubbed the 'real Indiana Jones' by the *Wall Street Journal* (and an 'ideological gangster' by the Soviet press) went one better by taking two elephants across the Alps, and this time across the Clapier pass.

Doctor Jack Wheeler is easily the most intriguing character you've never heard about. From an early age it was clear that he was going places – quite literally. Aged 12, precocious Jack was honoured in the White House by President Eisenhower as the Youngest Eagle Scout in history. By 14 he had climbed the Matterhorn; at 16 – the age at which my main hobbies included drinking two-litre bottles of White Lightning, developing chronic acne and failing miserably to kiss girls – Jack almost drowned while otherwise successfully swimming across the Hellespont; he was then adopted into a clan of headhunters in the Amazon. One year later, at the age I was sitting my A-levels and looking forward to a post-exam trip to Cornwall, he hunted and killed a man-eating tiger responsible for the deaths of twenty-odd tribespeople in Vietnam. When he was 19, Wheeler set up his first business, exporting cinnamon from south-east Asia.

Dr Wheeler has since led more than twenty expeditions to the Arctic Circle, including the first ever free-fall skydive at the North Pole (which he celebrated with a luncheon of Champagne and caviar on a polar ice cap). He has three 'first contacts' with tribes never before reached by the outside world, and has clocked visits to 193 of the 197 sovereign countries in the world (he will have bagged the remaining four – Libya, Tunisia, Mauritania and São Tomé – by the time the 2014 Giro reaches completion). If he didn't already have enough to wow dinner party guests with, he could always throw in the time he defeated both Vladimir Putin and his bodyguard in an arm wrestle. To top it off, he managed to marry a woman whose full name just about sums up his existence to a tee: Rebel Holiday. When, on their wedding day, his wife tossed her garter after the ceremony, it was Charlie Wilson, the swashbuckling Texas politician – and Jack's best man – who caught it.

Back in 1979, Jack, then a Californian philosopher in between his global jaunts of derring-do, decided to improve on Hoyte's expedition by doubling the elephant count and actually crossing the Clapier – the pass he too was convinced played host to Hannibal's army. His team included a 65-year-old American businessman (his financial backer) and his then-fiancée, a Parisian dancer from Las Vegas. It wouldn't have surprised me if there was a Japanese sumo wrestler and an Indian snake charmer thrown in there for good measure. Their route followed the Arc river and then went over the Clapier along a narrow rocky trail that Jack would later admit had probably been 'too dangerous' for the two elephants he had rented. They were apparently terrified of the 'fairly substantial' cliff on the side of the road, barely wide enough for a couple of horses let alone the world's largest mammal. A landslide on the Italian side made things more dicey. Wheeler and his adventurers had to place themselves between the elephants and the 100-foot drop-off to ensure that the animals didn't bolt as they edged down the trail inch by inch. Although his successful crossing was an 'extraordinary experience', looking back on it a couple of decades later Jack magnanimously admitted in an interview that he 'wouldn't do it again because of the chance of killing a wonderful animal'.

It was precisely this kind of danger that had animal rights activists up in arms when, in 1988, ramble-hungry English cricketing colossus

Ian Botham – just days after being sacked by his Australian club for manhandling a fellow passenger on a flight from Brisbane to Perth – decided to take not one, not two, but three elephants as companions during his own Hannibal Walk from Perpignan to Turin. When Batman, one of the hired circus elephants, went lame just 10 kilometres into the 800-kilometre trip, the activists – including Brigitte Bardot – went berserk. Botham duly told his critics to 'get stuffed'.

But the dynamic of the trip inevitably changed: the other two elephants were withdrawn on the grounds that they would refuse to work as a team without their companion. Instead, all three elephants were driven between the start and finish of each stage in a special air-conditioned transporter, accompanying Botham by foot for just a few hundred metres a day. Going over the Alps, the three elephants did get a chance to play in snow – and when Batman (clearly a pachyderm hypochondriac if ever there was one) picked up a cold, she was treated with half a bottle of brandy poured down her throat, which would have done little to appease the RSPCA.

Interestingly, Batman was just her nickname. The limping, booze-fuelled nellie was actually called Salammbô after the title character of Flaubert's unlikely follow-up novel to *Madame Bovary*. The book takes place in Carthage during the mercenary revolt following the First Punic War. With the city surrounded by bloodthirsty rebels – disgruntled at not being paid – a mass sacrifice of all Carthage's children is ordered by the city's rulers. Anxious to save his own son, Hamilcar Barca, the Punic leader, sends a slave child in place of his young son Hannibal – *the* Hannibal, and brother of the fictitious Salammbô. Keeping in line with Carthaginian customs, the enemy come to a sticky end: being crucified or trampled to death by elephants are the fates of some of the luckier of the defeated mercenaries. To surmise: Salammbô is a more evocative name for an elephant than Batman which, gender confusion aside, merely conjures up disturbing images of a special pachyderm

PVC suit – a cruel and unnecessary progression from Professor Hoyte's chic elephantine leather boots.

'Right, that's a big enough Hannibal detour. Let's return to the summit and get you guys back on your bikes,' said Sam after a quick team photo at the plaque. We squeezed back into the van and chugged up the hill, passing John and Kay grappling with the last major rise. Before sweeping by Terry on the closing straight we stumbled upon a chap who appeared to be taking on the Agnel on a fixed-wheel bike, and another long-haired hippy of a man – possibly Dutch – who gamely dragged a trailer behind his hybrid. Both, like Terry, received a rousing round of applause on arriving at the mountain-top border between France and Italy.

'Where's lunch?' asked Terry after vowing never to climb another Alpine peak in his life. The crazed look gone, normal service was resuming. 'This one defeated me last year and so I bloody well wasn't going to give up this time. But men my age shouldn't be doing things like this. I should be sitting on a beach with a piña colada. If it wasn't for Dylan, I wouldn't be seen dead on a bike. Although, at this rate, I will be seen dead on one – and entirely thanks to him.'

As Terry continued to grumble in an ever-increasing pool of sweat, I fetched my bike and clambered on to the border monument to strike a pose. With my back foot in France and my front foot in Italy, I stood defiantly on the granite block atop the 2,744-metre-high Agnel and pointed symbolically towards Monte Viso in the distance. That such a stance looked like I was greeting Italy with a right-wing fascist salute was unfortunate. To any onlooker (and there were a few), the fact that it was my left arm outstretched would have made me, at worst, a dyslexic fascist in figure-hugging clothing. Fortunately, most people would have been too busy looking at my see-through shorts.

It was the kind of bullish pose that Hannibal could well have adopted when delivering his men a rousing speech ahead of their descent. Morale was low. In the ten days it had taken to reach the roof of the Alps, the Carthaginians had lost ten thousand men. Never before had some of these mercenaries experienced such extreme cold; snow from the previous winter had yet to melt. Since setting off from the Iberian peninsula they had been on the march for five months. Finally, Roman territory was in sight. Both Livy and Polybius describe how Hannibal gestured towards the panorama of Italy below, reminding his dispirited troops of the fruitful plains of the Po valley and the friendly feelings of their Gaulish allies who inhabited those nearby lands.

I, too, looked eastwards towards the series of jagged peaks on the Italian side of the border, motivated primarily by the thought of food: the Piedmont slow-cook movement, the approaching truffle harvest, cured hams and chocolate, mountains of pasta and cheese-slathered pizzas as big as bike wheels. We had reached the final leg of our journey. All roads now led to Rome.

# COLLE DELL'AGNELLO TO GAVI

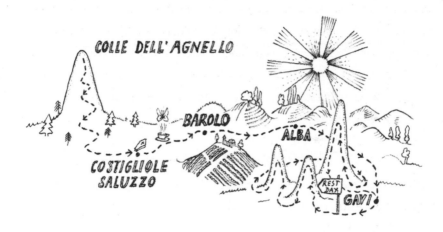

IT SEEMED THE MOST RESPECTFUL THING to do. Crowds had gathered outside the church, blocking the path. A bell tolled a single repeated dong. The hearse was ready, its boot open and awaiting the coffin being carried down the stone stairs by six men behind a priest clasping a microphone.

I could have tried to weave my way between the mourners. But many were teary or had their heads bowed, and this was a steep, gritty and narrow road leading to the top of the medieval hillside town of Costigliole Saluzzo. Colliding with a mourner at the funeral of a *grande formaggio* would have been a one-way ticket to my own interment. For there was definitely some *Sopranos* action going on. Those burly men in black suits and shades, for instance: clearly packing heat. So I did the sensible thing and pulled into the side of the road beside a large wall. I resisted the temptation to photograph the scene. But I still stood

239

out – the only lanky cyclist in multi-coloured garb not here to pay his respects to the dearly departed.

The coffin safely placed inside the hearse, the vehicle started to edge down the hill at a snail's pace. The priest chanted into the microphone from the passenger seat while the family and friends of the deceased shuffled along behind. It was a painfully slow process, comical almost, given that my destination was a mere handful of tantalizing metres further up the incline. Made worse by the knowledge that the plush Castello Rosso hotel had a pool, and I hadn't gone swimming since that impromptu dip in the Gard near Avignon.

At least I had had time to act. Anyone coming up the road now would meet the cortège head on and be forced to stop and turn just as the climb kicked up. I thought of Terry and Sharon, who I had passed not so long ago. Quite how they'd cope with such a chain of events was anyone's guess. I had visions of Terry ploughing into the hearse and getting himself arrested. The carabinieri of Piedmont were bound to be less accommodating than the comely policewomen of the sleepy Pyrenean foothills. His views on truncheons could change irrevocably.

But it was Sharon who came off worst. She trudged into the castle's leafy courtyard with her unbandaged knee covered in blood. They'd rounded the bend at the start of the climb just as the hearse appeared. Stopping suddenly, Sharon lost balance on the slope and was unable to click out of her pedals in time. A combination of grit and gravity did the damage; she now had a second gashed knee to even things out. The ghost of Michaela lived on. Miraculously, Terry didn't come a cropper. With his momentum gone, he had to push his bike up the last section and past what he probably thought was a wedding.

'Is there a bath?' he asked optimistically. There was no bath. Yet the bathroom was a whopper – larger than some of the bedrooms we had shared. Double doors led out to a balcony, from which a stone staircase stretched up to a private terrace atop a tower. A week's worth

*The lithe and slightly camp conqueror of the Col du Galibier.*

*Tour de France graffiti adorns the road on the ghostly Galibier.*

DEVANT CE ROCHER PASSERENT:
LES SOLDATS D'ANNIBAL AN 218 AV J-C.
LES LEGIONS ROMAINES DE CESAR 51 AV J-C
LE CHEVALIER BAYARD AOUT 1515
LE DVC DE LESDIGVIERES AOUT 1578
LE MARECHAL DE BELLEGARDE JANV 1579
LE DVC DE BERWICK · SEPT · 171
L'INFANT DON PHILIPPE D'ESPAGNE OCT 17

*Proof that 'Les Soldats d'Annibal' crossed the Alps via the Agnel pass?*

*An enormous elephant statue commemorating Hannibal's victory at the Trebbia.*

*The steep ascent of the mighty Galibier rises above the Col du Lautaret.*

Crossing the border atop the
Col Agnel.

A lonely mountain refuge on the highest
international pass of the Alps.

Bob stretches his seventy-year-
old legs on the Lautaret.

Gazing over Monte Viso:
all roads now lead to Rome.

*It wasn't just me that the Velosophy boys hung
out to dry on a daily basis.*

Light rest-day breakfast at the
Villa Sparina near Gavi.

*Making the most of the quiet
country roads in Piedmont.*

Veterans Bob and Terry cuddle up at Cavazzone.

Following the Velosophy blur over the Apennines and into Tuscany.

Atop the highest pass in the Apennines (L–R): Cam, Chris, Jason, Pete, Dave, Luke, Dylan, me.

*Starting the extra loop to Volterra after another hearty lunch in San Miniato.*

*My historic four cheeses and Parma ham pizza at Castell'Arquato.*

*Weary figures after a world champion deluge (L–R): Ash, Steve, Mark, Robin, me.*

Another storm brews during my solo breakaway in Tuscany.

Memories of family holidays at Casa Storta near Cortona.

Lake Trasimeno, site of Hannibal's bloody slaughter of the Roman army.

Edging ever nearer to our ultimate destination.

One final swim in Lake Bracciano.

Success where Hannibal failed: reaching Rome for a celebratory shot beside the Colosseum.

of festering kit washed in the basin with hotel shower gel, I adorned the balcony railing with these clean(er) garments dripping into the bushes below. Then off I went for that swim, picking up a couple of beers from the bar on the way back.

In matching white dressing gowns, Terry and I, like an old married couple, toasted our arrival in Italy as the sun went down, gazing over the fertile fruit plains of the Po valley from the scenic terrace of what was clearly the Castello Rosso's honeymoon suite.

On the south, Italian side of the mountain, the angelic Agnel becomes the bleating Agnello, a sheepish downhill ride all the way for 60 kilometres, which we broke up with a late picnic lunch overlooking the Lago di Castello in sleepy Pontechianale, and a coffee stop in sweltering Sampeyre.

Noticing that the Colle dell'Agnello was perceptibly steeper than the Agnel, I was relieved not to be tackling this climb in reverse – as Andy Schleck did en route to his Galibier win. Unlike the French side, the slopes are peppered with pine trees giving the pass a less mystical but more dramatic feel. The task of negotiating numerous tight bends at a double-digit downward gradient was intensified by the presence of various animals to dodge. Packs of sheep ambled leisurely along the road. Marmots scampered from one side to the other, seemingly attracted by fast-spinning wheels. A large cow slouched on the grassy verge, its bulk encroaching on the side of the lane with the kind of bovine abandon you'd expect to see in India, not Italy.

The Agnello has been known to topple even the best. On the Tour's first unscheduled visit in 2008, Spaniard Óscar Pereiro – the stand-in winner two years earlier following Floyd Landis's testosterone-fuelled rise and fall – plunged off the side of the road approaching one of these very same switchbacks. Sliding on the wet asphalt, Pereiro went over the barrier, tumbled 5 metres down a rocky embankment and through a tree, and landed on the road below in agony, taking a branch with him. He has a tattoo of the date – 20 July, 2008 – directly above the 25cm-long scar where doctors operated on his broken arm, reminding him of how lucky he was to avoid a worse fate.

Having scaled the 'Fence of Italy', Hannibal's army likewise suffered on the precipitous and slippery descent. Local barbarians weren't the problem – according to Polybius, only 'a few skulking marauders' offered resistance; the big issue was heavy snowfall, rocky avalanches, icy slopes and the presence of a gigantic boulder which blocked the mule path. For four days, the Carthaginians were stuck while scouts searched for an alternative route. Huddled together, the elephants slept standing up, as desperate men – the Numidians in particular – took shelter underneath their vast bulk (about as sensible as grabbing forty winks on a railway line, I'd have thought). The feted Numidians may have been recognized as the best light cavalry in the ancient world, but their habit of riding in the nude with only a leopardskin sash over the shoulder wasn't so effective in plummeting temperatures.

Eventually, Hannibal's engineers came up with an ingenious solution. Livy writes of bundles of vinegar-soaked firewood being tied round the boulder which, once lit, caused the rock to crack, aiding its removal by pickaxes. This, too, was at a cost – for vinegar was the Pot Belge of the Carthaginian army, a mild pick-me-up and painkiller which helped keep morale slightly above zero (unlike the temperatures). Seeing their rations of sour wine spilled all over rocks would be the equivalent of a professional cyclist in the late 1990s having to flush his doping stash down the loo during one of the late-night police raids that were so *de rigueur* at the time. Personally, I think the soldiers should have put a positive spin on things: if your tipple of choice is both flammable and potent enough to crack rocks, it's probably a good thing to keep it out of your stomach.

Emaciated, exhausted and looking every bit your average Tour rider, Hannibal's soldiers and pack animals soon made it to the pasture line where they could refuel and gather strength. It had taken fifteen days to cross the Alps – one day more than it had taken us to ride all the way from Catalonia. Hannibal's infantry had lost a third of its men during the crossing. Just 12,000 Africans and 8,000 Spaniards made it to the plains below. Six thousand cavalry survived the crossing, while none of Hannibal's thirty-seven elephants perished.

Crossing the Alps had given Hannibal and his army the same aura of invincibility that, two millennia later, cycling fans, cancer survivors and fawning media outlets would give to Lance Armstrong and his US Postal team. One sports columnist, Bernie Lincicome, lambasted the rumours of foul play that soured Armstrong's 'astonishing achievement' of winning the Tour in his return to the sport in 1999. 'There is no point in paying any mind to the drug insinuations directed at the Tour de France winner when his story is far more inspiring than petty slander,' he wrote in the *Chicago Tribune*. 'I mean, a guy beats cancer and the Alps. Did they give Hannibal a drug test?' Lincicome then suggested that Armstrong would even have won the race had he been forced to 'ride down the Champs Élysées with a priest and a poodle on his handlebars'.

Bernie was not alone in kowtowing to the inspiring Texan. Wet behind the ears and unaware of the Irish journalist David Walsh's brave attempts to expose the systematic doping behind Armstrong's empire, I remember writing an article entitled 'Lance's Positive Lieutenants' back in 2006 in which I lauded the 'perfect track record' of the 'most heavily tested rider in the history of the sport', concluding that it was the 'brilliance' of the seven-time Tour winner (and not something as nefarious as EPO) which was the 'drug that ran through the veins of US Postal'. A few years later – as the US federal vultures gathered – PR guru Alastair Campbell, of all people, greeted his hero's 2009 comeback with the assertion that 'he is still adding to the legend'. Writing in *The*

*Times*, Campbell reminded his readers of his favourite Armstrong quote: 'Losing and dying – it's the same thing'.

In Lance's world 'cheating and living' clearly went hand in hand, too. His first Tour victory in 1999 was seen at the time as one of the sport's greatest. While it would be followed by six more triumphs it also marked the start of a long struggle and countless battles that would ultimately result in the defeat and downfall of a man deemed untouchable. For Hannibal, crossing the Alps was also a mere stepping stone to bigger, more arduous challenges. It was one of the boldest military manoeuvres in history. But the war had only really just begun, and against an opposition capable of amassing three-quarters of a million troops against the invaders, the odds were almost as unfavourable as a contemporary Frenchman winning the Tour.

It felt as if someone had tried Hannibal's old vinegar trick on the road down to Costigliole Saluzzo. Deep rivets and cracks broke up the atrocious surface, running along like uneven tramlines primed to catch a wheel and send riders headlong into the asphalt. A clean strip ran perilously close to the verge – otherwise the safest bet was to ride in the centre of the road and stay alert for traffic coming in both directions. The net result was that we hurtled towards the Po valley rather po-faced.

Roddy was proving quite an asset. His uphill ability may have been rather shoddy, but my Australian companion's confidence rose now we were back on the zippy, flatter roads. On the gradual descent he picked a sensible line, only occasionally veering off dangerously into the path of oncoming traffic. When taking numerous pulls on the front, he was constantly alert and warning me of hazards on the road with slightly camp over-exaggerated gesticulations. There were times when he was so lively that he left me digging deep to fight back on.

The effort clearly got to him. Once alone (we had parted ways when I decided to nip off to a run-down town called Vernasca – primarily to clock the extra kilometre I needed to bag my daily hundred), Roddy pulled in for an ice cream at the first cafe he could find. That this was in an unsalutary place called Piasco – which smelled very much like it sounds – just a few kilometres from the final rise to the Castello Rosso, stressed the shift he had put in. Or perhaps merely underlined his astounding hunger for gelato.

Later that evening, Roddy and I spent much of the team's al fresco *aperitivo* shooting the breeze about his custom-made Dario Pegoretti bike. Having clocked up numerous hours affixed to the roof of the van, the flash red-and-white steel bike had finally got a decent run-out on the ride into Italy. Looking every bit the North Shore Sydney-sider in a long-sleeved white polo shirt (collar up) tucked into some beige chinos and with a red jumper draped over his broad shoulders, Roddy proudly recounted Pegoretti's impeccable CV as one of the great contemporary steel-frame builders.

'I remember reading an article about Pegoretti in a magazine back in 2001 and it blew my socks off,' he said. He ummed and ahhed about ordering a frame for years before taking a detour up to Pegoretti's workshop in the Dolomites while in Tuscany for a wedding, visiting en route an old friend who was a school teach-ah in Veron-ah (Roddy's honeyed Aussie tones could be a little harsh at times).

'Once I met Dario in person, I just fell for it hook, line and sink-ah.' In 2006 he was measured up in Sydney and then placed the order for a frame. He wanted a simple colour scheme ('You are almost forced by practising law to become very conservative') but Dario (an 'artisan hippy' who was 'at the other end of the spectrum') somehow convinced Roddy into opting for pearl white with a metallic fleck in the paint which, depending on the light, would emit a green or pink tinge. (I cannot emphasize enough how out of character this seemed.)

When Roddy's bike arrived in Sydney in late 2007 – following a delay while Pegoretti recovered from lymphoma – he would take it out on regular early-morning rides in Centennial Park, where I myself had first grappled with a road bike (with those sock-stuffed Speedos for protection). Roddy and his friends took post-training coffees in a nearby delicatessen at 7 a.m. 'The lady who owned the trattoria had some holy water from the Vatican and so we had a christening ceremony for the bike,' he said, now in full flow.

I found Roddy a real character. Behind the shy and introverted interior, there was an erudite guy who was passionate about his hobbies and had a lot to say. It was a pity that the others seemed less impressed. I sensed that he had been unjustly shunned by the other Australians on the tenuous grounds that he was a bit of a smarty pants. He told me once how one of the ladies in the group was unnecessarily aggressive towards him on his first day. I told him not to worry – that he had not been the only one to receive such frosty treatment. But he was clearly upset about it. As we spoke now on the terrace, there was a perceptible divide: us at one end of the table, the others swarming around plates of canapés that were never offered in our direction. Of course, I could feasibly have misunderstood blinkered hunger for mild malevolence.

It didn't help, though, that Roddy could easily be viewed as a cycling parvenu. When, for example, Bob turned up at breakfast wearing a La Vie Claire jersey, Roddy was quick to point out that it was not an original 'because it's clearly not the right shade of yellow for the Mondrian colour scheme'. This didn't go down too well with the others, who used it as a stick to beat a man whose sermonizing about the sport – not to mention his gadgetry and impeccable riding attire – was out of kilter with his farcical tendency to crack as soon as the going got tough. A conflicting shade of yellow didn't disguise the fact that Bob – twenty years Roddy's senior – had yet to seek solace in the van.

But it wasn't as clear-cut as that. As we tucked into our curious starter of baby squids stuffed with pistachios and spinach – clearly the result of a game of *Ready, Steady, Cook* in the kitchen – Roddy explained to me how he came late to cycling.

'Sailing was my sport – it still is. I did it professionally before I became a lawyer and continue at a high level today. I took up cycling as a way of building up my leg muscles for sailing. Before long I became hooked.' After a short-lived marriage broke down, Roddy moved to the Middle East in 2011 and his cycling duly suffered. He booked his place on our tour with a friend but found it hard to train in the desert, even when he shipped his Pegoretti out to Dubai. When his friend broke a leg in a skiing accident in Australia, Roddy was going to give up on the trip. But he came out despite illness and poor fitness to give it his best shot. 'We may return next year and have another crack. I feel I haven't really proved myself so far.'

After eating rich French food for the best part of two weeks, I was looking forward to some simple pasta dishes, but I'd have to wait a little longer. The curious squid-nut combo was followed by a thick, wholemeal tagliatelle with turbot, gurnard and prawns, which was rather stodgy and utterly tasteless. Oddly for seafood, the dish lacked salt. It also needed a kick and – Italians, forgive me – some Parmesan. While the other end of the table was being kept entertained by Richard and Simon's increasingly well-oiled double act, Roddy and I resumed our conversation about his bike.

It wasn't long before he had regrets about the wild paint scheme, pining for something more classic. But he was very particular – with his sights set on the vintage red and white of Eddy Merckx's old Faema team from the late 1960s. Such a job could not be done in Sydney or bike-friendly Melbourne, apparently. Instead, he'd been recommended a specialist shop in California which, in turn, used a painter based out in the Rocky Mountains. So Roddy duly shipped his bike across the Pacific to San Francisco, where it went on to Colorado.

Was that not a tad excessive? 'I was convinced they would do the best job so it was the right decision. But it was not without complication.' Shortly after he shipped the frame, Roddy made the switch to Dubai. He asked the shop in California to send the end product to a friend of his in Rimini so that he could have a bike in Europe for training. But irregularities with the paperwork meant the frame was held up in customs. Roddy was forced to stump up two thousand euros to smooth things over.

'How much did the frame cost in the first place?'

'Frame and forks, four and a half thousand dollars. Add to that the groupset, wheels, seat and stem – plus shipping costs, the repaint job and the custom fee – and it's more like ten thousand. But it's worth it. I bought all Dario's expertise and I think that's cheap. Plus there's a high degree of emotional attachment. It's a one-off, hand-made for me. A lot of carbon frames are mass produced in Taiwan. I wouldn't be seen dead on carbon fibre. I'm toying with getting a titanium frame as a back-up – not one of those gimmicky twisted ones that Sam has. But if I lost my current frame or it broke, I would definitely get a new steel Pegoretti.'

'What about a wooden one?' I asked provocatively, hoping Bob might hear. But he was too busy lapping up the raucous scenes as Richard and Simon cajoled a tipsy Terry into producing some classic material. He was currently explaining the bedrock of his happy marriage: 'My wife was after a passport and I was after exotic sex. It worked for a while.'

'This is just why I came back on the tour for a second year,' Bob guffawed as the waiters arrived and, rather unexpectedly, started handing out cotton bibs covered in cartoon cows. By now we were all (except teetotaller Bob) sufficiently lubricated to play along with the bibs – even though no one else in the restaurant had been offered them.

Curiously, when our mains arrived they did not even warrant a bib. The tender slices of rare veal on a sizzling slab of slate with a bowl of diced potatoes were quite delicious, but there was no sign of an accompanying sauce to legitimize such protective measures.

Perhaps, we concluded, the bibs were part of a game the waiters played with foreigners – either to entertain or to humiliate. It was interesting watching how the various characters around the table dealt with the situation. Sober Bob, for instance, refused to even wear his, while Roddy took his off rather quickly, revealing once he did so a small red stain left on his polo shirt by the very dish – the saucy seafood pasta – for which an earlier bib might have been welcome.

Dessert came in the form of tiramisu – or what would soon be known as Terrymisu, in the light of my room-mate's insatiable appetite for the sickly sweet, Marsala-infused Italian cake. Three of us still saw sense in sticking with the cow bibs. When Richard backed down, it was left to Melbourne John and me to have some kind of bib-off. Caving in under the pressure, John was out-bibbed by yours truly. But that wasn't the end of it. If the restaurant was indeed playing a game with us, then I would rise to the occasion. The bib stayed on as we rose from the table, and as I walked through the restaurant, past the hotel lobby and up to my room. And seeing that no one asked for it back, I kept it as a nice souvenir.

The honeymoon suite didn't get much action that night – although Terry ran the gamut of grunts and groans. Ear-plugged and content in the knowledge that an early Christmas present for my new nephew had been sourced, I dozed off trying to calculate the air miles of Roddy's bespoke frame. Italy to Australia to California to Colorado to Italy to Dubai to France . . . by my reckoning that was over 50,000 kilometres.

And still Roddy had yet to ride it the whole way up a mountain. Next year, perhaps.

There are worse ways to spend a warm weekend than riding through the rolling hills of Piedmont and sampling its wares. While Piemonte

– 'the foot of the mountains' – was the birthplace of modern unified Italy, you get the impression that the nation's largest mainland region could cope just fine on its own, *grazie mille*.

Piedmont boasts the source of Italy's greatest river, the Po, while its criss-crossing canals irrigate Europe's most important rice fields and fruit farms. Unspoilt medieval hilltop villages – often crowned by castles or filigreed by fortifications – preside over rolling hills wearing the green corduroy of some of the world's most prestigious vineyards, often surrounded by a hem of hazelnut trees. Italy's most culinary progressive region is responsible for a 'slow food' movement that sets it apart from its more traditional neighbours, while its capital, Turin, is the centre of Italian industry, its roads abuzz with locally built Fiats and its offices humming with Olivetti computers.

Safe in the knowledge that their region is responsible for gastronomic delights on every point of the spectrum, the Piedmontese can dip breadsticks into Nutella (thanks to those hazelnuts), shave pungent white truffles on to their pasta and take their pick of local vermouths – making me, with my vintage Cinzano kit, something of a passing celebrity. Children are kept in check with Kinder Surprises, while should any ambassador host a reception, a precariously balanced tray of the region's famous Ferrero Rocher chocolates can wow the guests – or perhaps they'd prefer a simple fruit salad of kiwis, apples and peaches grown on the plains? On weekends the people head into the mountains to ski, or go kayaking or trout fishing in the many rivers. And while taking a dip in the sea is not an option in the land-locked region, there's always the splendid lakes of the north.

With the area so self-contained, it's no surprise that tourism only plays a small fiddle in the ebb and flow of Piedmont's orchestral life cycle. As the classy *Cadogan Guide* states, 'If your Italy consists of Renaissance art, lemon groves and endless sunshine, you'd better do as Hannibal did and just pass right on through.' Although it wasn't plain sailing for our hero. Arriving with his army in a truly bedraggled state, Hannibal found his allies the Boii and Insubres as good as their word, which meant progression was quick. But another tribe, the Taurini, were not so accommodating. When they turned down Carthage's offer of a formal alliance, Hannibal blew a gasket, ordering his troops to level the Taurini's main settlement before executing all inhabitants. Nothing gains respect like a good bloodbath – especially when women and children are involved.

The locals were considerably more welcoming to our two-wheeled army and we had no need for such savage retribution. Our final stanza of the second leg of the tour was played out under hot autumnal sun, the early haze that gave a sheen to the flat plains or hugged the troughs of the emerald valleys replaced by a blue cloudless sky come midday. For the first time since setting off from Montseny two weeks previously, I put in back-to-back days without leg warmers, giving my pasty pins a chance to regain the tan that cruelly eloped with a sheet of warm wax back in Barcelona.

I was still unsure how I felt about the abrupt waxing of my legs. One upshot was that bedtime stroking yielded a distant reminder of what it was like to have a girlfriend (since taking up cycling, funnily enough, those had been few and far between – a decline inversely proportional to my growing collection of skimpy outfits). But that smoothness now seemed a lifetime away. Nocturnal rummages around the bedsheets – a rare extravagance given the Terry-shaped elephant in the room – were greeted with a slightly stubbly response: a reminder of that moment, a few months into a new relationship, when your better half lets things slip a little.

After the punishing crossing of the Alps we had all let things slip. The pace was considerably slower as we took in our surroundings and dedicated the weekend to enjoying the finer things in life. Once we hit the lush Langhe hills – the primary residence of the fabled

Nebbiolo grape – we became inescapably entwined with the region's strong viticultural traditions. Forget that the hills of Piedmont would be much prettier with fewer vines; they clearly wouldn't be as profitable or famous. Nor would our pit stops have been as much fun.

There's such a wealth of grapes in the area that the locals even use grappa as a disinfectant (at least, that was the impression I got when visiting the bathroom at our Saturday lunch stop in Monforte). Outside, eating a banana in the town square, an old man with a walrus moustache took a break from his weekend bike ride, his generous paunch held in place by a natty GSP Ferrero kit (otherwise known as Team Nutella), hugely out of place alongside his impeccable BMC Pro Machine (worth almost as much as Roddy's Pegoretti). The old boy had just seen me ride up the 30 per cent cobbled road to the historic crown of the town to blow away the cobwebs of lunch, and nodded in approval on my return. Like us, he was en route to Alba – where a warm and nutty ambrosial aroma pervades the streets as it wafts down from the Nutella factory just outside of town. After a brief ride together we parted ways, for just down the road we had a date in the cellars of Barolo's Castello Falletti for a spot of wine tasting.

Wine is to Barolo what chocolate spread and white truffles are to Alba. Big, powerful and tannic, Barolo is known as 'the king of wines' and is one of Italy's most esteemed dry, full-bodied reds. For a wine to get DOCG Barolo status it has to be grown from 100 per cent Nebbiolo grapes on south-facing vines within the eleven local municipalities. From sampling various vintages it is possible to detect the kind of soil the grapes have been cultivated in: sandy soil packing a fruitier bouquet than the more tannic offerings from clay. Slightly sozzled, we rode on, resisting the temptation to join a queue of Germans entering the nearby Corkscrew Museum on the Via Roma.

Richard and I burned off the alcohol with an undulating 35-kilometre extra loop taking in some of the punchy climbs that featured in stage 13 of the Giro earlier in the year. Manx sprinter Mark Cavendish managed to keep in touch over the highest point at Tre Cuni and took the win in nearby Cherasco – exactly a year after plundering the corresponding stage of the 2012 race just down the road in Cervere. With Richard's noble bulk contained by his ubiquitous Lampre jersey and my lanky self stretched out in the perma-slick colours of Cinzano, we were, if not in shape and stature, at least the sartorial envy of the locals.

The real Team Cinzano was a little-known Italian professional cycling outfit during the 1970s and early 1980s, made famous by their cameo appearance in the classic 1979 Oscar-winning coming-of-age story *Breaking Away*. Much to the delight of the film's lead character, Dave, a gifted young cyclist from rural Indiana besotted with all things Italian, Team Cinzano come to town to take part in a series of amateur races. Irked by the presence of Dave effortlessly latching onto their train and prattling on in their native Italian, the Cinzano boys resort to underhand tactics, eventually sending their unsuspecting tormentor flying into a ditch by thrusting a pump in his spokes. In what would prove an uncannily prophetic commentary on the state of cycling in the years to come, Dave, crumpled in a heap, concludes that everyone cheats – most notably the very people he worships.

I drew a line at jamming my pump into Richard's lightweight Canyon wheels, although, after the thorough workout he gave me on one particularly fast and sweeping descent, I was tempted to employ another shady Team Cinzano tactic on the subsequent vine-lined climb and use my companion to slingshot myself forward with a good old 'Belgian Push'. But there was no need: the savage gradient and laws of gravity resulted in me riding clear to toast another minor uphill triumph.

If Barolo is the red king then the exceptional Gavi di Gavi is the region's classy white queen. Delicate and dry, it's a wine made from the exclusive Cortese grape and produced only by a handful of wineries, including our home for the second rest day, the Villa Sparina in Monterotondo, where a celebratory dinner would include a quite outstanding risotto made with Gavi di Gavi and a tangy soft-ripened robiola cheese. The smell was enough to make you go giddy, while the taste – salty, rich and strong – evoked many a happy moment in the company of other creamy curds. That was not all: the tender chunks of beef that followed had been braised in Gavi wine for a precise 21 hours before gracing our plates. I would have waited double the time for such a giving dish.

Exquisite wine was not the only luxury that our Alpine crossing had momentarily called time upon; a proper coffee had become a distant memory stretching way back to those early days in Spain. Now in Italy, coffee stops became something of a bonanza – the country's gloriously bitter one-euro macchiatos going down like Bradley Wiggins on a wet descent. You could go anywhere and get an injection of caffeine of such performance-enhancing zeal that you'd be hard pressed getting it past Team Sky's zero-tolerance charter. Proof of this came when Sam led us to an unprepossessing cafe in a petrol station forecourt on the outskirts of the glum industrial town of Morozzo. It was great that he was breaking up our schlep across a flat and slightly drab agricultural plain – but did he have to take things this far?

And yet the coffee was unexpectedly fantastic. What's more, the ludicrous arrival of a dozen English-speaking cyclists of a predominantly mature age was a startling boon for the two busty waitresses used to spending their mornings being ogled by fat truckers. Not that there was an absence of ogling. Terry was not so quietly having a seizure, the birthmark on the side of his face no longer visible behind his blushes.

'I feel like I've died and gone to heaven,' he said to no one in particular.

'What's that, Terry?'

'I'm in love. Just look at her,' he said, giddily gesturing towards the curvy blonde in faux alligator-skin leggings and a black top low enough to reveal a butterfly tattooed upon her right DD breast. 'That girl over there is perfection.'

A second brew inevitably followed. 'This coffee's like Viagra. I haven't felt like this in years.'

Floyd Landis's record of thirteen consecutive cappuccinos in one sitting seemed very much under threat until Sam poured cold water on Terry's caffeine binge. But on the way out I approached the girls and put in an unexpected extra order. In a fit of giggles, they agreed to my request.

'Terry – get behind the bar. But take a tray to cover your privates. We're taking a photo!'

He didn't stop smiling all day.

Terry, it has to be said, was in his element now the mountains were behind us. In the continued absence of Dylan – still leading the corresponding group of Sydney club riders – his father had really come out of his shell. As our kilometre count rose so too did his alcohol consumption. No meal was complete until the retired dentist had gone off on a rant about toothpaste ('They never needed it in the old days'), the perceived merits of water births ('What do the experts know? Can they actually remember being born?') and, most frequently, his continued – and clearly exaggerated – subjugation at the hands of his tiny, yet clearly quite fiery, Mauritian wife ('Will she ever stop nagging?').

From their first night with us around the dinner table, Simon and Richard had seen how easy it was to coax a performance out of Terry. Here was a wind-up doll whose mechanism simply required ample lubrication and some gentle probing. And in Alba they put on the rubber gloves and got stuck in. But not before dropping the kind of bombshell worthy of a Christmas episode of *EastEnders* – or a Tour rest day in Pau.

I had gone for a pre-dinner stroll around the old town, taking in a performance of flag-waving and drumming put on by local children in medieval attire. (Should such a civilized event have taken place on a Saturday night in a similarly provincial town in England, it would have ended with a drunken brawl between youths using both flags and drums as weapons.) Bumping into Simon and Richard, we went for an Aperol spritz in the Piazza Garibaldi.

We ordered two of the bright orange concoctions – the same colour as Roddy's vintage San Pellegrino top – plus a vodka and tonic for Richard. The waiter clearly got a little confused on his way inside, and swiftly returned to confirm the order. He arrived five minutes later with two Irn-Bru-evoking spritzes and a gin and tonic. Embarrassment was etched over his face when, for a third time, Richard asked for vodka. The gin was apologetically whisked away and swiftly replaced. Then, a few more minutes later, the waiter returned with a plate of sliced focaccia. We were the ones who now looked confused. Was this a kind gesture for having fumbled our order?

'Given his track record, I reckon it's probably someone else's,' I said.

'I'm not sure if we should dig in. I half expect him to return and ask for it back,' said Simon.

'Before introducing us to his brother, a taxi driver just back from a massive detour to La Chalp,' quipped Richard.

'Ah, you ordered us an appetizer!' Beer in hand, Terry plonked himself down in the empty chair with the usual litany of moans – the human equivalent of a rusty gate creaking on its hinges. He was with Sam, who bravely joined us four Brits for a pre-dinner drink. Through mutual reminiscing about 'The Girl With The Butterfly Tattoo' the subject of wives and girlfriends came up – and Simon threw into the ring the first genuine shock of the whole tour.

'You know Tom Jones and Kay aren't an item?'

'Who's Tom Jones?' asked Sam, quizzically.

'Wait, wait, wait,' I said, ignoring Sam's ridiculous question. 'This is a lot to take on board. But first: Simon, I'm pleased – relieved, even – that you too think John looks like Tom Jones.'

'Tom Jones?' said Sam, still puzzled.

'He is *so* Tom Jones,' Simon giggled.

'I know! I told the others in the first week but they just looked at me strangely. But what's this about John and Kay not being together?'

'Tell me you're joking? You've been here since the start of the tour! You didn't seriously think they were a couple, did you?' Sam had a look of total bemusement on his face.

Richard was quick to jump to my defence: 'But *she's a lady* . . . And he's a *sex bomb* . . . It's an easy mistake to make.'

Talk about a bolt from the blue. It was like discovering Torvill and Dean weren't performing open axels or triple Salchows with one another off the ice. From the outset I just presumed that Kay was John's Delilah.

'But they share a room, wear matching kits, ride together every day . . .'

'Except they don't *ride* together,' said Simon.

'That sounds familiar,' said Terry, entering the fray with another sigh.

'Come on – they must be getting it on,' said Richard, before bursting out into song: '*Da da-da, da da-da! It's not unusual to have fun with anyone . . .*'

'Guys – you're ridiculous. Both John and Kay have partners at home. They're just good friends. I imagine they're sharing rooms because it's a damn lot cheaper,' interrupted Sam, the voice of reason. 'I booked all the accommodation and I can assure you that they have individual beds every night. And what's it with Tom Jones? They don't even look remotely alike!'

'They so do,' blurted Richard, before testing his baritone once again. '*Why, why, why* would you let your other half go on a month-long holiday in Europe with another person?'

He clearly wouldn't let it drop – although it was bleedingly obvious that this whole imaginary charade couldn't have been further away from, say, the real-life saucy antics of a certain Jacques Anquetil. The first man to win five Tours openly led something of a love rectangle between his wife, Janine, and her daughter from a previous marriage, Annie, with whom he himself had a daughter before fathering a son with Janine's daughter-in-law, Dominique. Try getting your head around that after a few too many Aperol spritzes . . .

Thinking back at the many times I had insisted on taking photos of John and Kay together – 'Come on, guys, get a bit closer!' – I inwardly cringed at having got it so wrong.

A small pause in proceedings was followed by Richard breaking the ice with a rather uncouth query that had admittedly also crossed my mind. 'I wonder what Tom Jones does when he needs a dump? It's bad enough when you're with your girlfriend or wife. But if you're just rooming with a friend – a lady friend . . .'

'That's why I'm always so late to breakfast. I have to wait until Terry's gone before I can settle down and see to my business.'

'That's kind of you, Felix. I'm afraid it's always the first thing I do once off the bike.'

'Yes, Terry. I know. I have to listen to the ordeal every day. I would cover my ears with an extra pillow, but they've always already been swiped.'

'Oh, do you like to sleep with an extra pillow too? I am sorry . . .'

The after-shocks of the grand divulgement having subsided, conversation inevitably moved on to our own relationships – or lack thereof. Simon, the silverback of our group, said he was newly single following a fling with a young lady from one of his spinning classes. Previously he'd been in a no-doubt colourful long-term relationship with someone who, as a girl, had lived with and worked for the ever-so-creepy eighties comedy duo The Krankies. Simon also had three children from a previous marriage: two daughters in their twenties and a 19-year-old son who was a professional golfer.

'He's always been sporty. I remember he once picked up a javelin on sports day and – despite recovering from a broken leg – smashed the school record with his first throw,' Simon said, adding with bogus self-deprecation: 'He clearly gets it from his mother.'

After a slight contemplative pause Terry replied, matter-of-factly: 'Oh, was she a javelin thrower?'

It was a classic Terry moment that had us all rolling in the aisles. What made it all the more hilarious was the total sincerity of his question. He started laughing along with us but had no idea why we found it funny. This incongruous naivety was at the complete opposite end of the spectrum to his usual over-the-top braggadocio where he – albeit egged on and aided by *molto vino rosso* – was in complete control.

Later on, during our meal around the block at La Duchessa, the best pizzeria in town, it was this side of Terry that he unleashed upon us. It was our first pizza since arriving in Italy and spirits were high. We ordered a whole range of different varieties and agreed to pick and choose along with some salads. To drink we had copious bottles of Barolo to which – now liberated from the yoke of our bikes – we could give our undying attention. Raising his glass of fizzy water, Bob proposed a toast to his wife, Sandy. 'She says hello to everyone. It's almost our forty-eighth wedding anniversary.'

'Forty-eight years!' exclaimed Terry. 'You don't get that long for murder. And at least in prison it's solitary confinement.' He downed his glass of wine, which Simon duly refilled.

'I just don't understand women,' he said, the whole table on tenterhooks. 'Mine's only five foot two and she's constantly beating me up. I have to leave the house just to get some peace and quiet.

'It's a constant struggle,' he added, with a cheeky grin and the kind of twinkle in his eye that didn't befit a man who was enduring any genuine hardship. 'Felix,' he addressed me as the first round of pizzas arrived. 'Stay single. Don't ever get married. Why would you ever want to put yourself through so much punishment?'

After taking a break for air – as well as some wine and a few slices of *quattro stagioni* – Terry shifted the subject on to more carnal matters, sharing rather a lot more information than you'd wager him offering were Dylan – or his wife, for that matter – present.

'I can't remember the last time we did it. Probably when Dylan was born. The more she deprives herself the more uptight she gets. And it's crazy because it was the one thing we were always good at. She moans like hell that I don't pay her enough attention. And when I do—'

'She moans like hell?'

Simon's comment had Richard in stitches. It was like watching *The Goon Show* perform live.

Meanwhile, Terry continued his improbable rant while tearing off a slice of truffle-oil-infused *margherita*.

'You know, I've even offered to pay but she's having nothing of it. Hahaha!' (When in full showman mode, Terry rarely resisted the temptation of providing the canned laughter to his solo sitcom.) Terry's subsequent declaration that he was contemplating divorce was proof enough that he was hamming things up for his baying audience. Towards the end of the trip he would eventually assure me in a moment of touching sobriety that, 'I'm only pulling your legs – I'm very happily married really and wouldn't get divorced in a million years. I have three amazing children, I've retired and now I'm a grandfather. What's not to like? Look at Dylan – he's the happiest man I know. And that only makes me happier.'

But back in Alba, Terry's circus continued as we paid a visit to a nearby ice-cream parlour. My trio of strawberry, lemon and Champagne pink grapefruit was, I concede, rather camp – but the three generous scoops were at least united in their fruitiness. For Terry, the rules of flavour pairing went out the window. His was the most bizarre flavour trifecta known to man: liquorice, melon and Terrymisu. Even the girl behind the counter had to bite her tongue.

Outside, as we licked our gelati while taking in the tremendous window display of the local barber (which, alongside the omnipresent posters of George Clooney and Brad Pitt as seen in hairdressers the world over, contained a quite splendid shrine to 1970s perms, bouffants and facial hair fads), Terry drew his final conclusion from a night of inebriation.

'I think I'm going to go gay for the next part of my life.'

Days later, I would catch him gazing at me during a pasta pit stop. 'You're really glowing today,' he told me (and the rest of the table). 'You've caught the sun and look very handsome.' That same night, we arrived at our hotel to find just the one double bed in our room. Yikes – what if he was being serious?

The alarm shrilly sounded. It was still dark outside. Terry's routine began in earnest: a shave and a succession of sobs and sighs from the shower; the noisy unpacking and repacking of his numerous plastic bags before the daily loading up of his camper's backpack. At some point during this sorry sideshow I squinted at my watch. It was only 6.30 a.m. I rolled over with a groan.

'Terry!'

'Oh no, what have I done now?'

'It's still dark outside . . . look at your watch again.'

'But I could have sworn I set it for half seven,' he said, realizing his mistake. 'Oh well, I'm up now. I might as well go and join Bob for breakfast.'

When I eventually stumbled downstairs to join the others the morning's misery was further compounded by a babble of tourists gathering with stale intent at the breakfast bar. It was rush hour and a bottleneck of hungry Germans around the cheese and ham counter was causing minor mayhem. Expectations high after the bright orange yolks of the Castello Rosso's sumptuous soft boiled eggs, breakfast at Alba's Hotel I Castelli was a philistine experience: a return to packaged snacks and hot beverages delivered with deafening clangour via the single nozzle of a solitary machine.

With eight short but sharp climbs on the agenda, our second day in Piedmont was hardly the typical Sunday day of rest. An early setback saw me suffer the ignominy of stumbling on to the pavement of a town right in front of an old lady, who promptly burst into a fit of cackling. She continued to goad me as I fumbled with my chain, which had slipped off and wedged itself between the cassette and frame. Payback, perhaps, for those column inches spent taunting Andy Schleck about his infamous chain drop in the Pyrenees in the 2010 Tour.

It happened when Schleck launched an attack near the summit of the Port de Balès climb. Seeing the yellow jersey stutter to the side of the road, Alberto Contador pressed on with two others – later drawing scorn from Schleck, who claimed the Spaniard should have done the sporting thing and waited. Despite a frantic descent, Schleck came home 39 seconds behind Contador, who took the race lead. Contador admitted to the press afterwards that it was a 'delicate situation' but stressed his conviction that '30 seconds won't change the race'. A week later, Contador rode into Paris in yellow to beat Schleck by 39 seconds.

'My stomach is full of anger,' the spindly Luxembourger admitted. When it later turned out that Contador's own stomach was full of contaminated beef, it was Schleck, the resultant de facto winner, who had the last laugh.

Seeing me struggle, both Terry and Sharon took pity and, unlike

Alberto, waited. We then snuck off for a coffee so I could wash my oily hands. The treat was on Terry by way of an apology for the early wake-up call. We indulged in some morale-boosting mini ice-cream pots – wild berry for Sharon, chocolate orange for me, and tiramisu (what else?) for Terry – before I sauntered into the market to replenish my snack pouch with a bag of wine gums.

The remainder of the final day of the second leg of the tour was largely uneventful compared to the significant revelations of the night before. I still felt mortified for having thought for so long that John and Kay were married, consumed by pangs of guilt for not having ascertained this through polite conversation. It was an honest mistake – and assuming they were a couple from the start, it wasn't as if I was looking for evidence of the contrary. That, after all, would have been weirder than the misunderstanding in the first place. But it still took some getting used to. When I later spotted John answering a call of nature beside the road as Kay – wearing a matching Team Australia kit – kept watch, I had to forcibly remind myself that she was doing so not as doting wife but faithful friend.

My perplexed mind was thankfully distracted by a field of pigs mooching around in a huddle. Female pigs used to be integral to locating truffles in the region's soil: the ingots of priceless pungency produce a chemical almost identical to a sex pheromone found in boar saliva (the same chemical, incidentally, that men secrete in their underarm sweat). Such is the power of their snouts, sows can sniff out these 'white diamonds' as far as three feet underground. But a law in 1985 banned the use of truffle hogs in Italy – primarily because of their natural porcine propensity to gobble up the prized nuggets as soon as they had trotted them out of the ground. In the absence of horny, hungry hogs on heat, truffle hunting went to the dogs – quite literally.

Obediently trained truffle hounds are now used – and in Italy, one particular breed sets the standard: the Lagotto Romagnolo. The curly-coated water dogs were duck retrievers until the draining of the northern marshes in the early twentieth century led to a decline in duck hunting and the end of the traditional role of these hard-working, cheerful mutts. But the Lagotto's infallible sense of smell – coupled with their doggy disinterest in eating the fancy fungi – made them the ideal candidates to replace pigs in the cut-throat world of truffling. Prized truffle hounds can fetch up to £6,000 each at auction, making the Lagotto – the only pure-bred dog on the planet specifically recognized for its phenomenal truffling instincts – one of the world's most expensive breeds.

The spa town of Acqui Terme welcomed us for lunch – a caprese salad and a plate of ravioli in the central square, a truffle's throw from the octagonal pavilion underneath which a sulphuric spring bubbles out of the ground amid diabolical pillars of steam, scalding the hands of inadvisedly curious tourists. (Luckily there was some soothing hand cream for Terry in the bus.)

The Giro has come to Acqui Terme just twice, with an Italian winner on both occasions. In 1937 Quirico Bernacchi took the spoils days before contracting typhoid after drinking from a puddle. Eighteen years later, the race returned with victory for sprinter Alessandro Fantini who, the previous year, had famously finished a brutal stage in the Dolomites wearing a leather jacket for protection from the sub-zero temperature brought about by a freak snowstorm. Like many riders, Fantini had earlier hitched a lift in a car – a course of action (along with hot baths en route) actively encouraged by the desperate race officials to stem the rampaging tide of withdrawals. In fact, stage winner Charly Gaul, whose morose features made him a dead-ringer for Droopy the dog, was practically the only rider who eschewed motored assistance. 'The Angel of the Mountains' was in short sleeves as he turned his disproportionately stumpy legs up the snow-buffeted Monte Bondone to seize the *maglia rosa* on a day which, *L'Équipe* wrote, 'surpassed anything seen before in terms of pain, suffering and difficulty'.

Four years after his victory in Acqui Terme, Fantini fractured his skull in a crash during the Tour of Germany. After tests in hospital, doctors concluded that the 29-year-old had suffered a brain haemorrhage moments before his crash. They couldn't operate because of the high levels of amphetamines in his body. He died two days later. The moral of the story – as Lance Armstrong might say – is pretty clear: avoid wearing leather.

Towering over the ramshackle riverside town below, the imposing eighteenth-century fortress at Gavi can be seen from quite a distance and helped Richard and me find our bearings as we neared the completion of the stage. Both our Garmins had run out of juice and so we slowed to wait for our domestiques, Bob and Bernadette.

Before the second rest day and two successive nights of luxury in the peaceful Villa Sparina, one final obstacle: a rasping climb through dense woodland to the hamlet of Monterotondo – five minutes of sustained lactic-guzzling activity akin to ten lashes of the whip. With 1,700 kilometres now in the legs after sixteen consecutive days in the saddle, I rode clear of my companions to cement my place at the top of the standings. The pink jersey would stay on my shoulders heading into the final leg of our ride to Rome.

The delicious robiola risotto and braised beef combo that awaited us that evening was capped by generous bowls of home-made vanilla ice cream with a variety of toppings. Preceded by Italian breads, cured meats and ample *aperitivos*, it was a meal to guarantee a good night's sleep. Terry and I even had the luxury of separate bedrooms in our plush living quarters, giving us both some welcome time apart (my tendency to stay up late working and rise in a foul mood must have tested Terry's patience by now). We did, however, still share a bathroom – accessible only via my room – which led to a couple of heart-in-mouth moments as Terry traipsed past my bed in search of the loo, fumbling his way in the dark.

Shortly after my fifth slice of mortadella at breakfast the next morning our numbers were depleted by numerous deserters. Melbourne John and Roddy's ten days with us were over, while long weekenders Simon and Richard had to return to the hustle and bustle of London. On a positive note, we would soon be buttressed by the select core of the hardened troupe of Sydney club riders entering the fray, alongside the welcome return of Dylan. Despite its early sedentary promise, my rest day was not entirely restful. There may have been nothing as appealing as the Ventoux on the horizon, but I was still eager to keep the legs turning – even if I stopped short at putting in a full hundred klicks.

While most of our group chose to mooch around the narrow, cobbled streets of Gavi during the day, Bob and I opted to stay back at the hotel and take it easy: he to do some outdoor reading (a few chapters of Edgar Allan Poe, no doubt, washed down with a carton of orange juice) and me a little work on the veranda. As we later grazed on a light lunch of mushroom tortellini and steak tartare on the terrace overlooking the villa's vineyards, I was tempted to ditch my riding plans – especially after a glass of sweet and musky Asti Spumante, the local sparkling wine. But having returned to my room for a snooze, my limbs were stirred by the scenes playing out in the courtyard below, from where a series of cries and expletives came as a slowly increasing number of fatigued figures gathered on bikes.

'Jeez, that last bit was hard as.'

'My legs turned to shit on the sixth ramp.'

'D'you see Dave? The fat fuck blew to pieces before the first bend.'

'Pete, who won? Please tell me it wasn't the frigging dead possum again . . .'

The Velosophy splinter group being chaperoned by Dylan had arrived with a typical jejune Antipodean swagger. Evidence of their exertions forced me up and into my Cinzano top and lime-green shorts. Creeping out the back door to avoid any confrontation, I set off for a 30-kilometre cruise towards the nearby town of Novi Ligure – a place that is to Italian cycling what sick pilgrims are to Lourdes.

Home of 'The Novi Runt' Costante Girardengo, the bustling town boasts a museum dedicated to the diminutive rider and his fellow Italian great, Fausto Coppi. Back in his heyday in the 1920s, Girardengo was the first cycling star to be declared a *campionissimo* – or champion of champions, the nickname now usually associated with Coppi. If, as was claimed, Girardengo was more popular in Italy than Mussolini, he certainly wasn't doing the prime minister any favours in his bid to get the nation's trains running on time: such was the public esteem towards the nine-time national champion, it was decreed that all passing express trains should stop in his home town – an honour usually reserved for heads of state.

For his part, Coppi was brought up in nearby Castellania, leaving school at the age of 13 to work for a butcher in Novi Ligure. On top of the 15-kilometre ride to and from work, Coppi spent most of his days delivering salamis and prosciutto on his bike before being taken under the wing of a former-boxer-cum-cycling-masseur who was a regular at the delicatessen. When he won his first race at the age of 15, Coppi's reward was 20 lire and a salami sandwich – a bit of a rubbish prize considering he spent his days couriering the damned things in his knapsack. *Bradley Wiggins – here's your prize: a pair of fake sideburns!* The advice given to Coppi on his professional debut in Tuscany in 1939 was clear: 'Follow Gino Bartali!' That he did throughout his career until, in a spray of Perrier on the Galibier, he eventually surpassed the one other Italian rider with a claim to true *campionissimo* status.

Marble busts of both Girardengo and Coppi are on display outside Novi Ligure's Museo dei Campionissimi – the largest bike museum in the world. This being a quiet mid-September Monday afternoon, the museum was shut and my plans for a spot of culture derailed. Instead, I rode the undulating road back to Gavi and tackled the crazily steep lane up to the fortress to watch the sun set over the jagged horizon. This extra uphill excursion to the last Napoleonic stronghold in northern Italy meant I had to forgo a tour of the Villa Sparina wine cellars while I freshened up for dinner. Having already enjoyed the culinary wizardry of the hotel kitchen, we conceded our table at the restaurant to the animated Velosophy gang while our streamlined team of seven stalwarts – Bob, Bernadette, Terry, Sharon, John, Kay and myself – headed back to Gavi with Sam to eat in what appeared to be the only open establishment. Tough and sinewy, my bone-heavy rabbit stew boasted about as much flesh as a braised leg of Chris Froome, while the accompanying broccoli had clearly been on the boil for as long as Froome's trigger-happy girlfriend, whose Twitter spat with Mrs Wiggins during the 2012 Tour made ripples in the pages of the *Daily Mail*. As we ate, Sam filled us in on the Carthaginian army's early movements in northern Italy.

Around 70 kilometres north of Novi Ligure, Hannibal's march on Rome had entered a new dawn. News of the Taurini massacre had spread like wildfire. Still leading his own troops towards the Po after having set sail from Marseille, the Roman consul Publius Cornelius Scipio was perplexed at the alacrity of Hannibal's Alpine crossing. For his part, Hannibal was equally baffled that Publius's army had made their round trip so quickly.

But spare a thought for the people of Rome, who were still under the illusion that *both* armies were in Spain. Imagine the bewilderment and alarm of the Senate on discovering that Hannibal had not simply crossed Europe's largest natural barrier, but had routed the Roman army in battle at the river Ticinus, a tributary of the Po.

For this is indeed what happened when the two sides finally came head to head on Italian soil. Before the confrontation, Hannibal had roused his men through novel means: offering certain Gallic prisoners the chance of freedom through various bouts of armed combat among themselves. Think of it as a grown-up version of *The Hunger Games* for the second century BC. Hannibal felt his men would better understand the challenges ahead by watching the suffering of those they had already conquered. You could say that I was working along similar lines of motivation on deciding to get off my arse and start cycling some of the routes tackled by the professionals – although I was not in the habit of strangling Bob with an inner tube or cleating Bernadette to death.

Just before leading his men into battle, Hannibal called them together for some final words of encouragement. He then hoisted up a lamb in one hand and, uttering a prayer to the gods, dashed the animal's brains out with a stone; a sacrifice that would have got the thumbs-up from *bon viveur* Jacques Anquetil, who famously spent the rest day of the 1964 Tour stuffing his face with barbecued lamb at a VIP party in Andorra. The next day Anquetil's form was so woeful, the defending champion was dropped on the first climb. At the summit, his directeur sportif gave him a make-or-break bidon of Champagne in a bid to clear his indigestion. It worked. 'Maître Jacques' caught up with his principal rival Raymond Poulidor and stayed on course for a record fifth win.

There was no Champagne but you can imagine Hannibal granting his army extra rations of sour wine following their rousing victory at the Ticinus. The swift-moving Numidian horsemen were the stars of the show, making up for their poor performance at the Rhône and doing a Richie Porte-esque job for their team leader. To make matters worse for the Romans, Publius was badly wounded and would have died were it not for a last-ditch rescue by his 17-year-old son, the future Scipio Africanus, the man who ultimately proved to be Hannibal's nemesis.

# GAVI TO CASTELNUOVO DI GARFAGNANA

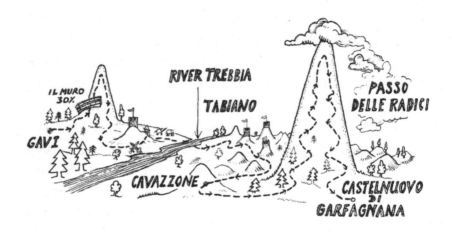

VELOSOPHY – PRONOUNCED *VE-LOSS-UH-FEE*, or, across the Atlantic Ocean, *vello-sophie* – is the rational investigation of the truths and principles of being, knowledge or conduct in relation to the bicycle; to wit, the philosophy of bikes, or 'the way of the bike'. It is also the name of a bike club and retail store in Sydney. Velosophy – both concept and entity – was about to play a huge role in shaking up the foundations of my tour, forcing me to break out of my comfort zone and start riding aggressively. Almost anyone can tick off 100 kilometres a day at a leisurely pace, taking in the surroundings and pausing for croissants stuffed with custard, chocolate or warm marmalade. What I was doing on the roads of Spain (custard), France (chocolate) and Italy (warm marmalade – *marmalada*: divine) hardly made me special. As we edged nearer to

Rome, friends and family were congratulating me on a daily basis as if I were on the verge of an extraordinary accomplishment, when in truth I'd merely spent large swathes of successive days sweating in the saddle. It *was* a truly epic adventure on two wheels – but not one which necessarily excluded most people on grounds of fitness. Some of our group were a living testimony to the fact that being out of shape or not even that bike savvy was no valid reason to forgo such a pedal-powered culinary extravaganza.

Sure, my chronic knee problems were of considerable early concern and jeopardized my progress. And I had pushed myself with additional climbs up and down Mont Ventoux, Alpe d'Huez (twice) and the Galibier – more often than not in quite horrific weather. Then there were all those extra loops carried out to feed my curiosity and top up the mileage. This was more than most people could achieve on a bike – but considerably less than many dedicated riders manage on a regular basis. Besides a few rounds in the big ring with Sam, Bob and Bernadette (two of whom were roughly double my age), I had ridden very much within myself. There had been more of a competitive edge to my eating than there had been in the saddle.

That was all about to change.

Throughout our week in the Alps, Dylan had been updating Sam about his progress with a dozen hardened Australian club riders who were following our exact route one day behind. They were beasts who would devour the roads, he said, stopping for lunch for but a handful of minutes before pressing on at a ferocious pace. They would race relentlessly. There was banter, rivalry and camaraderie. Everything was done as a unit. They were in it together to ride it together. But that didn't stop each one wanting to be first over every climb or into each town.

Half of this Velosophy splinter group – including my Ventoux descending partner, Alan – headed back Down Under after one night at Gavi. Six extreme Velosophers, however, would join our motley crew of ramshackle riders for four days as we weaved our way out of Piedmont, across the southern tip of Lombardy, into the rustic and rugged Emilia-Romagna and over the Apennines into northern Tuscany. The hallowed Velosophy Six would then head off to nearby Florence to catch the men's road race of the 2013 World Championships, which was starting in Lucca before finishing with ten circuits around the Tuscan capital.

Two weeks of conditioning and finding my form had been building up to this: a chance to pit myself against some serious cyclists – guys who had churned the pedals all their adult life and who lived and breathed for the sport. Things were about to get serious.

At breakfast on the opening day of the third and final leg, an inevitable stand-off ensued. By now we had all grown familiar with one another and our little routines. We were aware of the extra bodies of brash masculinity in Lycra, downing glasses of blood-orange juice and filling their traps with cereal, yoghurt, fresh fruit, warm pastries, thin slices of heavenly Italian ham and so-wrong-it's-right slithers of pungent processed mortadella. But with formal introductions yet to be made, both parties complied with a game of feigned ignorance.

Outside, our group readied for the day's ride – a rolling 103 kilometres through the Oltrepò Pavese to the banks of the river Trebbia. But as Bob and Bernadette led the way, Dylan drew me aside for a word. 'Hold back and join Sam with the others today, mate. You'll enjoy riding with the boys . . .'

Boys they certainly seemed to be. A long-haired chap with a near-full 'sleeve' tattoo on his right arm and a large skull grinning from his right calf was busy entertaining his friends by reciting lines from episodes of *South Park*.

'How would you like to suck my balls?' he said as I proffered my hand. Not words I would use to greet someone for the first time, but so be it.

This was Pete, second in command (or 'Operations Director') of Velosophy Bikes but clearly the team's designated road captain/resident joker. His hair lank and face unshaven, Pete was slighter and shorter than the rest, possessor of a trim and toned climber's physique, not to mention an astounding vocal range when it came to high-pitched cartoon buffoonery.

Three others – including Chris, the owner of the self-proclaimed 'hottest bicycle retail store in Australia', who held a passing resemblance to Stifler from the American Pie film franchise – were powerhouse criterium-style racers with muscly glutes, bulging thighs and legs as smooth as they were sturdy. Dave, a comparatively portly pilot controversially clad in civvies, sat in the van alongside Dylan, a trifle under the weather. 'I've done eight consecutive days. I need a break,' he said. I resisted telling him I had now notched seventeen.

Amid much back-slapping and bravado they tweaked their bikes, adjusted their saddles, pumped their tyres and thumped their chests. A few cursory 'hellos' only enhanced the general feeling of intimidation. These were alpha males of the worse sort – Australian – and collectively oozing with enough testosterone to fill the boot of Willy Voet's car. I was about as macho as Frank Spencer in a pair of Y-fronts – a milquetoast mumbler of meek Englishness to their assertive Aussie brawn and cocksure hardihood. Lanky, spindly and now hairier in the leg, I felt even more out of place than Andy Schleck pumping iron at a World's Strongest Man competition.

Their terrorizing collectivity enhanced by impeccable matching kits, they were ready to dish out an abject humbling to the skittish punter who made a grave error in not leaving with his friends.

My fears are confirmed almost instantly when I lose touch within moments of setting off. A couple of bends into a winding descent and they're gone – a red light at an intersection down in the valley my early saviour.

'Blimey, they're fast,' I whisper to Sam as the light flicks green.

'Don't worry: you'll get them in the hills – and there are loads of hills today.'

A few flat kilometres follow, during which I take last place in the Velosophy train. Our Garmins beep to indicate a left turn and the road starts to edge uphill. I have twenty-odd metres to close before I can latch on to my companions, who have bunched up considerably. Having regained contact, the strangest thing happens. I'm checking my speed and slowing. It actually becomes a bit of a chore and so I start to edge through the gaps towards the front. But still I find myself riding very much with the handbrake on. Wary of touching wheels or causing a spill, I take up position on the front of our group. The tide has turned.

The gradient of the remaining 2 kilometres is fairly paltry and I feel no need to drop into the small ring. In London I commute on a single speed so I've grown accustomed to feeling a bit of resistance in my strokes. But I avoid using the biggest sprocket at the back and crossing the chain. This, I'm told, is a recipe for disaster, causing unnecessary damage to cassette teeth and chain. Anyhow, my knees finally feel up to it so I continue at a slower cadence but faster pace than the others. Sensing an awkwardness in having to turn round and slow up I decide to just ride off at my own rhythm.

Before I know it I've opened up some space between me and the others. This is rather delicate. Slowing now would require an explanation. Peering back would acknowledge what's happening and may be perceived as a goad. So I keep turning the pedals in denial. I can hear 'Easy, tiger' from behind but I can't pick out what else is being said.

There's no denying that I feel rather self-conscious. I don't want to be seen as making a statement when I'm doing nothing of the sort.

I'm merely riding how I've always ridden. Curiously, this is much faster than these guys, who are clearly much better than me, can take.

I conjure up some excuses to roll out later.

How about: *If I ride too slowly my knees start to hurt*? Not good. It implies that I view their pace as inferior, which it is, but which is not the point. I don't want to appear to be confrontational.

*I knew I needed an advantage going over the summit or I'd never see you guys again today*? That's better. I'm being complimentary *and* modest. But they might see through it. Worse, they might think I'm taking the piss.

*I thought you were playing a game with me*? Hmm . . . does that not suggest that I can only comprehend such a lowly pace within the context of a practical joke? That could be twisted.

Blimey, this seems unnecessary. I shouldn't be looking for a way to explain my reasoning for riding clear of the same guys who completely rinsed me on the opening downhill.

But I can't stop thinking about what might be going through their minds. Chris, for instance. How might he explain this unexpected scenario?

*So, we were riding up the first climb when the English guy suddenly appeared from nowhere. He'd been struggling a bit before but he let rip as soon as the road went up. We all thought he was doing some interval training because he was churning a real heavy gear. I looked at Pete. He shook his head and shrugged his shoulders. We let him go. He seemed on a mission. What was that all about? Perhaps he wanted to prove something after we dropped him on the downhill? I heard him say he's a bike journo. Covers the big races. So he must know his stuff. He's the tallest dude I've seen on a bike. All skin and bones too. Better suited to the climbs than some of us. Although Pete will put him in his place later today. Sam said he rode Alpe d'Huez twice last week. And with dodgy knees. It's no surprise he fucked them up if he rides crazy gears like that at 10 in the morning. It's not as if he's new to cycling – he should know that by now. Unless he was doing some interval training. Who knows?*

By the time I'd crested the summit I'd passed John and Kay, Sharon and Terry, Bob and Bernadette, and also Steve. Steve was a friend of Dylan's brother-in-law who had done the opening leg of the Hannibal tour last year. He'd come out this year to help with guiding and van duties, replacing James who was on his way back to Morzine. Tall, blond and strapping, Steve resembled the cricketer Freddie Flintoff, so we'll forgive him for struggling on the steep stuff.

Steve was a couple of years younger than me but not the youngest of the new arrivals. That accolade went to Jason, a bike sales rep from the suburbs of Sydney, who was only 27. Nicknamed 'dead possum' because of his uncanny ability to feign weakness before launching a spitting attack, Jason was an utter bike junkie – and the best sprinter of the Velosophy troupe by far. In their ongoing game where every town sign doubled up as an intermediate sprint, more often than not Jason would take the spoils. This was the case when we hurtled down the back of that first climb. I had stopped to take photos of both the view and my companions (another excuse: *I wanted to ride ahead to get a good movement shot of you guys crossing the summit*) when Jason exploded in a threesome with Pete and Chris, adding another notch to his bedpost.

The trio missed the turn-off, leaving our numbers depleted when we tackled the next incline: a one-kilometre lung-buster called, rather menacingly, *Il Muro* – 'the Wall'. Kicking up to a fiendish 30 per cent, the road zigzagged through trees, each relenting bend followed by an ever steeper slog where uphill slaloming was the only alternative to total standstill. Needless to say, I was no longer in the big ring. I cracked on because the others cracked up, mentally calling out for a sherpa and an oxygen mask as I crested the summit a gasping wreck, my companions eventually trickling their way to the crown of what was the unforeseen king of our trip's entire collection of climbs.

It took more than a few coffees to steady the nerves in the small town of Brignano. Jason even ordered a slice of pizza once he and the other tearaways found their way to our first pit stop. Across the road, someone had painted 'IL CAMPIONISSIMO' on the side of a tumble-down barn. We were, after all, just a few kilometres away from Fausto Coppi's birth-town of Castellania.

'Who's Coppi?' asked Jason when I relayed the significance of the graffiti as we rolled out of town.

'Just some guy who won the Giro five times and the Tour twice. The champion of champions . . .'

'Never heard of him.' And then he was off – for Jason had a tendency to sprint for the out-of-town signs too.

I found it quite staggering that someone who was so bike smart would not have heard of such a legend of the sport. But was it any more bizarre, say, than me not fully comprehending the intricacies of bicycle gearing? For me, everything I did on a bike followed a decade of watching it on TV and covering pro races for work. Jason's love of cycling wasn't steeped in history or dependent on prior knowledge; it didn't have to be affirmed by the actions of others. His travelling to the World Championships was more about getting four extra days in the saddle than watching others race for a rainbow jersey.

Normal service resumed on a long drag through a neglected valley once we'd crossed into Lombardy. Here the Velosophy train left the station with me still grappling with my bags on the platform. For the best part of 10 kilometres I struggled to hold on, finally giving up when an echelon formed. If Chris and Cameron were also feeling the pinch, then I didn't stand much chance.

'I just can't keep up with you guys. The pace is infernal,' I told Cam
– the oldest of the group, but the fastest descender. Almost suddenly I
was left to rue the apparent phoniness of my statement when the road
finally dealt me a favourable hand: no sooner had I opened my trap,
than I'd swallowed up and spat out Cam on the next climb. I reeled
them in one by one until it was just Pete left ahead. When I rounded
him, I felt put out in a way only an Englishman could be: by the guilt
that he may have felt I should be feeling.

*That's right. We drag you along across the valley and then as soon as the road
tilts upwards, you're off. There's gratitude for you.*

It wasn't like that, though. I hadn't been close enough to the back-
runner's wheel to benefit from the slipstream. They all took it in turns
pulling on the front but I never got close enough to take the baton.
Perhaps they didn't know this. That was what got at me. I didn't want
to get a reputation. And look – Pete's clearly pissed off because there he
goes . . .

With the group trailing in our wake, Pete's attacked. He's done so
at just the right moment: a false flat before a final little dig and then a
long plateau ahead. Even if I were to close the gap, he'd burn me soon
after. No option but to ease up. There's a Pete-shaped blur every now
and then, as I emerge from one bend and he enters the next, but it's no
use.

I see him minutes later waiting at a crossroads in a hamlet called
Valverde. 'I missed the turning and rode about four kilometres further
up the road,' he says when the others arrive. I don't question this
obvious embellishment.

Pete and I will move beyond (largely imagined) verbal gamesmanship
on the final climb of the day after a light *pranzo* of cured meats and fresh
ricotta and spinach agnolotti with sage and butter. When Chris tells the

delighted owner of the roadside restaurant that it's the best pasta he's ever tasted, it's no lie. But it's a line he'll have to repeat to the chef at our hotel later that evening when we're treated to the exact same two dishes ahead of a bonus round of red kidney bean gnocchi soup and a plentiful main of guineafowl and veal with potatoes. Stomachs would not be rumbling in Italy.

Sandwiched between these two sensational meals was my coming-of-age ride against Pete. We'd entered the unmanicured Emilia-Romagna region famous for the Parmigiano-Reggiano whose fruity, peppery nuttiness was so liberally grated across our melt-in-the-mouth agnolotti. This is a region unspoilt by the heavy touristic demands of its more southerly counterpart Tuscany. Once the largest bastion of Communism outside the Soviet sphere, Emilia-Romagna is said to have the best soil in Italy – and beside the narrow roads ploughed fields stretched out towards the blue horizon.

Disoriented by lunch and the afternoon sun, after successfully shedding their timid hanger-on the Australian flat-road bullies missed the turning on to the showdown climb so started with a handicap. The road clung to a ridge and stretched upwards for around 3 kilometres. It was hardly a second *Muro* but the gradient certainly posed questions after such a heavy feed. I had about 50 metres to play with over the pursuing Velosophers. Only Bob rode ahead, the last of the 'others' to succumb to the laws of natural selection.

As I draw up alongside Bob, we look back and see the Antipodean chasing group lurking with intent after ditching Bernadette et al. My American mentor offers me some touching words of encouragement. 'You're doing us proud, Felix. You're taking it to those guys and showing them what you've got. Now make sure you make it to the top first.'

Thanking Bob, I press on, invigorated by his kind comments. I'm doing this one for the team – that's our team, the Hannibal tour originals. Yet I'm distracted by the mesmerizing beauty of the blue sky set against the patchwork green and brown fields. A familiar impulse hampers my progress as I slow to take some photos.

A minute or two passes before I hear a rider come on to my wheel, hawk loudly and spit. I'm just about to make some quip about Bob's resurgence when I look to my left and see that it's not a wooden Renovo alongside my trusty Felt but a spotless Look boasting the famous La Vie Claire Mondrian colour scheme that would have made Roddy jump for a yellow colour chart. I say 'Hey' but Pete doesn't reply. He's looking ahead and keeping a steady pace in an elegant style that doesn't befit a man with such shaggy hair and gauche body art. He has no time for pleasantries. His legs are doing the talking.

Before he gets the chance to edge ahead, I increase my own tempo and open a gap. I'm sure it's not a pretty sight, but it seems to be effective. Without deigning to look back, I step on the pedals for a series of sprightly surges. Sensing I've shed my rival, the tourist chronicler inside yet again gets the better of me. I want a photo of those rolling fields and the lone tree emerging from the palette of brown. And when the road jerks to the right, I look back and there's no sign of Pete as I whip out my camera.

Wow, I've cracked him. I won't deny it – the elation is pretty high.

I ease up. Then – BAM! – a huge wake-up call. Appearing from nowhere, Pete powers past. I could have sworn he wasn't there just now. He must have been in the shade of those trees when I looked back.

The next instant is vital. Leave it a split second too long and I could be forced to give up. But I react fast and reel him in.

Swish! There's more yo-yoing going on here upon this sun-bathed Italian hillside than an entire school playground.

Swoosh! Once again Pete pulls clear, his unzipped shirt hanging heavy with human truffle juice. The crazed sockets of the multi-coloured skull stare out from his right calf. I'm being taunted by a tattoo. A tattoo of something that's not even alive. This won't do.

Pete's out of the saddle now and laying it on thicker than a Gewiss team time trial up the Mur de Huy. The summit's only a few hundred metres away. A penny for his thoughts . . .

*He got a surprise when I came to his wheel. Man, I couldn't sit back and do nothing. He's been attacking on the hills all day. Time for me to show him who's boss. The old dude didn't do him any favours. Told me I stood no chance in catching him. Said Felix was the 'best'. Talk about motivation. As I came level I thought I'd give him a warning. Spitting seemed the right thing to do. It's what I'm doing now – spitting on his chances. To be fair, he responded well. He's got some stamina when he's not taking photos. Always stopping and starting. Never any continued momentum. Somehow he didn't see me when he looked back at the bend. I rode on. Couldn't take my eyes off his bleeding saddlepack. It's fucking enormous. The guy's carrying a tent. And what about his bulging back pockets? God knows what he's got stuffed down them. And don't get me started on that lame Velcro pouch on his top tube. Talk about punter. He looks ridiculous. It's doubly tragic because he's got skills on the bike. You see, here he is again. Fuck! He's doing a Chris bloody Froome on the wrong side of the road. Guy has balls. Shit, he's done me.*

Do him, I did. Gloriously so. Shifting down a gear in the back, I put in the kind of high-cadence, saddle squat of an attack that would have made the incumbent yellow jersey green with envy. More elbows and knees than a Bavarian barbecue.

Both timing and exploitation of circumstances were key: my last throw of the dice came just as we approached a severely riveted part of the road. Taking a frivolous line on the left-hand, cleaner side of the road meant any approaching vehicle from beyond a semi-blind bend would have forced me into a) the ploughed field, or b) its bonnet. But it would have forced Pete to use a cluster of potholes as the platform of any response. So I took the calculated risk. We hadn't met a car all afternoon.

Kapow! With the momentum in my favour, I surged round the bend and saw the road flattening out in front of me. I gave it one last dig to be sure before coming to rest at an intersection just beyond the summit. Game, set, match to the wildcard.

'Well done, mate, you had me there,' said Pete. 'That was pretty epic. I thought I'd done enough but your legs were just too strong.' Still exhilarated from the climb, I was moved by Pete's words. Coming from such an accomplished rider – and a man from whom I had sensed wholly fictitious hostility – they meant a lot to this relative newcomer.

We'd barely gulped down a few sips of water when we heard the rev of the van, which emerged around the last corner with Jason in tow. His textbook wing-mirror 'sticky bidon' was enough to pip Luke – a retail CEO about to make the sideways shift from lingerie to barbecues – to the summit. Both Luke and Jason enquired who had won our duel; both were surprised by the answer.

Later that afternoon, as hotel staff switched that double bed for two singles in mine and Terry's room, Dylan and I chatted in the shadow of the tumbledown tower of San Martino. Following my easing up on the final descent, I had ridden home at my own steady pace when I spotted the tower on the side of the road. The ancient hamlet also contained a church and the ruins of a castle. Definitely worth a gander, I thought, not yet clocking that this was to be our noble accommodation for the night, beside the autumn trickle of the river Trebbia.

'You rode unbelievably today,' said Dylan. 'The Velosophy boys were extremely impressed. Surprised, even.' He may have further flattered my ego were it not for a request from the haughty Count of San Martino for the van to be moved from his field of vision. Apparently it was blocking the view of the courtyard from his sitting room.

Outnumbered and obliged to rely on tactical nous, forcing the battle to take place on the enemy's least favourable terrain: Hannibal and I had rather a lot in common. A few kilometres north of the Torre di San Martino, on the banks of the river Trebbia near modern-day Piacenza, the first major battle of the Second Punic War took place around the winter solstice in 218 BC. Following their defeat in the cavalry skirmish at Ticinus a month earlier, the Romans were eager to get back on the front foot.

Tiberius Sempronius Longus, the second consul, had arrived with an army from Sicily to help his wounded counterpart, Publius Scipio. To call Longus short-sighted and impetuous would be to do scant justice to the likes of Eddie the Eagle and other gloriously impulsive myopic adventurers. With election season just around the corner, Longus was eager to end his consulship with a splash – and victory over the foreign invader would have been a one-way ticket to glory. Think of all the talks he could give, the dinner invitations, the Roman lecture circuit and forum consultancy roles . . . Longus could have been Tony Blair in a toga, cleaning up in every way possible once out of office.

While Publius urged caution, favouring consolidation and soldier training during the cold winter months, Longus was up for going all out. Imagine a directeur sportif sending his riders up the road without any food or gels, ordering them to put in numerous attacks on the first climb of a mammoth mountain stage hampered by snow and cold temperatures: this analogy only partially conveys the tactical hash Longus would make. But with Publius still licking his wounds, the ambitious consul sniffed an opportunity to seize the limelight. Buoyed by a flurry of victories in minor cavalry scuffles in what Ernest Hemingway would one day describe as 'the most beautiful valley in the world', Longus readied his men for battle.

Of course, Hannibal was fully aware of the situation. He had bluffed his way into puffing up Longus's self-confidence and he was now about to play him like a record.

The ambush came on one bitterly cold December morning. Hannibal had sent 2,000 horsemen and infantry to lie in wait under the control of his brother Mago. He then ordered the rest of the Numidian cavalry to cross the Trebbia and provoke the Roman camp before dawn. Although his men had not eaten, Longus took the bait and retaliated. When the Numidians withdrew to the other side of the bank, Longus told his infantry to wade through the icy waters and fight – like a British field marshal ordering his men to go over the top into no-man's-land. Cold, drenched and hungry, the Roman soldiers were lured into the trap. Once across they were pulverized by Mago's men – the brotherly plan coming off in a way that even the Schleck siblings could never fathom.

Hannibal's elephants joined the attack from the flanks, tearing into the infantry and wreaking complete havoc. Some of the Roman soldiers were so cold from crossing the river they were unable to unsheathe their swords in battle. One bonus of losing all sensations in your limbs: you don't feel a thing when they are severed and stabbed at by the enemy. An estimated 28,000 men died from the Roman army of 40,000 – against paltry Carthaginian losses of 4,500 from 30,000.

Longus tried the famous old chestnut of blaming a poor performance on extreme weather conditions (something the Schlecks excel at). But the people of Rome soon learned the humiliating truth of the crushing defeat. 'Hannibal ad portas!' exclaimed trembling senators. The enemy leader henceforth became the bogeyman of the ancient world, with Roman parents for years telling their misbehaving children that Hannibal was lurking on the other side of the door.

Nearby the alleged battle site of the Trebbia – at an ugly crossroads and surrounded by a flimsy green metal mesh to deter non-existent vandals – there stands a giant bronze sculpture of an elephant. The lifesize pachyderm is being driven by a mahout while two Carthaginian soldiers stand in a howdah attached to the creature's back with chains.

Never before had I seen such a wonderful monument in such a drab, unlikely place. It was a bit like a Tour champion hanging his framed yellow jersey on the wall of the closet under his stairs.

Having survived the brutal Alpine crossing, twenty-nine of Hannibal's thirty-seven war elephants died at the Trebbia. Of the eight survivors, only one made it through the harsh winter that followed. Deprived of his totemic beasts, Hannibal regrouped and saw out the remainder of the colder months near Piacenza before venturing south towards the Apennines. On the back of individual ignominious defeats, Publius and Longus retreated with their tails between their legs, to be replaced by the newly elected consuls in January – like washed-up stars voted out of the *Celebrity Big Brother* house.

After a spell of bloody activity, the ensuing lull in the Second Punic War was mirrored by my own position as we also edged south towards the backbone of Italy. I laid the blame for this unscheduled truce with Velosophy firmly at Hannibal's door. For had I not insisted on a post-breakfast detour to inspect this statue of one of his elephants, then who knows the kind of destruction I might have inflicted upon the rattled enemy peloton. I certainly missed latching on to their train on the lengthy uphill haul that preceded the highest of seven climbs on the day's menu. It felt as if the ghosts of Hannibal's deceased thirty-six elephants were all blowing their trunks in unison as I fought a debilitating headwind to arrive at the foot of the 800-metre peak in a right old mess.

Once on to the remote track that coiled up the climb, I made my first sighting. It'd been a soul-searching solitary traipse for 35 kilometres since breakfast, during which my legs had been bitten to pieces (Hemingway didn't mention the mozzies). As I caught close (but not *that* close) friends John and Kay I enquired about the Velosophy group. 'Oh, they passed us a long time ago,' said Kay. Terry and Sharon, being paced along by Steve, delivered the same news: long gone. Joining Bob and Bernadette for a coffee (and a Coke, ice cream and some biscuits – all of which curdled something rotten inside) at a cafe over the summit, I was informed by my scouts that they were 'probably well on their way to lunch by now'.

I felt like Hannibal tracking the Roman army, only to be told at every settlement that the enemy had passed through just moments earlier. A solo pursuit of half a dozen elite riders was almost as futile as a Team Europcar break in a Grand Tour. Best sit up, take in the scenery and have a day off. Although, unless you had a fetish for ploughed fields there was not much geological eye-candy to get the blood flowing.

It was while squinting through a set of electricity pylons at a sprawling cement factory that I almost rode into a colossal ditch which had apparently formed when half the road recently subsided into a gully. The nearby town of Lugagnano Val d'Arda – unorthodoxly located between the above factory and a hill half consumed by open-cast mining – was about as bleak as you can get; a place, I contend, even the annual hosting of Miss Italia could not reprieve. I half expected it to be twinned with Chernobyl. A tradition of pretzel-making aside, the most interesting thing about Lugagnano Val d'Arda is the surname of its mayor, Papamarenghi.

The mayor of nearby Castell'Arquato clearly has a much better job, even if his name, Rocchetta, is not such a delight. Mercifully, as we approached the charming hillside town, the roads improved and the countryside looked prosperous again. Perhaps the local MP resides nearby, I thought. The narrow cobbled streets of the old Roman stronghold led under a series of archways to a splendid town square boasting a church, a thirteenth-century palace and a sixteenth-century fortress with four imposing bastions. It was like Tuscany without the crowds: sleepy, unspoilt and gratefully neglected. Lunch was a do-it-yourself affair at a local pizzeria where I treated myself to a *quattro formaggi con prosciutto crudo*. After all, the chase was well and truly off: the Velosophy Six had refuelled in a flash, leaving almost an hour earlier.

It was not a day of total saddle solitude. Dylan and I joined forces in the afternoon and a post-*pranzo* call of nature proved a real eye-opener.

'Do you always do it the traditional way?' asked Dylan after I'd completed the usual process of delving deep, yanking up, pulling down and ahhhing-out.

'Is there another way?'

'Next time try feeding it through one of your leg holes. You get much better purchase. And there's not so much leakage afterwards.'

Unsure whether or not this was a nod to the numerous times I had left a dark speck at the end of the minute hand of my bib short's tick-tocking bulge, I agreed to give it a go. It irrefutably made gravitational sense – although some of my shorts were quite tight around the thigh and I doubted the feasibility of such an unorthodox operation.

Dylan was recovering from a squash-related knee injury and so eased up on a series of hairpin ramps inside the demanding final 20 kilometres. From the highest point of the rolling hills the four bastions of Castell'Arquato could be seen in the distance, as well as myriad other towers and steeples. We must have left Signor Rocchetta's patch because the roads were once again thoroughly crappy: at times just a couple of metres wide, they crumbled away at the edges, more distressed than Bradley Wiggins on a mountain trek without fags, a leashed dog or an umbrella. Astonishingly, I had avoided puncturing since the opening day in Spain, but my luck must have been running out.

Surrounded by ploughed fields so chalky they resembled Saharan sand dunes rising into the sky, after another trademark off-piste loop I cycled the final undulating kilometres on my own. The road became so ridiculous – both in gradient and quality – that I suspected Dylan and Sam had reconfigured my GPS and were playing some kind of practical joke. It wasn't until I passed Kay keeping guard as John took another leak (the traditional method) that my mind was put at rest. By the time the roaming peacocks greeted my arrival at the Antico Borgo di Tabiano Castello – yet another castle-themed palatial bolt-hole – the Velosophers had already taken their ice baths, full body massages, acupuncture and whatever else it was they did with needles in the evenings to recuperate. They had indeed rolled in around 2 p.m. – just as I savoured the last slice of that historic pizza.

Swings and roundabouts. I'd had a good day even without the element of competition that had recently widened my scope and altered my parameters. Granted, I might have been denied a spot of bike jousting, but I had learned the best way to unsheathe my sword – and such a skill could prove invaluable in the grand scheme of things.

No fewer than eight punchy climbs meant that battle well and truly recommenced the next day, as we cycle-surfed our way over the rolling land waves south of Parma. Things went downhill from the outset: the Velosophy Six and Sam cruising away on the drops as I made a typically ham-fisted attempt to stay in touch. We regrouped on the flat roads in the valley, where the locals out for a leisurely Thursday morning spin didn't know what hit them. One chap we passed managed to latch on to my wheel at the back and got a complimentary first-class ticket on the Velosophy Express.

But then a tight left-hander and the first climb: a small one-kilometre wall which didn't so much defeat as de-cleat me. Galumphing out of the saddle to respond to a synchronized dig from Sam and Jason, my right foot slipped out of the pedal and scraped across the asphalt. 'Woah, epic save!' someone said as I avoided a tumble, unwittingly re-clipped on the next revolution and continued the attack: one of my most embarrassing moments on a bike morphing instantaneously into a rare flash of adroitness. Back in the small ring to steady the ship, I soared past Sam, himself grappling with a chain issue, before deflating Jason with a piercing dig to plunder the win. One–nil.

Jason was sufficiently piqued to launch his attack much earlier on the next climb, a sweeping affair with several large bends before a gradual twisting finale. I'd started from the back after being skinned on the previous short descent. Dave was the first rider I reached as Jason rode clear of his fellow Argonauts. It was the first time Dave and I had experienced each other in Lycra, after his rest and my solo efforts the following day. He gave me a knowing nod as I waltzed past.

*He caught me at the start of the climb and said he was going after Jason. I heard Felix was tidy on the hills but he almost stacked it on the first climb. Hardly a surprise given the state of his cleats. He showed them to us this morning at the hotel. They were worn clean through. Pete said both shoes would unclip from the pedal under too much pressure – and what d'you know? Fair play with the recovery, though. That was awesome. Top marks. Shame he descends like a girl. And he pees in a weird way too. I saw him do it through the leg hole earlier in the day. Made a right mess of his shorts. He's a bastard to pass on the downhills because he's way too stiff and careers all over the road. Never on the drops. But going up – well, I stand no chance. From what I've seen, he's very strong. Churns a big, heavy gear. But he's carrying no weight – all arms, legs and wings. He's got no official king of the mountains jersey but he's certainly got polka dot legs – those mozzie bites look horrific. Such a Pom! Now let's see if he catches Jason. Think he may have left it too late . . .*

I formed a chasing trio with Sam and Pete, who soon dropped back. Sam and I went shoulder to shoulder before he eased up. 'I can't keep this up. You're going to have to go soon though, or it'll be too late.' Despite Sam's words, I had everything under control. If I was going to cross the Rubicon, I had to bide my time – and according to my Garmin it was still too early. It was paramount to avoid shooting my bolt and being out-sprinted by Jason and his Jack-in-the-box thighs. So I kept him there, reeled him in slowly, conserved a little energy, and then went for the jugular – denying Jason the Golden Fleece. Two–nil and sitting pretty.

The third climb was more clear-cut but perhaps the most satisfying – for I had an audience. With Pete in tow, I thundered past most of the Hannibal B Team, who had left the hotel a full forty minutes ahead of us. Only Bob and Bernadette remained up the road as I took off the safety catch and shot to the summit. Three–nil before half-time. The opposition reeling. Game as good as over.

But then the referee blew the whistle. With the boy Lowe in the ascendency, the match was controversially postponed – to be replayed in a different venue.

We had just reached the foot of the fourth climb, past a sign reminding drivers to affix chains to their tyres in the winter months (an idea of how steep some of these roads were). There had been a regrouping on the descent and I was beside Sam when his phone rang.

'What, totally closed? So you recommend we turn back and make a detour?'

It was Dylan calling from the van. He'd driven ahead and discovered that the entire pass was being dug up and resurfaced. Having already gone so far, Bob and Bernadette had gamely pressed on rather than turning back, pushing their bikes over some of the more wayward parts. But Dylan recommended we took a diversion through the valley – replacing two ascents with 20 kilometres on the flat. The Velosophy boys were ecstatic. I was gutted. It was like telling Michael Rasmussen that a mountain stage had been replaced with a flat team time trial. Because that's what it became – a Velosophy race against the clock with me clinging on for dear life.

There was no let-up. From the word 'go' they formed a line and surged ahead, full throttle, their legs spinning in unison like wind turbines in a hurricane. My problem was that I never quite managed to join the train. Like a scene from a movie, I was running along the platform with my arms outstretched, but never got quite close enough to jump on to the last carriage as it chugged out of the station. There were always a few metres between us. I completely buried myself trying to close the gap, but one foal versus six thoroughbreds had an inevitable outcome.

The gap stretched to 5 metres, then 10, then 20. Like a spring pulled beyond its elastic limit, there was no slinking back now. Up ahead I saw a cyclist in South African colours become engulfed by the front of the train. As I dropped further behind, this man slipped into the position I'd vacated. I'd been replaced by a random. Time to slacken the pace and call off the chase.

At our rescheduled lunch stop there was no sign of Velosophy. They'd simply disappeared.

'What happened to you guys?' I asked Cam when I finally rolled home following an enthusiastic extra loop in the hills.

'Mate, we had the best experience. We caught an old boy and he asked if he could join so we told him to latch on at the back. He must have been in his late sixties or early seventies – but he still made some big pulls on the front. He was seriously strong for his age – lean with some serious quads on him. He asked us where we were going. We said Traversetolo and he started laughing. "That's my home town," he said. He asked us if we had any plans for lunch. We said no and he invited us to his home. Look, here's a picture.'

Gazing out from the photo, surrounded by six grinning Aussies, was the man in the South African jersey: the guy who took my place in the train.

'We got to his house and his wife made us some sandwiches with

Parma ham. She'd just baked a cake so we had that with coffee. Then Angelo – that was his name – said he had something to show us. He led us to the back of his house and opened a door to his workshop. It was unreal. He had his own private museum with around fifty bikes on display. It was like Aladdin's cave. There were rows of old steel bikes – Bianchis, Colnagos, De Rosas . . . you name it – in all the colours of the rainbow. Some of them were a hundred years old. He even had a green and orange Legnano that Fausto Coppi – you know him? – used to train on.'

Cam showed me pictures from Angelo's bike grotto. The walls were covered with black-and-white images of the greats. There were race numbers, medals, bike tools and trophies littered everywhere. In one picture, Angelo's weatherbeaten face smiled in front of a framed yellow jersey belonging to Gino Bartali.

'When we left we asked Angelo how much we owed him for lunch. He just waved us away. "It's my pleasure. You guys have a passion for cycling and that's payment enough. When I come to Australia you can take me out for lunch." He then led us out of town and told us where to go. I never met a nicer bloke. He was a real character, such a twinkle in his eye.'

What a great story. The guys had met the Italian Bob – someone who was even more of a cycling nut than our aged American friend. In fact, Angelo made Bob's collection of sixteen bikes seem small fry, something of an excessive amateur rather than a professional collector. There was a pang of regret inside my stomach. If only I had fought just a little bit harder to get back on the train then I could have seen all this with my own eyes.

'Yeah, sorry, mate. We thought you were with us but when we looked around, you'd vanished. You know how Jason and Pete are – they were riding real hard and the pace was pretty high. What did you get up to in the end? The others got back ages ago . . .'

I told him about our ropey ciabatta toastie in Traversetolo's only open cafe and how the owner couldn't comprehend why we would ever choose passing through such a place on a bike holiday (he was from Rome and clearly didn't think much of his adopted hometown). By now Chris had come to join us as we awaited our tour of the traditional balsamic vinegar factory that was adjoined to the *agriturismo* at Cavazzone.

'I was keen to do some more climbing and avoid the busy flat roads so I headed back into the hills.'

'You love your climbing,' said Chris. 'I was talking to the others and we decided that you were some kind of freak, inverse cyclist. You find the hard things easy and the easy things hard.'

'Keeping up with you guys on the flat isn't that easy.'

'We weren't going that fast today! Even Angelo managed to hold on. Did Cam tell you about Angelo? He was pretty goddamn awesome. You just need to push yourself a bit further. I've noticed that you tend to leave a gap. Get closer and we'd just drag you along.'

'But I don't trust my reaction speed. And on the downhills, I'm too worried about stacking.'

'I watched you descend today and you're a bundle of nerves. You have to relax. And you shouldn't ride on the hoods. That's just lazy. Get Cam to give you some lessons tomorrow – he'll sort you out.'

Bernadette joined the fray and asked about my afternoon detour. I told them all about the numerous castles that reminded me of the Cathar strongholds in Languedoc; about the succession of isolated ridges and the rays of low sun catching the grooves of some perplexing eroded rock formations; about the smiley old men on mountain bikes whom I passed and who all wished me well; and about the incongruous Tibetan Buddhist sanctuary whose wind chimes mingled with the rustling of horse chestnut leaves in an eerie hidden valley.

'You're really making the most of this trip, Felix. Good onya!'

Ever since Bernadette insisted upon calling me Bradley Wiggins for the first days of the tour, she and I had had our fair few differences. For her part, I think she never forgave me for absent-mindedly failing to inquire after her own health one morning within a second of her asking me how I was. 'I'm fine, by the way – thanks for asking,' she had said, cutting me off before walking away just as I was telling her about the pain in my knee. For my part, I felt particularly aggrieved to be labelled rude when I seemed to spend most meals bending over backwards to refill the water and wine glasses of all those around me. But now we were well into the third week, a mutual burying of the hatchet seemed to have happened – and thankfully, not in each other's skulls. We were certainly on good terms as Tommaso, the oldest son of the family and heir to his father's prosperous *agriturismo* empire, led us into a dark room filled with rows of wooden barrels of varying size.

Tommaso talked us all through the intricate balsamic vinegar production line at Cavazzone, amusing us with his special Cockney-Scottish twang that came from stints working in Glasgow and north London. While 'Tommy' explained how the grape juice was cooked down to *mosto cotto* – thick syrup – I sagely nodded, hopefully disguising the fact that, well, it had never occurred to me before that balsamic was actually made from the same fruit as wine. The boiling process over, activity shifts from a special laboratory to the dank, cavernous room where we stood, an acidic redolence percolating the air. This is where the magic happens, as the balsamic is aged in five wooden barrels of decreasing sizes. Cocooned in oak, juniper, chestnut and cherry, the balsamic is aged for at least twelve years, shifted through the procession of barrels using the old suck-and-spit method favoured by petrol-pilfering thieves.

We contrasted the aromas of the younger and older barrels – the alcohol-heavy head of the former totally transformed by the time it reached the end of the line. Tommy told us that there were some barrelled balsamics in the room that had survived both world wars, before revealing a top trade secret: 'We never empty or clean the barrels.' A tactic my flatmate back in London seems to apply on a daily basis to our kitchen.

'Now it is a-time for you to sample the a-may-a-zing balsamico,' said Tommy. 'For your din-nar tonight ev-ary dish has been a-created around balsamico.'

One of the Velosophy boys described the exquisite Parmesan soufflé with crispy pancetta and six-to-eight-year-old balsamic as a 'posh eggs and bacon', but that hardly did justice to what was arguably one of the most delicious starters of the entire trip. It was followed by some balsamic tasting. When we sampled a teaspoon of thick and immensely sweet 25-year balsamic I suggested – half in jest – that it might go well with ice cream. 'There's no way I'm going to eat any kind of dessert that comes with vinegar,' said Bob, refusing to get into the spirit of things. Around an hour later, he was one of the first to demolish his panna cotta drizzled with the region's black gold. 'I have to say – that was kinda nice,' he acquiesced.

Before dessert came a subtle balsamic and onion risotto and our main of pig cheeks and necks braised in balsamic gravy (which tasted nicer than it sounds). The wine, thankfully, was not vinegary – a velvety Tuscan Sangiovese – although we did kick things off with some sparkling red Lambrusco – refreshing, eminently drinkable, yet baulked at by most. While 'Lambrusco' never took off as a baby name in Essex, the wine is very much a relic of the 1980s when it was as unfairly tarnished as Chardonnay would become two decades later. Perhaps inevitably maligned as the fruit punch of wines, good Lambrusco is still deemed by most an oxymoron, in the same vein as a climbing Cavendish, a fat Froome or a polite Wiggins. I didn't mind it, to be honest. Fizzy and frothy, it may well be the industrial balsamico of vino but it got the thumbs up for novelty value – and it was a blast from the past that wouldn't be outdone until we were served, some days later, Chianti in straw-wrapped bottles.

Wired and buzzing in bed later that evening (I knew the espresso balsamico was a bad idea), the hypothetical historical implications of balsamic swamped my mind. Had traditional balsamic been invented back in the third century BC then perhaps it would have made as big an impact on the Carthaginian army's recuperation process as, say, EPO did on cycling in the 1990s. Sour wine vinegar may have been viewed – and scorned accordingly – as a primitive pick-me-up of a bygone era. There's certainly no way Hannibal's men would have relinquished their rations of balsamic in a bid to burn cracks in rocks. The Alpine crossing might never have happened.

The final showdown with Velosophy was a team affair: myself, Sam and Dylan forming a Ride & Seek triumvirate against the steely sextet. A couple of smaller climbs featured before a lengthy slog up and over the Apennines via the Passo delle Radici, an ascent unused in the Giro since 1976, when it had a category-two status despite rising to 1,529 metres. The rules were simple: a point for each town sign; the highest tally come Tuscany wins.

Once again, the day started with a descent – and during a brief ceasefire Cam came good on his promise of downhill tuition. The oldest of the bunch, Cam worked in the construction industry in some kind of government role. But motorcycles were his main passion. From an early age he rode them, built them and took them apart. It was riding motorbikes that got him into riding a road bike. If there was anyone you wanted to teach you about cycling fast downhill, it was Cam.

'First things first – always descend on the drops.'

I made the switch and tensed up instantly. For me this was like walking out to bat against Mitchell Johnson without a cricket box.

*He's about as rigid as a weightlifter's stomach. He's got to relax or he'll over-shoot or over-brake. For his sake, I hope he hasn't come into cycling too late to get over his hang-ups with speed.*

Cam talked me through picking the right line, weight distribution, body position and braking techniques. Although I did my best to put everything into practice it became rapidly clear that twenty days of turning my knuckles white on the descents had virtually incapacitated my brake pads.

'Knowing when and how to brake is the key to mastering descents,' he said.

This was probably my cue to tell him that my pads – like my cleats – had practically been worn right through, particularly the rear pad.

*He'll struggle with brakes like that. You can hear that they're completely gone. He's a lovely guy, Felix, but he's way out of his comfort zone. He's a decent climber but in a race he'd lose more time going down than he'd gain going up. Look, he's all back and no front. Hasn't anyone told him that's a bad habit?*

'Downhill riding really should be done 90 per cent on the front brake.'

Ah, that might explain my near miss the last time I tried to ride on the drops, back on Ventoux. But it's hardly an uncommon error: when Chris Froome rode one of his first Under-23 races in Europe – the 2007 Giro delle Regioni – he crashed four times on the opening stage. Apparently he admitted afterwards that he'd always ridden downhill using the back brake as master. Anyway, six years later Froome won the Tour. In six years I'll be 38 – which leaves me with more than enough time to win the Vuelta and get a contract with Lampre.

*Alan said Felix almost stacked on Ventoux when his back wheel locked up. It'll happen again if he doesn't work on feathering those front brakes. And look at his balance. He's more wobbly than Luke's backside.*

'You have to compensate by shifting your weight back while applying pressure on to the pedal with your outside foot, which should be straight through the apex of the corner.'

When I tried to imitate Cam it was worse than even my feeble attempts at karaoke. It didn't help that I had no confidence when hunched in such an aerodynamic position, primed to be knocked off balance.

*He doesn't seem very aware of his surroundings. He's got to get out of his own bubble.*

'Always look ahead into the bends. If there's no vehicle coming then take the easier line, anticipate the corner.'

This was all too much to take on board. I'd need to replace my pads before I felt comfortable trying out some of these techniques. It was already tricky enough being away from the familiar curves of the handlebar hoods. Luckily we'd run out of downhill and so the lesson was over. Our session meant Cam and I had to fight back to rejoin the others ahead of the opening climb – and a chance for pupil to become teacher.

'Go for it, Felix!' shouted Sam as Jason latched on to my wheel after I'd used my momentum to attack from the outset. What followed was a big ring battle of attrition between Jason and me as we matched each other stroke for stroke. As every turn in the road brought fresh expectation of a town sign, neither of us dared to drop into the small ring. We would need all the teeth we could get in the event of a sprint.

*So here we are again . . . Yesterday Felix got the better of me so I won't let that happen again. I knew he'd attack on the climb. They're already a few points down and they know they'll never take us in a flat sprint. He's still in the big ring and has a few gears to play with on the back. Talk about extra punishment. And what's it with the bright green shorts? Did he lose a bet or something? Why do they have 'Saddles' written across them, too? Right, time for the old party trick. I think I'll drop down and see how he responds to a slower pace. No doubt with relief.*

When Jason started dawdling it seemed like a truce was on the cards. We had a buffer over the others. It was just a question of whether a settlement worthy of signage came our way. So far, so bleak. Just a few houses but nothing to sprint for. So I took a break from the big ring myself and eased up accordingly.

Bloody dead possum. He only went and caught me out with the oldest trick in the book. Around the next corner there was a town – and off Jason went in a flash.

At coffee we were already five–one down and defeat looked a certainty. Dylan and Sam drew me to one side and said I should go on the offensive in anticipation of the next hilltop town. That was all very well, but before the road went up I had to bust a gut getting back in touch following another downhill. Luke had already attacked so my first job was to nullify his threat.

Moments earlier in the cafe there had been some mild dissent within the Velosophy ranks. Despite their healthy lead, tempers had flared when Luke – with supreme unknowing comedic agility as he tried to squeeze through a small gap between Pete's chair and the table – upturned his team-mate's macchiato with his backside, scalding his crotch. When Luke insisted that he'd underestimated the size of the gap, the others said this was irrefutable proof that his bottom had ballooned since the start of the trip. To be fair, it was quite a rotund posterior.

Certainly something to focus upon as I turned the pedals in pursuit.

Having caught Luke atop a ridge there was no arsing about on my part. It was onwards but not yet upwards for the road rolled along a plateau, gifting me two points as I passed through two hamlets to slash the deficit. But then Pete caught me on the long downhill and showed no intention of letting up. It was the last time we'd see him before our rapid yet sapid lunch of black truffle tortellini in the town of Frassinoro, halfway up the Passo delle Radici.

We left the restaurant just as the likes of Sharon, John and Kay were trickling in. Terry was even further back, suffering with backache and a cold. He'd been off colour for a few days now – a far cry from the Terry who entertained us so masterfully in Alba. At first we thought he had reined in his antics to avoid further embarrassment to Dylan, but in reality he'd been keeping mum about severe back pain. Later that evening the smile would return to Terry's face at the dinner table after an hour at the mercy of a Russian masseur named Sergei. Just as the young Scipio had pulled his father Publius from the fire, Dylan had pulled some strings and come to the rescue of his old man.

Before Sergei could work his magic, we had the small matter of scaling the Apennines. As our leading group resumed battle with the Radici pass, Cam and Dylan were the first to crack – blaming their sluggishness on the large slices of strawberry ice-cream cake we had all devoured to combat the lingering taste of truffle. Because of its fabled aphrodisiac qualities and penetrating aroma, the Epicureans used to liken the scent of black truffles to the sheets of a brothel bed – something I'd recommend expunging from your mind the next time you find yourself tucking into a plateful of spaghetti al tartufo nero.

Perhaps trying to flee such bawdy thoughts, Jason quickly pinged off the front – so early that he was soon forgotten. I fumbled briefly with a futile pursuit before becoming distracted by the glorious autumn leaves, slowing to take a photo, and allowing Pete, Chris, Dave and

Luke back into the fold. My relentless search for imagery meant I was constantly easing up and chasing back on. When it clicked that the summit was less than a kilometre away, I shimmied clear to cover a move by Luke, who had opened up a gap.

It was tough going. Luke was much stronger than I expected. About to give up, the sight of some serious signage on the summit less than 100 metres away spurred me on. We were about to move from Emilia-Romagna to Tuscany, swapping the province of Modena for Lucca. Surely these signs were worth more than a mere town sign? A new region should be at least 10 points. Beating Luke to it could secure a victory for our bedraggled team . . .

*I thought I'd done enough to shut the guys up about my fat arse but then Felix came from nowhere, rounded me effortlessly and punched the air in celebration. Man, he's strong. When he told me on the first night that he'd been riding for less than a year my mouth dropped. For such a newcomer he's got some serious skills. But still – didn't he realize that Jason had already won?*

It was only after raising my arms over the summit that I looked down and saw Jason sitting on a bar terrace with his feet up. 'Pretty pleased with your second place, hey?' Damn the dead possum.

What I could have really done with after all that climbing was a cold drink. Serendipitous, then, that a sign pointing up the hill and into a misty tree-lined chasm read 'San Pellegrino'. Could this be the source of the world-famous bubbly water? Surely too good an opportunity to miss. Besides, the alternative was to ride for a couple of minutes downhill before being abandoned by the Velosophy crew and having to play catch-up for the remaining 29 kilometres towards the mouthful that is Castelnuovo di Garfagnana.

None of the others had the bottle for an extra foray uphill. Their transfer to Florence was in a few hours and the sun that shone bright on the other side of the Apennines had vanished. We were enveloped in dense cloud. The temperature had plummeted so much that jackets came on for the first time since freewheeling down the Col Agnel. There was time for a few team photos and then they were gone, hurtling off at breakneck speed – a speed that would live up to its name were I to try to replicate it.

Alongside the road to San Pellegrino at regular intervals there were numbered plaques representing – I soon deciphered – the fourteen Stations of the Cross. Now, I'm not one to compare my toils to those of the figurehead of Christianity but, like Jesus, I was certainly taking one for the team. As I cut through the mist on this dismal excuse for a road it certainly felt as if I was burdened with an immense weight (the fig bread in my back pocket was rather heavy). No one would cast lots for my sweaty clothes, nor would my achievements earn even the thorniest of crowns, but I would get a metaphorical spear to the side on discovering, up top, that this was not the spring of the classiest of fizzy waters.

That San Pellegrino was in the Dolomites. This one was merely the highest inhabited town in the Apennines – an isolated place that belonged simultaneously to two parishes, two provinces and two regions, and home to one of the most ancient shrines in Italy, dedicated to Saint Peregrine. Legend has it that the seventh-century hermit was the son of the king of Scotland, but gave up his wealth to tame wild beasts (as you do) and live in a hollow beech tree in these hills while overcoming the evil forces of the Devil. When he popped his clogs both the Emilians and Tuscans claimed the right to his relics. To decide the outcome of this dispute, his body was placed on a cart drawn by two wild bulls, one from Modena and one from Lucca. The bulls (perhaps former pupils of Peregrine) bounded off, stopping exactly on the border between the two provinces. The bulls refusing to budge, it was decided that this would be the site for a church and sanctuary housing Peregrine's remains.

If only it was the patron saint of pizza whose body had been dragged up here, I thought. That would have been my kind of sanctuary.

I would have stopped to take in the wonderful views over the Apuan alps that the village's thirty-eight inhabitants regularly enjoy, but the mist was so dense I had to make do with the artist's impression on an information board while being barked at by a ferocious hound (the taming of wild beasts in these parts has clearly gone downhill since Peregrine's time).

Downhill I went, too, all the way to the bustling town of Castelnuovo. To get there, the long descent looped its way through dense, atmospheric woodland and past the fairly rubbish-looking ski resort of Casone, with its three rickety drag lifts and as many intermediate runs. The road was empty and the views nostalgically Pyrenean.

Eating paninis in the hotel lobby were the Velosophy boys awaiting their transfer to Florence. It had been an enlightening four days riding with these serious bike enthusiasts. They'd taught me a lot and injected a competitive edge into the tour that had previously been lacking. Once I overcame my initial trepidation, I'd like to think that I had made an impression too.

'It's been an absolute pleasure riding with you,' said Pete with an outstretched hand. 'Forget all those downhill tips Cam gave you or we won't stand a chance next time.'

'Yeah, please don't get any better,' added Chris as I edged off for a shower.

'And keep taking photos – it gets you off our back and gives us a little breather,' said Luke.

Lurking around the corner in the hotel lobby, Bob was sitting on a sofa writing his daily newsletter for his family in the States. 'You know, they're right,' he said. 'If you'd have started cycling earlier you'd be winning amateur races by now – and I mean that.'

Now I'm naturally suspicious of compliments and after so much misguided praise and flattery I really needed to take a lie-down and plan ways of getting back on an even keel with some grade-A self-flagellation. Supposing I had – with my long legs, naturally gangly frame and calf shave-ability – made it as a minor professional domestique, then my peak years (in real, as opposed to Horner, terms) would have coincided with the back end of the supposed dark ages. Would I have been one of the guys who doped merely to get a contract next season, or would my abuse have put me on the podiums and on the receiving end of kisses from the kind of beautiful girls whose bottoms Terry and I can only dream of pinching?

I'd probably have not doped at all – not simply because of my scaredy-cat law-abidingness or innate stinginess but primarily by dint of not being deemed worthy of dope. Fill a toy car up with petrol and it won't win a Grand Prix. Besides, I'd have been a rubbish doper. The sight of blood often causes me to faint – I almost passed out just *reading* Tyler Hamilton's book – and even the thought of a needle is enough to make me go green. Of course, needles have made the very best cyclists go green – just ask Erik Zabel, who won six Tour de France points jerseys off the back of EPO injections. But that's the point. Such achievements would be beyond me. Like Eros Poli, I'd be remembered only for being tall and coming last in the Giro – and every other race I'd enter.

But supposing there was a smidgen of truth in what the others were saying – that they were genuinely taken aback by my ability on a bike after less than a year in the saddle. Then what? What if I were to cut down on the cakes, do the right training, forgo the photographic interludes, learn how to pee convincingly using *all* the approved methods? My answer? Well, it just won't happen. Old habits die hard; I'm in my early thirties now and cycling will never have such a control over my life that it dictates which foods I avoid and landscapes I should not snap.

Is it even worth dwelling on the question of how good I could have been on a bike? I quite like being the half-decent amateur: better than some, worse than many, constantly pushing myself to pedal that bit faster, ride that bit further, testing my untempled body's limits up back-breaking climbs and down punishing descents, taking in the wonders of the world from the saddle – but very much the gentleman rouleur rather than some crazed and delusional wannabe pro in a Team Sky replica kit, pretending to be Wiggo on the way to work.

# CASTELNUOVO TO LAKE BRACCIANO

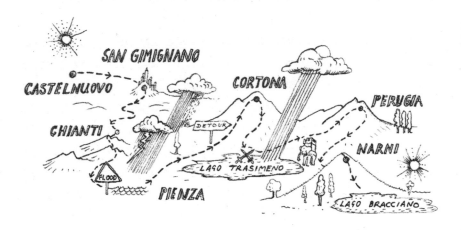

THE BLACK HORSE STOOD IN THE middle of the field with its head sagged and legs partially buckled. Relentless rain had turned the ploughed field into a quagmire of sloppy clay, the horse into an embodiment of equine dejection. However wretched we felt from being demonstrably pulverized by the elements for the past few hours, this horse's lot was far worse.

Only five of us had turned down the van's offer of salvation. As tempting as the open door and dry seats had been, what was the point? Further saturation was no longer possible. Imagine a power shower equipped with fancy body jets continuously emitting tepid water from all angles. This was what we had in store. It was ridiculously, boisterously, painfully, laughably wet. But we were in it together and determined to arrive at our monastic accommodation for the night having not thrown in the drenched towel.

Two days earlier I had been the only one of the tour stalwarts to join Sam on a zippy ride down the Serchio river from Castelnuovo and across the chaotic Arno valley, clocking up the best part of 90 kilometres before meeting the rest of the group – including three new arrivals for the final push – at San Miniato for lunch. I wasn't prepared to render that ride irrelevant by now hoisting the white flag just three days away from Rome.

So I rallied to the cause as we took refuge from the rain in a flimsy wooden garage at the gates of the Borgo San Felice in Chianti. Munching on a slightly soggy wild boar salami sandwich, I managed to talk Steve and the tour's three new recruits into joining me as we headed into what, rather ominously, looked to be the eye of the storm. Together we made up a team of five British bulldogs. Father and son combo Terry and Dylan – the only remaining Brits in the group – had entered the van with their tails between their legs, joining the fair-weather Antipodean contingent (Bernadette, Sharon, John and Kay) and Team USA's Bob (who, heralding from Seattle, should really be used to such downpours).

The next three hours would be like surviving twelve rounds in the ring with a meteorological Muhammad Ali.

Thick, bulbous drops of rain jabbed at my lips, nose and face, while blustery winds pelted my sides like a series of body shots. Jets of spray from the rare vehicles venturing out served some unforgivably low blows. Rivers of mud flowing off the fields and across the road came like hooks. A flash flood in the town of Arbia was a sucker punch that knocked down one of our men. An avoidable collision with a stationary Steve hit me like an uppercut. Two punchy climbs near Siena had us all on the ropes.

And seeing that pathetic horse hit home like a haymaker.

But we were determined to go the distance – which was more than could be said of other, more illustrious British bicyclists in the area. For not far away the World Championships men's road race was coming to its conclusion in similarly dismal conditions, with only a risible 61 riders from a start list of 208 making it to the finish in Florence. The entire British squad – including former world champion Mark Cavendish and the two previous Tour winners, Bradley Wiggins and Chris Froome – had sought the warm refuge of their team bus with over 100 kilometres left to ride.

This abject British capitulation had fans up in arms, with many accusing the nation's top cyclists of acting like a bunch of overpaid, prima donna footballers.

I might have agreed were it not for the salient fact that one of my four companions on that sodden day in the saddle was a former Premier League star renowned for his tough tackling and no-nonsense approach to the beautiful game: Hull City legend, Ian Ashbee.

Before I came to be sharing pleasantries with a man whom, no doubt, I had – along with about 58,000 other Arsenal fans – abused relentlessly ('Ash' had captained Hull City the day the newly promoted side beat my team 2–1 at the Emirates in 2008), there was that small matter of those 55-odd matutinal miles before San Miniato.

It was Saturday. We had entered the fourth week of the tour and there were some weary legs. Given the hectic nature of the roads around the plains to the east of Lucca the offer of a shuttle bus from Castelnuovo had been thrown on the breakfast table alongside the crimson-coloured blood orange juice that had become our daily Hannibal nectar. As I was the only person keen to ride, Sam agreed to keep me company. Our initial plan had been to take a more direct but arduous route back over the Apennines. But we were making such good progress on the fast road hugging the Serchio that we decided to continue down the valley, soon passing the wonderful eleventh-century Ponte della Maddalena. Commissioned by Matilda of Tuscany – one of the rare medieval women remembered for her military accomplishments (she was also, poor girl, forced into a marriage with her sinisterly named step-brother, Godfrey the Hunchback) – the bridge was a vital crossing for the Via Francigena pilgrimage route and had clear echoes of the Pont du Diable at Olargues.

The closer we got to Lucca – the old stomping ground of the dastardly doping doctor Michele Ferrari – the more cyclists we passed, heading up to the hills on their weekend rides. Shortly after a warm *marmalada* pit stop we left the Serchio and cut across flat agricultural plains on a series of dull, straight roads through an increasingly insalubrious industrial sprawl. With cars and lorries jostling for position on the busy roads, it soon became apparent why the others were sitting this one out. Picturesque sights were inversely proportional to the amount of roadkill we were forced to dodge: one single stretch of road alone included two dogs (although one might have been a badly decomposed boar), a cat, a pair of rodents, one snake (possibly the infamous Tuscan viper) and a pigeon.

Frequently we passed signs advertising the area's most popular gentlemen's clubs, of which there were an alarming array – including the ubiquitous American Bar with its catchy slogan 'Lap Dance Sexy Restaurant'. Mincing in a layby at the exit of a petrol station, two ladies of the night, dolled up in unreasonably revealing dresses, were flaunting their wares to potential customers. I was just trying to word an opportune joke with the punchline 'fill her up' when a car sped past at close proximity forcing Sam to brake and me, riding right in his wheel, to avoid a collision by tumbling into the grass verge, grazing my knee and adding to the roadkill count by apparently squashing a slug (my saddle post bore the sticky remains for the rest of the day).

Such was our stellar progress that we stopped for a second coffee at the pretty town of Fucecchio on the banks of the Arno river. Back in Hannibal's day the plain we had just crossed was still marshland, not to be drained until Renaissance times. After the harsh winter of 218/217 BC Hannibal decided to seek out a more reliable base further south but found the eastern and western routes blocked by armies belonging to the two new consuls, Gaius Flaminius Nepos and Gnaeus Servilius Geminus. Taking a more central route, the Carthaginian army crossed the Apennines into Etruria without much drama before Hannibal decided to catch the Romans unawares by crossing the Arno swamps. It was a decision that backfired dramatically: his men spent four days and three nights wading through bogs unable to find anywhere to set up camp. Horses lost their shoes in the mud and many soldiers and pack animals perished.

While Hannibal had the luxury of riding the only remaining elephant – a huge Asian bull named Surus – he was nevertheless afflicted with conjunctivitis, which he failed to treat, resulting in blindness in one eye.

On learning this fact from Sam as we sipped macchiatos under the Tuscan sun I felt even closer to the Hannibal myth. For I, too, was effectively blinded in one eye following a childhood incident with my brother involving a home-made bow, a sharpened garden cane and an unfortunate ricochet off a rock.

'You made that up!' said Sam in disbelief.

'I swear it's true – just look here,' I replied, proffering my right eye, the pupil of which (on close inspection) runs into the fortuitously dark brown iris like the burst yolk of a fried egg.

'I can still see but it's why I squint in the sun,' I said.

His own vision restricted, Hannibal would spend more and more time atop Surus so he could overlook the terrain and survey battlefields. The one-tusked Surus ('The Syrian') was described by the Roman historian Cato as the bravest elephant of the entire Punic army. He wore a red cloak and was fitted with a shield and a howdah on his back. There are even stories of Surus trampling on the heads of Roman sympathizers later in the long fifteen-year conflict with Rome. It certainly seems that the right elephant had survived the cold winter.

On we pressed to the hilltop town of San Miniato, the Tuscan residence of many an emperor. After more than 80 kilometres covering largely flat terrain, the punchy climb to the historic centre was a leg-stinger of the kind Sam formerly excelled in until my stamina started to shine through in the Alps. After a leisurely gander, we freewheeled down the southern side of the town to meet the others at our lunch rendezvous. New boys Ash, Mark and Robin were assembling their bikes on the green lawn of the Ristorante Il Convio.

Mark and Dylan were old friends from their time on the professional squash circuit. Having hung up his Dunlop Green Flashes, Mark took over control of the family designer watch business in Hull and asked Ash to join once he retired from professional football in 2012.

A combative midfielder capable of scoring the odd screamer, Ash spent nine years of his career at Hull City and is the only footballer in history to have captained the same side in all four divisions of English football, from bottom to top – not bad considering he was sent off on his debut. Given the average footballer's insatiable thirst for all things bling, plus the respect Ash gleaned from opponents and team-mates alike during a long career, having someone with his credentials and contacts at a flash watch and glitzy jewellery business was a no-brainer. A Brummie by birth, Ash became Hull's heartbeat during his time at the club despite never being capped by England (you could say the Three Lions refused to accept into their brood the fiercest Tiger of them all). Except for his adopted hometown, Ash could walk pretty much anywhere and remain unrecognized – the kind of success enjoyed by the members of Coldplay who aren't Chris Martin. Or French cyclists not called Thomas Voeckler.

Gorging on a well-earned lunch of thick pici spaghetti with arrabbiata sauce and a side of baked aubergines with Grana Padano and truffle oil, I tried to play it cool with our new high-profile arrivals. Not wanting to reveal that I had been to the kind of school which favoured hockey over football, I clearly overlooked the fact that, a) just opening my mouth was evidence enough, and b) they were so laid-back they really didn't care.

Happy-go-lucky Ash was just relieved to be able to ride a bike at all. Back in 2005 he was diagnosed with a rare degenerative bone condition in the femur. Surgery involved drilling fourteen holes in the bone to stimulate regrowth, the outcome of the operation threatening not only his career but his ability to walk again. Luckily, it was a success. Ash played for another five seasons before ligament damage in his knee finally prompted him to call it a day. 'The doctor told me that cycling was the best thing for rehabilitation so I came out last year with Mark. We enjoyed it so much we're back for more.' Joining them for a few days in the saddle was their flame-haired friend Robin, an architect and the most solid rider of the trio.

Not keen to overdo things on the opening afternoon, Ash decided to catch up with Bob and Terry in the main group for the ride to San Gimignano. As clouds began to gather, myself, Dylan, Mark and Robin went on a detour towards the taciturn and grey Etruscan stronghold of Volterra. Getting there involved an undulating ride over an eerie, barren landscape more lunar than the summit of Mont Ventoux. The soil in these parts is a thin clay – good pasture land but not conducive to growing vines or olive trees. In fact, the area around Volterra is one of Italy's richest mining regions: vast salt pans lie to the west and the famous Metal Hills stretch out to the south. Sulphur, alum and alabaster are also found around the town the Etruscans named Velathri. Volterra itself is perched on a steep hill with a flat top, the sides of which are riddled with *balze* – barren, eroded chalk ravines that probably originated as mining cuts. Subsequent landslides through the ages have swallowed up ancient Christian churches and Etruscan ruins alike.

With legs eager to let rip after a flight from the UK, Robin led the way up the savage climb to the city centre, which momentarily peaked at 25 per cent as we crept past the cemetery and medieval city walls. We barely had time for some gelati before continuing on our way to San Gimignano, which we reached after the sun had set. It had been a tricky final phase during which my morning exertions had caught up with me and I dropped back off the pace. Bolstered by the sight of the remaining fourteen towers that give Italy's best preserved medieval city its inimitable skyline, I managed to reel in Mark on the final uphill slog after some adept downhill drafting – rather pleasingly – in the wake of a Sky TV delivery van.

Waiting with a round of beers in the bar opposite our hotel was Ash, well lubricated and still in his cycling kit. We raised a glass to my 168.5 kilometres in the saddle – the longest day by anyone in the entire tour – before the focus switched to just how I could replace the 5,000 calories I'd burned since setting off with Sam in the early hours. The hills around San Miniato are home to the famous Tuscan totem tubers – white truffles which local legend has it, are spawned by lightning bolts hitting damp soil among the region's oak trees. Gram per gram, these earthy, odoriferous gourmet delicacies are the most expensive comestible in the world. Rich, creamy and just about perched on the right side of overwhelming, my pici carbonara with gratings of white tartufi and Grana Padano would have been fit for the very best of truffle hogs were it not for the presence of delicately smoked cubes of pancetta.

Local porcini mushrooms, also in season, found their way on to my plate, joining forces in a rich sauce atop juicy, rare slices of *controfiletto*.

Such decadence across two courses was chaperoned to my stomach by a glass of deep ruby red Brunello di Montalcino, the Chris Horner of Italian wines (visibly limpid, brilliant and persistent, Brunello's ability to age well is renowned, although doubts have been raised about the provenance of certain past blends leading to inevitable contract disputes with suppliers). The 2007 vintage that we sampled alongside our less revered table wine was deemed one of the most exciting since the start of the millennium, praised in a way only wine can be for its 'ethereal balsam notes of eucalyptus, hummus, dried fruit and dried mint'. Terry, our resident sommelier, described it in more accessible terms as 'bloody terrific'.

The next morning, the first drops started to fall shortly after I trickled eastwards out of the Town of Fine Towers some distance behind the others. I'd visited San Gimignano before as a child but the previous day's late arrival scuppered any chances of daylight nosing around. So up I rode through the cobbled streets to the sloped Piazza della Cisterna, named after the town's grand marble well which stands in the middle of the main square.

Signor Dondoli, the four-time gelato World Champion, stood in his doorway chatting to a friend. His acclaimed gelateria has been visited through the years by the likes of prominent after-dinner speaker Tony Blair, film director Franco Zeffirelli, actress Dame Judi Dench and pukka chef entrepreneur Jamie Oliver. Photos of these luminaries adorn the walls of his mini flavour palace alongside the smiling faces of at least six former Miss Italias. Dondoli's outré ice cream offerings were even reported to have extracted a rare public smile from bearded sourpuss Alexander Solzhenitsyn, the Russian writer. With a zesty panna cotta being broken down by a post-dinner Peroni with the boys, I'd forgone the opportunity to sample some of Dondoli's finest the night before.

Although the temptation was now huge, I just couldn't justify a gelato so early in the day after yet another scene-setting breakfast.

In peak season San Gimignano attracts more than three times the town's population of 7,500 in day-trippers. The delicatessen on the street outside our hotel had already opened its doors, guarded by two stuffed wild boars wearing spectacles. Crowds were starting to gather in the main square as I managed to squeeze five towers in one photo. Back in San Gimignano's medieval prime there were seventy-two towers stretching up to 70 metres high – essentially the result of incessant family rivalries and the feud between the Pope-supporting Guelphs and the Emperor-loving Ghibellines (the size of one's tower being a telling status symbol). As I followed the signs to Poggibonsi I thought how the current fad for ridiculously tall skyscrapers the world over was essentially the Guelphs vs Ghibellines Mark II: a totally ludicrous dick-swinging contest, but carried out on a global scale.

We were heading into the hilly Chianti region and my mind turned to the World Championships road race. It was Sunday and as I rode up the long but gentle climb to Castellina in Chianti the peloton would have been rolling out of Lucca to start the 272-kilometre undulating race to Florence. The severe weather that hampered the majority of the race had yet to reach these more southerly parts of Tuscany but it was only a matter of time. There had been occasional drizzle all morning, and the views down over the Elsa valley, of cypress trees, poplars and parasol pines, of the trademark Tuscan rolling hills topped with vineyards and olive groves and large villas with ornate driveways, were not as picture-postcard perfect as usual.

When Hannibal passed through these parts he deliberately ravaged the agriculturally rich Chianti region where the consul Flaminius and his army were stationed. Like Sempronius Longus before him, Flaminius had a reputation of impetuousness and arrogance. Sensing an opportunity, Hannibal went out of his way to goad the consul as he planned the next phase of his attempted destruction of Rome.

Today, Chianti is best known for its rich and full-bodied red wine, famously paired with human liver and fava beans by a certain Hannibal Lecter. If Chianti is the Bordeaux of Italy then Chianti Classico is its Saint-Émilion in terms of prestige. Blessed with extremely fertile soils, the sub-region produces premium, medium-bodied wines under the iconic *gallo nero* – black rooster – label. I know this because my friend Rowan proudly sports a Chianti Classico cycling kit that he picked up a few years ago: the same kit that still adorns various shop windows on the main street in Castellina.

The eleven o'clock bells rang out to encourage a number of umbrella-bearing locals to attend the Sunday mass. A sudden downpour curtailed my snooping around town and I joined the others in a bar just as Ash, Mark, Robin and Dylan rolled up, lagging somewhat behind after getting lost in the purlieus of Poggibonsi. Inside, we weren't the only cyclists taking refuge: a group of three Americans propped up the bar in bright Lycra, one of whom sported a pair of brown loafers. 'I refuse to accept we're from the same country,' said Bob through gritted teeth.

The weather deteriorated further as we made the sweeping descent through Radda and Gaiole in Chianti, the latter voted Europe's most idyllic place to live by *Forbes* magazine in 2008 (the man in brown loafers could no doubt have told you that). While Gaiole has a rich cycling tradition, even we – with over 2,000 kilometres on the clock since leaving Spain – would not have been welcome had we rolled through town exactly a week later. The problem would be with our contemporary bikes and attire, for taking place on the first Sunday of October since 1997 in Gaiole in Chianti and the surrounding area is a bike race like none other: L'Eroica – 'The Heroic'.

Anyone entering the period-cycling *gran fondo* must do so with a vintage, pre-1987 bike with a steel frame and toe-clip pedals. Merino wool jerseys, leather shoes, small-peak caps and other sartorial throwbacks from a bygone golden era must also be on display, tight figure-hugging Lycra an even bigger faux pas than going full polka dot in the Tour, à la Pierre Rolland. The actual race takes place over numerous sections of ancient, bone-jarring gravel tracks gentlemanly interspersed with regular lavish buffet stops. Here, sports drinks step aside for coffee and Chianti while cheese and cured meats take precedence over energy bars and gels; those wishing for a full musette can feast on rich beef stew followed by jam tarts and other locally baked goodies.

Riders have the option of three different routes of varying length and difficulty. Capturing the ethos of L'Eroica perfectly, the longest – a fearsome 205 kilometres – is so demanding that anyone finishing within twelve hours is awarded a huge picnic hamper filled with enough edible delights to stir the grave of Jacques Anquetil. Although it wouldn't be surprising if the few who manage this feat were forced to strap the prize to straw panniers and haul it over the last few kilometres of pot-holed dirt tracks.

Such was the success of L'Eroica that a professional version was set up in 2007 and is now known as the Strade Bianche – after the white gravel roads. The race runs every year in March, usually starting in Gaiole in Chianti before taking on eight sections of *strade bianche* en route to a grand finale in Siena's Piazza del Campo. The winner in 2013 was Moreno Moser, the young Italian who months later would crest Alpe d'Huez in first position after the first of those back-to-back ascents in the Tour.

Spoilsportingly, the professional race does not adhere to the worthy traditions of the amateur Eroica. Riders aren't forced to carry spare inner tubes wrapped under their arms and teams don't even get into the spirit of things by issuing their squad with limited-edition vintage wool jerseys. Given the location of the finish line in Siena – where twice a year the bareback horse race Il Palio (a contest so brutal it makes the Grand National look like a pony club) takes place between seasoned jockeys representing each of the city's districts – the organizers are clearly missing a trick. The spectacle of a peloton of riders having to discard their saddles and seat posts on the outskirts of Siena before undertaking an unorthodox and upright final lap over uneven flagstones would be second to none.

On designing our itinerary, Sam and Dylan had clearly not envisioned such calamitous weather when giving us the option of an extra 20-kilometre loop over some of these fabled chalk tracks. In the event of considerable rainfall, the *strade bianche* take on a whole new dynamic, caking riders not in white dust but a thick layer of brown mud – much like 'the Hell of the North' that is the cobblestone classic Paris–Roubaix. Indeed, it was in scenes more reminiscent of a Flanders Classic than a Grand Tour that Cadel Evans won a sodden stage 7 in the 2010 Giro after the route passed over a number of these gravel segments inside the closing 30 kilometres. On a day where the scheduled climb up to Volterra was scrapped because of a freak landslide, viewers were hard pressed to pick out Evans's iridescent rainbow stripes as the Australian world champion broke clear on the final climb into Montalcino to take the spoils. It allegedly took Evans days to clean out the road residue from the generous cleft in his chin.

Relinquishing all thoughts of a sludgy detour, we at least remained faithful to the Eroica ideology in the form of a bountiful lunchtime spread. While we huddled under the rickety tractor garage outside the vineyard that allegedly turned down a purchase offer from Roman Abramovich, thunder started to growl overhead and sporadic flashes lit up the grey sky. Some 60 kilometres north in Florence the rain-soaked battle for the rainbow stripes was in full swing.

'There's no way I'm going to let a little rain stop me from riding the whole way to Rome,' I said with defiance.

'I'll come with you,' said Steve. 'It's not as if we can get any wetter anyway.'

'Well, if you two are doing it then we'll come along too,' said Robin, speaking for himself, Mark and Ash.

'We will?' said Ash.

'Any more takers?' I asked. But the others were practically already in the van. There's courage and there's stupidity. What we were about to do clearly, in their eyes, fell under the latter umbrella. 'Just us five Brits, then.'

'I'd make it six but I should keep Dad company,' said Dylan, playing his Get Out Of Jail Free card. Although he had chirped up a little since his session with Sergei the masseur, Terry was still a little fragile.

Funnily enough, it was just about now that the British grasp on the World Championships was waning. Mark Cavendish and his team-mates had controlled the peloton on the waterlogged ride from Lucca to Florence, but once the first of ten 16.5-kilometre circuits got under way, the Italians upped the ante considerably. By the time the fourth circuit was completed, the entire British team was drying off in the team bus. When Team GB manager Rod Ellingworth labelled Cavendish's performance as 'average' it was actually a compliment of sorts. 'The other guys were well below average,' he added.

If the torrential showers that hampered the lion's share of the men's road race gave way later on to clear skies and, well, a rainbow for Portugal's Rui Costa, then that was apparently because all the foul weather had shifted south and chosen to engulf our ratty yet more resilient troupe of amateur home-grown riders.

After fifteen minutes hanging around and waiting for a rain break that didn't come, we said a prayer and set off. The folly of our undertaking became rapidly apparent as we rode along an exposed ridge that swept down towards the Arbia valley, our faces angled against stinging jets of water that came at us with the same kind of velocity and intent that sees water cannons blast the trousers off football hooligans. Despite his tough-man image on the pitch, our own footballer, Ash, screamed a whimpering falsetto every time lightning flashed overhead.

'Just think of all the white truffles sprouting in the soil,' I cried with Panglossian perseverance. But my words were drowned out by a deafening drum and roaring cackle that almost instantaneously followed the latest bright bolt – evidence enough that we were very much at the epicentre of this meteorological mayhem.

Mindful of lightning's penchant for striking the tallest object, I rode stooped over the handlebars. Steve was rather perplexed by this anti-self-truffling tactic, claiming we'd be saved by our rubber tyres. When I told him that this rubber ruse was an urban myth, a look of doubt crept over his face. On the reminder that he was the only one of us crazy enough to ride a metal bike through a thunderstorm, he cowered in the saddle more than anyone.

Shortly after setting off, the support van pulled up beside us at an intersection. 'Sure you won't change your mind? It's another 50 kilometres to the finish,' said Sam from behind the wheel.

'I think we're through the worst of it. We'll see you there,' I replied. 'Just make sure Terry doesn't use up all the hot water . . .'

On entering Arbia we were greeted by rampaging fountains gushing vertically out of burst manholes whose metal covers had been ferociously blown aside. Visibility was minimal so it was all we could do to focus on the next few metres of road. Then, suddenly, the road disappeared. So, too, did half our wheels and our feet. It took a couple of seconds to realize just what was happening. Robin and I rode on through the flooded street but Ash panicked, clicked out of his pedals and dismounted. He now waded through the mass of water, his legs totally submerged below the knees. Most mollycoddled footballers would have thrown the bidons out of their cages by now – but not Ash. 'I love it,' he said. 'Reminds me of home games at the KC stadium.'

We regrouped on the other side of the flash flood outside a chaotic cafe. An elderly German couple on a tandem had sensibly called it a day and sat inside drinking hot chocolate. We looked at each other searchingly. It was Robin who broke the silence. 'If we stop for a warm drink now we'll never get going again. Let's crack on.'

When Hannibal's men marched through the Arno marshes for four days, Polybius claims they did so 'through a land that was under water'. Unknowingly, we had pretty much recreated those scenes. Although the flooding never got worse than the deluge that engulfed the streets of Arbia, the deserted roads, free from traffic, often became shallow flowing rivers. If scaling Ventoux had been like pedalling through sauerkraut, this was like taking on a cassoulet. Uphill segments saw us fighting the gradient as well as riding against the current, while descents became a challenge of dodging debris and curtailing speed – not an easy task when your brake pads are non-existent (stupidly, I had yet to replace them).

Every now and then the rain eased and the clouds ahead appeared a fairer shade of grey. 'It looks to be clearing,' I would say with faux sagacity before the next round of water cannon was fired. 'Will you stop saying that!' implored Mark on the fourth occasion a break in the rain looked on the cards. It made no difference: we were doomed whether I opened my mouth or not.

There reached a point when it all became rather invigorating – in a ho-hum, Spirit of the Blitz, tally-ho kind of way. None of us would usually have even considered riding in such pitiful conditions – but we were strangely content with the chain of events that placed us here, with no option but to battle on through a monsoon. The unprecedented nature of the whole escapade was as much a means of unification as it was demoralization. Were we alone, each one of us would have given up at lunch. But together, we rolled up our sleeves, soldiered on and made do with a quite ghastly situation. Dare I say it, soon it all became quite fun, forcing us to laugh out loud at the sheer preposterousness of our predicament.

Never in my wildest dreams – when I embarked on my quest to turn from writer to rider – did I envisage a scenario that included me, a former Premier League footballer, atrocious flash floods in Tuscany, booming thunder and cackling lightning, and the most forlorn-looking horse in history.

That horse captured to a tee the utter uselessness of trying to combat the elements. It stood there in total subjugation to the gods above, accepting of everything and anything. Unfettered and free to roam, the horse had specifically chosen to place itself in the least protected part of the entire field – if not in open invitation to a misery-ending bolt of lightning then at least in a vain attempt to elicit pity from the Being upstairs in control of the climatic taps. As cold and sodden as we were, every pedal stroke took us closer to a resolution. But this horse's immediate-to-mid-term future lay in the exact place it skulked: in the middle of a muddy field with no visible end in sight. Try to move, and perhaps it would succumb to the same fate as Hannibal's pack animals in the Arno swamps.

Psychologically, our decision to ride on became both a defiance and a matter of honour. We were doing it because we could – because we had the choice. Because it was far better than standing still. Infinitely better than giving up. We also had no say in the matter now that the van had driven on to our home for the evening. As hellish as it got, however, all of us, deep down, were pleased to be there.

Of course, those three hours of scuba-cycling did not completely play out on the crest of a wave. Careering into Steve as I looked over my shoulder was fairly unfortunate – as was copping a face full of liquid dirt, sprayed from one of the few cars still out on the road. There comes a time even in moments of perverse pleasure where enough is enough. That happened, funnily enough, once the rain finally morphed into a mere drizzle on the lumpy approach to the former monastery that was housing us for the night.

Just as the weather had cleared up in Florence, so too were we granted a bit of respite at the end of our ordeal. On the last climb of the day, with around 3 kilometres remaining, I dropped the others on the feisty 10 per cent section that immediately followed a nippy descent (having no brakes was an advantage here). In Florence it was Spain's Joaquim Rodríguez who put in an attack from the decisive five-man break on the final lap of the men's road race. Inside the final kilometre Rodríguez was pegged back by Portugal's Rui Costa, a double stage winner in the Tour two months earlier, who evaded the grasp of J-Rod's team-mate Alejandro Valverde before ultimately proving the stronger in the two-man sprint for the rainbow jersey after almost seven and a half hours of racing.

It was a case of close but no cigar for the man they call 'Purito', who added yet another bridesmaid's performance to recent runner-up berths in Grand Tours. After bawling his eyes out on the podium, a forlorn Rodríguez told reporters: 'Clearly this is Purito's destiny – to lose the Giro by a whisker, then the Vuelta and now the Worlds.'

There were no late counter-attacks in my race. Puckered and empty, I managed to negotiate the monastery's muddy driveway (giving us a taste of *strade bianche* after all) to secure the token victory. But we're all winners today, I thought as I clambered the metaphorical podium staircase leading up to the historic *agriturismo* at Sant'Anna in Camprena.

As for Rui Costa, he became the first Portuguese cyclist to be crowned World Champion – and with it the chance to finally step out of the shadows of his famous former footballer namesake. It also secured a second successive Portuguese sportsman of the year title over prolific Real Madrid marksman Ronaldo. Cycling 2, Football 0. This was the latest redemptive stepping stone for the 27-year-old since returning from a shortened suspension for a positive test for a banned stimulant in 2010, which he blamed on a contaminated supplement.

This is cycling, after all; the spectre of doping is never too far away. Football, of course, is '100 per cent clean' – as Ronaldo once claimed. 'It's a collective sport and so there's no need to dope to improve performance,' the 2013 Ballon d'Or winner said, just one week after Dr Eufemiano Fuentes admitted to a Spanish court that footballers, too, were among his previous clients.

A thin layer of low cloud filled the troughs of the Val d'Orcia and the top of faraway Monte Amiata, Tuscany's highest peak, was obscured. The retreating rain meant we could enjoy an *aperitivo* in the mani-cured grounds of the former Benedictine monastery, which was used as a location in the film *The English Patient*. The idyllic Val d'Orcia has strong cinematic credentials, having also formed the dreamy country-side paradise where Russell Crowe's character returns home too late to save his family in *Gladiator*. The group was in good spirits that night – five of us following our nautically themed excursion, and the others after an unscheduled afternoon off spent dozing in the old monk cells or taking in the magnificent frescoes by Antonio 'Il Sodoma' Bazzi in the refectory.

The movie theme continued into dinner when the spitting image of towering butler Lurch from *The Addams Family* entered the grand, yellow-walled dining room brandishing huge bowls of peasant salad (tomatoes, breadcrumbs, olive oil, onions, salad leaves and celery). Without a word, the lofty waiter with angular features returned with platters of cured meats and salami. Famished from a day braving the elements – and oblivious to what other delights (if any) were being prepared by Uncle Fester and Morticia in the kitchen next door – I went overboard with three large helpings.

Halfway through my third plateful, Lurch tantalized our taste buds by placing a bowl of Parmesan on the table, followed, at his next cameo, by considerable portions of gnocchi with fresh pesto. Clearly an observant chap, Lurch returned ten minutes later with a large serving dish and enquired – with the raising of a solitary eyebrow – whether anyone would like seconds, his gaze inexplicably falling on me.

Seeing that my first gnocchi of the tour was scrumptious in its simplicity, it would have been sad to see it go to waste. And with this being but a run-down former monastery, surely a second bowl of gnocchi was all that separated me from dessert and bed. But no! Out came plates of roast chicken (with the kind of crispy, salty skin so revered in Italy) and coarse pork sausages, alongside some exceedingly good roast potatoes. I was so stuffed that a pudding of apple cake (alas, more cake than apple) only performed a minor role in my stomach's nocturnal workout.

Sleep was fraught and stuttered ahead of my final solo mission before Rome: a nostalgic off-piste detour to visit an area in Tuscany where I'd spent many a summer holiday as a child. It was the third-to-last day of the tour and my twenty-fourth successive day of pedalling. It was also the stage I had been looking forward to most in the past few weeks – a chance to ride over familiar roads and take a stroll down memory lane.

With an extra 45 kilometres of wistful sentimentality spliced to my schedule, I set off fractionally ahead of the others to reach nearby Pienza – an ode to Renaissance town-planning and the current capital of Italian sheep cheese – by 9 a.m. The sun was starting to break through a haze of puffy clouds as I pressed on to the gastronomic hilltop haven of Montepulciano, home of the highly prized and unusually powerful Vino Nobile (known as 'The Red Infuriator' in my household).

Although I had a busy agenda I couldn't resist extending my circumbendibus through the town gates and up the narrow cobbled streets to the main square. It's a route Chris Froome knows well: his first ever European win came in the historic centre of Montepulciano back in the 2007 Giro delle Regioni, the Under-23 race (won that year by Rui Costa, no less) where the unknown Kenyan (with more water behind his ears than a bathing elephant) was first touted to be a star of the future (despite those opening-day downhill tumbles).

I was too busy grappling with the gradient to notice the unusual clock tower on the main street on the way up. But it soon came flooding back when I took in my surroundings on the way down. In charge of time-keeping atop the tower is a clockwork Pulcinella – Italy's equivalent of Mr Punch, a Neapolitan clodhopper named after a young chicken due to his beaklike nose and disoriented dimwittedness. Entrusting such a purposeful task to someone so notoriously feckless may seem like an enterprise fraught with risk – akin to employing Bradley Wiggins as a pre-watershed children's TV presenter – but good old Pulcinella has been ding-donging for several hundred years now, a functioning piece of tongue-in-cheek architecture extraordinaire.

While tempted to await his eleven o'clock performance from a caffeine-themed vantage point, I could hear Cortona calling.

As a family, we started our love affair with the Etruscan hilltop town long before the book (and subsequent film) *Under the Tuscan Sun* made Cortona the must-see destination for American tourists, language students, artists and writers looking to find their inner Italian by drinking straw-encased bottles of Chianti and mingling predominantly with their fellow countrymen. That set us apart from other fans. In cycling terms: we liked Peter Sagan before he started pinching bottoms; Laurent Jalabert in his pre-polka dot, green jersey phase; and Phil Liggett when he actually seemed to know which sport he was commentating on.

Stopping at the Monday market at Montepulciano Stazione at the bottom of the hill, I filled up my candy pouch (velcroed back on to the top tube now that the naysaying Velosophy boys had gone) and started the long slog across the Chiana valley, passing numerous other cyclists en route. The approach to Camucia, a busy town on the plain directly below Cortona, is dead straight and, despite the lofty town walls still catching shafts of sunlight, I could see grey thunderclouds gathering overhead. It started to rain halfway up the meandering ascent, as I approached the already heavily weatherbeaten Chiesa di Santa Maria delle Grazie – known to our family simply as the 'John Melvin church' after an artist friend of my parents who once painted it.

Once under the ancient arch in the city walls, I found the paved road that rises at a God-awful gradient to the Piazza della Repubblica shorter than I'd remembered but still the work of the Devil. Mindful of the public conveniences halfway up, I held my breath and gave the expected waft a wide berth. As teenagers my brothers and I would explore the town's precipitous streets, discussing the merits of a stage finish being held in Cortona and presuming the alleyways to be too inaccessible. Little did we know that it had already happened – in 1982, when Mike Wilson became the first Australian to win a stage in the Giro. Christened Micheal (he believes his mother misspelt his name on the birth certificate), Wilson was riding his debut Grand Tour in his first season in Europe and managed to teach fellow neo-pro Laurent Fignon a rare lesson in only the second stage of the race – despite being reprimanded by his team for breaking rules by eating an ice cream the night before. The Australian rookie would get the better of 'The Professor' again one year later in the final stage of the Vuelta – not bad for a rider more revered in Italy than his home country, someone most people see as incapable of even spelling his own name correctly.

In 1986, two months before we first came to stay near Cortona, the opening stage of the Tirreno–Adriatico week-long race saw two men go shoulder to shoulder up the same narrow Via Guelfa to Cortona's main square before sweeping into the Piazza Signorelli for a seemingly slow-motion sprint finish. Italian journeyman Luciano Rabottini –

father of Matteo, the young climber who burst on to the scene with an Alpine victory in the 2012 Giro – snared the victory. The escapees were carelessly granted so much leeway by the peloton that Rabottini would keep the race lead all the way to the finish, securing an unlikely overall win. Such a scenario is often called an *échappée à la Walkowiak* in France, after one-hit-wonder Roger Walkowiak, winner of the 1956 Tour off the back of an unlikely break in stage 7 that involved thirty-one riders finishing 18 minutes clear. In the five other Tours the Frenchman raced during his career, a lowly forty-seventh place was the best he could muster.

I headed straight to the Piazza Signorelli to write some postcards over coffee at Bar La Posta. Drizzle turned to torrential showers and I was forced inside as scenes of utter chaos played out on the terrace: umbrellas were blown out of their holders and water gushed down the sloping flagstones from the theatre. I took the opportunity to enquire after Angelo and Mirelle – the former owners of the bar – who first met me when I was a wee fat boy nicknamed 'Huff'. As luck had it, they still lived in a flat above. Once the rain had stopped I rang the doorbell and Mirelle came down. Despite her initial claims to have 'no idea' who I was, she eventually came round.

'But you were much smaller the last time I saw you – and it looks like you are a professional cyclist now.' I filled her in about my epic ride and it was with regret that I had to turn down the offer of lunch upstairs with Angelo. The road to Perugia was long and I still had old haunts to visit (including the Ristorante La Tufa, in nearby Ossaia, with its legendary four cheeses pasta). 'You'd better go now, then, while the rain has stopped,' she said before I clipped in and took off.

At the end of the Via Nazionale, the only street in town with no gradient, I stopped to gaze over the agricultural plains from the Piazza Garibaldi, scanning the horizon for the edge of lake Trasimeno, usually visible on a clear day. The largest lake in Italy south of the Po,

Trasimeno was the sight of one of the bloodiest massacres in Roman history. Unsurprisingly, our man Hannibal, after passing through this very town, was the author of the carnage.

Having laid waste to the prized Chianti region that the consul Flaminius had been expressly sent to protect, Hannibal lured his hot-headed rival into a pitched battle on the banks of the lake. Hiding the bulk of his army on the higher ground in a defile between the hills and the shore, Hannibal attacked Flaminius's left flank and provoked a hasty pursuit early on the morning of 21 June 217 BC. With a dense mist making visibility poor, the Romans did not see the danger until it was too late – Hannibal's textbook ambush resulting in the brutal slaying of around 15,000 legionaries, including Flaminius himself. Not all the deaths came from the swords of Carthage: many Roman troops retreated into the waters of the lake, where they drowned in their heavy armour – or, to quote Polybius, where they 'perished in a shameful and still more pitiable manner'.

Staring defeat in the face, six thousand more troops surrendered to Carthage. By subsequently sending the Italian prisoners home but holding the Romans in fierce captivity, Hannibal's message was clear: his fight was not with Italy but with Rome's hegemony and for the freedom of Italy. Three days later, the second consul, Geminus, arrived with reinforcements but saw his cavalry annihilated by Hannibal's Numidian horsemen in another surprise attack. Rome, it seemed, was teetering on the brink.

Before pedalling the flat 15 kilometres to Trasimeno my sappy detour led me to the hillside villa where my family used to stay all those summers ago. The sun's reappearance caused steam to rise from the wet surface of the road as I cycled through the village of Pergo and up into the hills. Casa Storta was the same as always – just shut down for the approaching winter. The front gates were locked but I managed to sneak through the hedge and have a snoop. Being there – beside the covered pool surrounded by cypresses and a single parasol pine, overlooking rows of tomato plants and olive groves – had a visual Proustian effect on me, swamping my mind with dreamy reminiscences in the same way that hearing Phil Liggett's incredulous cries of 'It's Stephen Roche!' as the Irishman emerges through the mist of La Plagne will always produce a woolgathering swell of youthful reflection.

While exploring the grounds, I munched on a juicy fig plucked from a tree beside the same ditch where Julia Melvin – John's wife – once took a head-cracking, but thankfully not fatal tumble. My stomach suddenly stirred by the sweet flesh (of the fig), I was pulled from these rampaging waves of reverie. It was past 2 p.m. and waiters 'Steve Davis' and 'Rocky' at La Tufa – named so because of their long-since-expired (and, in all likelihood, totally-imaginary-from-the-outset) resemblance to the monosyllabic snooker player and Sylvester Stallone (an unlikely combo if ever there was one) – would not be serving the kitchen's creamy *fusilli ai quattro formaggi* for much longer (presuming, of course, that both doppelgänger waiters still worked at the restaurant in the first place).

Alas, the summer months now over, I arrived to find that La Tufa's doors weren't open for lunch. The Steve and Rocky showdown would have to wait for another year. It was not an entirely useless diversion, however, for on the wall in the main street of the village an inscription reads: 'This place bears the name of Ossaia, from the bones of those unfortunate men whom Hannibal slew here.' If the whitened bones of the Roman troops are apparent in the name of Ossaia (from *ossa*, bone), then the plentiful blood of the slaughtered legionaries, which legend says ran in torrents for three days, is recalled in the name of the nearby hamlet Sanguineto.

Perched on the side of the hill overlooking the lake – and back on the official route following my lengthy detour – Sanguineto was the next port of call after a decidedly joyless toasted sandwich at the station café in Terontola (an act of desperation that became the culinary low-point of the tour – as shameful as the Romans' abject performance on the banks of Trasimeno). By now I had crossed into Umbria and a billowing UFO of a cloud that resembled something from a Hollywood disaster movie grew exponentially over the valley, seemingly with me directly in its sights. The whole of the lake was engulfed in the kind of grey gloom that must have hung over Rome following one of her darkest days. Above the larger of two islands – where my 12-year-old self once badgered TV panel-show host Angus Deayton for a photo (I remember that he had huge, cyclist's calves) – a mini tornado strove to swirl. Sweeping over the lake like the shadow of a cloud passing across a green meadow on a summer's day, a wall of rain advanced like Hannibal's army.

Utterly drenched for a second afternoon running, and now some two hours behind schedule, I decided to skip most of the historical information boards dotted around the alleged battlefield, stopping only on the spot where Flaminius was supposedly slain: run through by a lance, arms strung up, and then decapitated by Ducarius, a skilled Celtic horseman from the Insubres tribe. In the centre of the hamlet of Sanguineto (the 'Blood River') a sombre plaque reads: 'Here played out the inevitable fate of one of the largest battles ever seen in the Mediterranean, which allowed Hannibal of Carthage to vent his unbridled hatred towards Rome.'

Someone for whom the concept of rivers of blood certainly strikes a nerve is prolific Danish doper Michael Rasmussen. In early 2013, the man known as 'The Chicken' admitted he had used PEDs throughout his professional career, listing, with admirable sang-froid, EPO, growth hormones, insulin, testosterone, cortisone and blood doping as part of his race preparation. In his warts-and-all autobiography later in the year – in which Rasmussen didn't so much spit in the soup as spew forth a decade's worth of lukewarm chowder – the former Rabobank rider confirmed that he had used a notorious blood bank in Vienna to store the fruits of his labour.

When the Austrian doping scandal of the 2006 Winter Olympics broke, the clinic had to act fast. 'One night in February the doctors threw all the frozen blood from the athletes into the Danube. There went all my Tour de France wins,' Rasmussen wrote. 'If my blood wasn't in the Danube, I would have won three Alpine stages in a row and reached Paris one day before everybody else,' he boasted. Instead, the wiry whippet had to settle for one stage win, a second successive polka-dot jersey (which he accepted on the podium with his newly born baby) and eighteenth place overall. Rumour has it the fish in the Danube were swimming pretty fast that week. In fact, there was pandemonium at the annual Bratislava angling tournament a little further downstream, with mutant salmons ripped with third-generation EPO turning the tables on their catchers.

Rasmussen's book is a veritable goldmine of doping titbits, including his plan – allegedly concocted with then-Rabobank doctor Geert Leinders, whose subsequent employment at Team Sky raised even the most heavily Botoxed of eyebrows – to dope with his father's blood (something even Rasmussen felt was 'stepping over the line'). Quite how transfusing the blood of a 65-year-old into your body would facilitate record ascents of Alpe d'Huez remains a mystery – unless Rasmussen senior had spent large swathes of that February swimming in the Danube. On discovering his dad was a different blood group, Rasmussen stooped to another low: in what he downplayed as 'a foolish experiment', the Chicken tried doping with synthetic canine blood in what sounds like some kind of veterinary nightmare.

Despite such grippingly lurid revelations, the Chicken's stock has fallen in Denmark. At a book signing event for *Yellow Fever* at a provincial town west of Copenhagen only three people showed up –

two of whom allegedly thought they were celebrating the release of an X-rated travel guide to Southeast Asia. When Rasmussen resorted to entering Denmark's equivalent of *Dancing with the Stars*, the public soon tired of his Funky Chicken, were unconvinced by his Red Danube Waltz and then finally kicked him out for his Mexican Fandango.

Talking of which, I was soon dancing on the pedals on the main climb of the day – the twisting but not-so-tortuous rise to Castel Rigone on the high road to Perugia. Following my lunchtime debacle I had treated myself to a humongous ice cream from the lakeside town of Passignano. Reminiscing about childhood trips out on pedal boats on the shallow lake Napoleon so desperately wanted to drain, I left the Umbrian Riviera a satisfied yet shivering wreck. The effort required on the punchy 8 per cent mid-section of the climb soon had me warmed up, and a smile returned as the sun broke through the clouds and brought a new lease of life to the spell-binding surface of the lake they call 'the mirror of Umbria'.

A wondrously secluded 10-kilometre descent through mystical fog towards the next valley preceded a series of stinging ramps leading up to the famous university town of Perugia, whose steep narrow streets and high walls led to total GPS meltdown. Negotiating the baffling one-way system in the knowledge that the others were already enjoying their dinner provoked some rather fruity language before I eventually located the hotel in a side street off the famous Corso Vannucci, not far away from the grand Palazzo dei Priori, whose top-floor art gallery holds a rather graphic painting of Saint Sebastian being used as an archery pin cushion which caused me to faint when I was 12. (Despite being fired upon until he resembled a bloody sea urchin, Sebastian is said to have survived his ordeal – only to be swiftly clubbed to death on the emperor Diocletian's orders.)

Three medieval popes reportedly died in Perugia – a town, according to the travel writer H.V. Morton, perfect for assassinations. Two of these holy men were poisoned, while one simply stuffed his gut with too many Trasimeno eels. Perhaps fortunately, there was no freshwater fish for me that night – just a large helping of gnocchi Gorgonzola e speck, a no-nonsense pizza *quattro stagioni* and a well-earned Birra Moretti. After such a personal trip down memory lane I was actually pleased to be on my own to compose my thoughts and take stock of the situation. Just two days separated me from the walls of Rome as the completion of my debut Grand Tour loomed. Riding in such familiar surroundings had made me feel very much at home – and the thought of being off the bike and back into a very different daily routine filled me with pangs of anxiety. Couldn't this trip just go on for ever?

News of the Trasimeno massacre in 217 BC sent a ripple of panic through the streets of Rome. When one of the praetors finally climbed on to the speaker's rostrum in the Senate to deliver the news, he could only lay down the truth in the most prosaic of manners: 'We have been defeated in a great battle.' Hannibal, by contrast, was on a bigger winning streak than 'The Cannibal' in his pomp. With a jubilant Carthage promising more support for the campaigns in both Spain and in Italy, Rome was forced to take drastic measures. With one consul dead and another trapped, the Romans shook the foundations of their Republican ideology by appointing a dictator.

Assuming the emergency mantle of temporary commander-in-chief on a short six-month pay-as-you-go contract was a much-maligned chap called Quintus Fabius Maximus, father of the attritional 'Fabian strategy' later so successfully (yet scornfully) employed by 'wheel-sucking' riders in the mould of Cadel Evans. All things considered, Fabius's tactic was quite sensible, really: avoid having your army trounced by the superior military machine of Carthage by simply refusing to fight.

But the Roman people were enraged, branding Fabius the 'Great

Delayer', or *cunctator* – which sounds like something an irate Bradley Wiggins might call a enquiring journalist. Having dined out on decades of successful aggressive military action, the Roman people viewed Fabius's actions of shadowing and containing the enemy as cowardly and, well, un-Roman. A cycling analogy springs to mind: fickle fans who complain about their sport being riddled with doping but then lament when races are not as explosive as they were back in the good ol' days.

While the Romans were busy granting autocratic powers to the man who refused to satisfy their lust for blood, Hannibal led his flagging army out of Umbria towards the clement Adriatic coast for some much-needed recuperation.

'Shouldn't we stick to Hannibal's route and delay our ride into Rome for a while?' I asked Sam as we readied to leave Perugia on the penultimate day of the tour.

'Not unless you're prepared to ride around southern Italy in circles for the next seven years.'

As much as I was angling for a prolongation of our adventure, even that seemed a little excessive. And they called Fabius the Great Delayer?

'Ah. Rome it is, then.'

But not yet. First up we were heading to yet another bustling Umbrian hilltop town, Narni, perched on the cliffs above a narrow canyon of the river Nera and overlooking, alas, both the main autostrada to Rome and the local electro-carbon plant. Bob was sporting the familiar green, white and red colours of the old 7-Eleven American cycling team, which later morphed into the Motorola set-up responsible for the early successes of a certain Lance Armstrong. How responsible, we may never know.

In 1985 another American in 7-Eleven colours bravely staved off the peloton as he lumped up the hill into the centre of Perugia to take an unlikely win in his maiden Giro. Twenty-five-year-old Ron Kiefel –

who earlier in the season had swung an arm at Bernard Hinault during an in-the-saddle scuffle – became the first American to win a stage of a Grand Tour on what was the last time Perugia hosted a Giro finish. The stage that day started in the Abruzzan town of L'Aquila, devastated by an earthquake in 2009 that killed more than three hundred people. Tremors and earthquakes are frequent in this part of Italy – and as we made our way along the flat Umbrian plain towards Bevagna we were flanked on our left by hillside towns such as Assisi, Spello and Foligno, all badly damaged by two shattering quakes in 1997.

On the rolling roads out of Perugia I rode alongside Bernadette for the first time in a while. When she told me about the bad shoulder that had plagued her since the start – and threatened her continued practice as a chiropractor – I once again felt bad for having whinged so incessantly about my own poor knees in the opening week. Bernadette and I had already turned the page but I now sensed that we had started an entirely new chapter. I felt we were completing the tour with mutual respect and admiration for one another. It was certainly a weight off my shoulders – not that I wanted to rub this in at all.

Our main challenge that morning was neither weather nor gradient (the sun had returned and our route largely pancake flat) but an infestation of flying ants. The whole plain teemed with the buggers – and judging by the amount trapped in my arm hairs, it was no bad thing that my legs were still sparsely covered. Being the sole sporter of a retro cycling cap below my helmet, my barnet was the only one not swarming with vermin when we stopped for coffee in the dramatic Piazza Silvestri at Bevagna. This compact walled town was also hit by earthquakes in 1997, and the impressive Romanesque church of San Silvestro was restored thanks to funds raised by Prince Charles, who is said to have a villa in the area.

Earthquakes are not the only threat to the town's cultural treasures and charm: in 2005 the mayor of Bevagna issued a decree declaring pigeons a health risk after the town's medieval monuments became encrusted with festering bird droppings. When the church bells stopped ringing because of the accumulation of dead, rancid pigeons and their muck, Bevagna residents were granted permission to shoot the feathered pests in approved hunting grounds outside the city centre. Two rules stood out: pigeon carcasses could not be left lying around or brought home to eat.

Pigeon-free, the bar terrace was teeming with custom as a cantankerous waitress struggled to keep up with our order. 'She's not a scratch on the butterfly girl,' Terry said to me once Bernadette, Sharon and Kay had tottered off for a peek at the church. 'I didn't want to say while the ladies were around but she's definitely on her period,' he added in a half-whisper. It was nice to see Terry reacquainted with his marginally misogynistic mojo after being so down in the dumps for a few days. A barometer of the group, Terry's morale had become intricately linked with the general attitude of the tour, his high spirits rubbing off on us all. Bob was in good humour too, despite a puncture on the plain.

'My pump was playing up so I tried using a gas canister,' he said. 'I pulled the trigger on the gun but nothing happened.'

'That must happen often for a man of your age, eh, Bob?' I replied to the amusement of the others.

'Rats! I guess I set myself up for that one. You jest, but there's no history of sexual dysfunction in the Berg family. In fact, my dad was quite open about his, er, abilities. I'll never forget what he once told me when he was not much older than I am today: "I remember what to do but I forgot the reason why."'

'He's lucky,' said Terry. 'I don't even remember what I'm meant to do any more.'

'For the next two days, Terry, that's fine by me,' I said as we rolled out of town. So far, his threat to 'go gay' had remained just that: a threat.

But who knew what might happen with the excitement of reaching our final destination . . .

A couple of testing climbs preceded our lunch stop and the town of Bastardo added an obvious photo opportunity. It was here that Mark and Ash mysteriously vanished, the truth of their disappearance only becoming apparent as we tucked into our pasta *pranzo* (I went for the four cheeses gnocchi to make up for the cruel letdown at La Tufa the day before).

'We snuck off for an ice cream at a bar we went to last year,' said Mark. 'Ash remembered that it had a really cute bargirl but she wasn't there any more.' The two shared a glance and laughed before an awkward silence. Perhaps there was more to Bastardo's name than we all thought?

Robin and I were the only two up for the extra loop, Terry expressing a rare interest but pulling out at the eleventh hour with the desultory remark that his 'piles' wouldn't let him. The circuit took us past fields of sunflowers, colonnades of cypresses and some mercilessly severe ramps in and around the ancient hill fort town of Amelia. At one point my GPS indicated we had broken the 30 per cent barrier – a figure more in sync with my school performances at maths rather than an acceptable gradient to tackle by bike. Having often been distanced by Robin on some of the longer climbs over the past couple of days, it was a welcome boon to see my long legs come out on top on every ascent, including the final prickly incline to Narni.

'The past few days have been brilliant,' said Robin as we took a gelato time-out in Amelia. 'I can only imagine how incredible it must have been to do the entire ride from Barcelona. You're a lucky guy – what you've done is every cyclist's dream.' He was right – it was and is and forever will be.

C.S. Lewis named his imaginary land of Narnia after coming across the alluringly sounding Narni in an old atlas as a child. Come to think of it, our ride to Narni had seen us pass lions aplenty (frequent road-side garden centres had many Aslan-esque statues on display), a witch in the form of that curmudgeonly barmaid and, in mine and Terry's room, a wardrobe so large it could well have concealed an imaginary world. For Ash, Mark and Robin, the final slog up to the higgledy-piggledy central square had been their last battle: as we rode on to lake Bracciano the next day, they would be on a flight home.

Mark and Ash were propped up on the terrace of the hotel bar with two beers waiting as Robin and I completed our circuit. 'We were going to get showered and changed but as soon as we saw the view we couldn't help ourselves,' said Mark, gesturing towards a group of passing girls. To be fair, they had a point: Narni seemed to have an unexpectedly high population of extremely attractive women. Every now and then, Ash would comically pause what he was saying to nod towards a passing girl and say out loud: 'You'll do.' On one occasion, Robin disagreed, mockingly claiming that the lady in question was a '1664' – 'Sixteen from behind but sixty-four once you see her face.' Thankfully, I took my leave before discovering what a 'Hoegaarden' was.

That evening we had the only real dud meal of the entire tour, a bizarrely eclectic set menu that seemed to have hinged on using up the remaining scraps of the restaurant's pantry. A peppery but plain barley risotto was as chewy as the cured rind of crispy ham which adorned the top of a lump of buttery mash that made up our curious antipasti. A type of lasagne pillow filled with meat so gristly I can only assume it once belonged to one of Bevagna's dwindling pigeon population preceded some sinewy scraps of veal accompanied by a salad so salty and tired it must have been washed in the nearest sea port and then transported 80 kilometres inland by bike via some bumpy segments of *strade bianche*.

'This reminds me of the time I ate bow-wow burgers in Tibet,' said Bob, recalling his 100-day expedition in the Himalayas from the 1980s.

'I remember quite clearly that there were three fluffy black puppies when we arrived in the last village before the Everest base camp. The food at this guest house was truly atrocious – in particular the mystery meat. On the second day, one of our team members noticed that the puppy population of the village had dropped significantly.' Bob allegedly survived the last day or two on peanuts and Coke alone. 'To this day I'm not sure if I ate dog but the circumstantial evidence makes a compelling argument,' he said as a rich chocolate mousse arrived, partially making amends for the previous kitchen disasters.

'Don't worry – there are no dogs in Narni,' said Ash.

'Just loads of fit birds,' added Mark, right on cue.

After dinner Sam, Steve and I walked it off in the murky backstreets before joining Ash and the boys for a serious drinking session in the bar. The food may have been culinarily questionable, but the evening had been a jolly affair thanks to the presence of Mark's father, Ian, and his Italian girlfriend. When Ian split up from his wife a few years ago he had found readjusting a bit of a struggle. Then, out of the blue, he handed over the reins of the family jewellery business to Mark and moved out to the nearby town of Terni, dubbed the Manchester of Italy and twinned with Hannibal's quasi-home town of Cartagena. It was in this City of Lovers (Terni's patron saint is Saint Valentine) that Ian found a new lease of life. 'Just look at him over there in his shirt, blazer and cravat,' said Mark as we propped up the bar. 'He never used to dress like that in England. He's totally reinvented himself and I'm so happy that he's found what he's looking for out here.'

Our collective drink of choice that night was neither Kronenbourg 1664, nor Hoegaarden, but Aperol spritz, that highly drinkable, luminous orange cocktail combining Prosecco and the Campari-lite liqueur. 'I love this drink. It makes me feel . . . educated,' Ash, in skinny jeans and a pair of fluorescent yellow flip-flops, confided to me in his endearing Brummie accent. With everyone on the sauce, this was a good opportunity to garner some gossip from one of English football's biggest unsung heroes. Who, for instance, was the nicest opponent he came up against during his career?

'John Terry, without a doubt. The press give him a hard time but he's a top geezer. I remember after we played them at Stamford Bridge and he came into the dressing room to wish us well after the game. We'd got hammered but he said we played with a lot of fight and said if we continued like that we'd avoid relegation. Lovely guy, JT.'

What about dressing-room pranks – what kind of hijinks did he and his team-mates get up to?

'The usual stuff,' Ash said, shrugging his shoulders. 'Shitting in the communal bath, putting Deep Heat into people's pants, bumming . . . only kidding. Nothing like that. To be fair, football's changed a lot since I started out. There was a time when the young players felt honoured to clean your boots. Nowadays all that kind of thing has been phased out. It's a big shame, Felix.'

Perhaps demonstrating his yearning for the good ol' days, Ash then dug out his phone while Mark had his back turned at the bar. 'Last weekend he got really drunk. Look what we did . . .'

Before I had time to think I suddenly came face to face with a snap of an inebriated Mark, out cold and slumped in a heap, his forehead adorned with something that made me momentarily recall that stray dog in Céret. Let's just say that while Ash was renowned for his tough tackling on the pitch, his actual tackle did showcase his undeniable soft side.

'Don't tell him I showed you that,' he said, tapping his nose as Mark returned to the fold with another round of Aperol spritzes.

'Here you go, guys. Last round for me. I'm still suffering the after effects from that session last weekend, Ash.'

I bet you are, I thought.

That night my dreams were dark and tormented, indiscriminately involving Terry reenacting that beastly photo stream with Sergei the masseur.

The peculiar buzzing noise emitted by my front tyre on every rotation of the wheel had me fearing the tour would end as it started – with a puncture. I pulled to the side of the busy road that climbed out of the gorge below Civita Castellana for closer inspection. The valve had broken but there was no audible hissing so on I pressed. Once the road flattened the noise magically vanished, never to return. The inner tube would have to be changed – but it would get me the remaining 35 kilometres to lake Bracciano, our final port of call.

Like the remnants of a winter Sunday afternoon, there was a distinct feeling of finality about proceedings. We'd lost the cheery presence of Ash, Mark and Robin and we all knew that the early morning wake-up calls, large breakfasts and pre-stage briefings we'd grown so accustomed to would tomorrow be replaced by handshakes, final goodbyes and a return to our much-neglected civvies. Even the route had an end-of-term feel to it: my twenty-sixth consecutive day in the saddle would be a shorter 70 kilometre ride with no clear scope for extra circuits to take the tally up to the three figures I'd managed for the most part throughout.

All roads now did, indeed, lead to Rome, the Italian capital's name featuring on every signpost of every intersection. We'd climbed out of Narni on the old via Flaminia – the former Roman road joining Rome to Rimini, built, in happier times, by the impulsive consul Flaminius, before he lost his head at Trasimeno – and then descended into Lazio to cross the mighty Tiber, and the mightier Autostrada A1, the 'Motorway of the Sun'. Aware that the final sands of my saddle time were passing through the Hannibalic hourglass, I gave my thighs a thorough workout by soaring ahead, the last dash of a serial lone escapee.

After a final coffee stop in Civita Castellana we pressed on to the town of Nepi and its medieval city walls and Roman aqueduct, leaving the busy road to join some dirt tracks past woodland and fields of horses. The cobalt blue waters of Bracciano – the favourite holiday spot for many a Roman emperor – shimmered nearby as we dropped through the national park that surrounds its shores. Soon joining the road which hugs the shore, it became clear why this lake remains one of the biggest summertime tourist attractions on the outskirts of Rome.

I was now on to the final few kilometres of the tour but something was bugging me. Deep down it didn't feel right for me to be leading the group into the town of Anguillara Sabazia, rather than the two riders who had spent the majority of the last month plugging away off the front: Bob and Bernadette. Slowing to take some photos of parasol pines towering above a row of colourful bobbing boats, I allowed the indefatigable duo to ride clear and take the glory, Bob eventually beating Bernadette in a two-way sprint to punch his ticket in pole position. Sharon and Terry also passed, fittingly finishing the tour side by side, while I rolled in some minutes before John and Kay brought home the lanterne rouge.

Spotting a pier jutting out into the water, I rode straight past everyone gathering by the van, bunny-hopped on to the wooden structure and pedalled to the end. Stripped down to my bib shorts, I then clambered over the barriers and plunged into the clear waters below. Our final day was the hottest of the lot – and soon all the men joined me for a refreshing swim while the ladies made a beeline for the local gelateria.

There followed a quite delicious celebratory lunch on the terrace of a pretty restaurant beside the water's edge. Dylan took the reins and in his perfectly enunciated Italian ordered a fine spread with an emphasis on local produce from the lake and the sea. Mussels marinaded in oil, garlic and lemon, and a salad of octopus and squid jostled for position on our plates beside crispy bruschetta topped with juicy tomatoes. This was succeeded by two quite brilliant pasta dishes – one with local fish, tomatoes and olives, and another with anchovies and capers. Having raised our glasses of wine for a toast I then broached a subject that had been bugging me.

'So, who's going to join me for the final 30 kilometre ride into Rome?' After all, it did seem a shame that having cycled so bloody far it would not be mountains or foul weather that derailed my quest to reach Rome, but the busy commuter belt of the Italian capital.

'Riding across the Lucca valley with you was bad enough but there's no way we're going to take on the Roman rush-hour traffic by bike – especially after a meal like that,' said Sam.

'Come on, Sam, don't be a spoilsport,' I said. 'See it as one last extra loop that will help me nail those triple figures for the final time.'

'If you're going to do it you'd better get your bike off the roof of the van,' said Dylan. 'But, honestly, I wouldn't recommend it. In fact, I'm not going to allow it.'

Once my mind was made up for me, it was a relief not having to face the main roads which, through the van window in an hour or so, did admittedly look as appealing as cycling Paris–Roubaix on a Penny Farthing.

'I suppose we never actually rode out towards Montseny on day one and so there is a precedent to this bookending negligence in our remit to ride from Barcelona to Rome,' I said, trying to be philosophical. 'But I do concede that it would be a shame to get run over by a Fiat Uno so close to our ultimate destination.'

'I think we can all be forgiven for not riding the last bit given the circumstances,' said Bob.

'Yes, you're right,' I said, before raising my eyebrows in faux rebuke. 'But whether or not some of us can be forgiven for sitting out the heavy drizzle the other day is another matter. It must be galling for you to have fallen short for a second successive year, eh, Bob?'

'Rats! Don't remind me! Now I'll have to come back and ride the route for a third time.' A situation I think Bob had probably engineered.

'Look at it differently,' Sam said, ever the diplomat. 'You should hardly see it as a failure because Hannibal never actually made it to Rome either.'

## EPILOGUE

# ROME

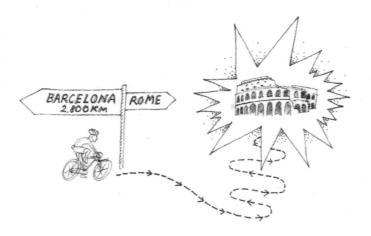

I<small>F</small> H<small>ANNIBAL</small> <small>FAILED</small> <small>TO</small> <small>MARCH</small> <small>THROUGH</small> the gates of Rome it was perhaps because taking Rome by force did not appear to have been one of his key objectives. No clearer did this become than in the immediate aftermath of the Battle of Cannae, where the Carthaginians had mighty Rome in their sights but their leader, like Bob, couldn't pull the trigger.

Exasperated by Fabius's delaying tactics, the Romans had elected two new consuls in January 216 BC. The first, Paullus, was an advocate of the old Fabian approach of containing Hannibal's army, while the second, Varro, was determined to force the enemy into open battle. To make matters more intriguing, both consuls joined the bolstered Roman army on the campaign trail, with each man given ultimate command on alternate days. In essence, this was like Dave Brailsford telling Bradley Wiggins and Chris Froome that they would divvy up daily leadership of

Team Sky during the Tour de France: appealing for neutrals, a disaster for anyone with any sense.

Despite being considerably outnumbered outside the small Apulian town of Cannae in August that year, Hannibal was architect of Rome's most comprehensive defeat. Luring the enemy forward, Hannibal simultaneously attacked both flanks with his cavalry. This supreme double envelopment is still celebrated today as the greatest tactical feat in military history. Encircled and annihilated within a single stroke, the Romans were killed at a rate of six hundred a minute. Such was the enemy's numerical advantage that Hannibal even ordered his men to slash the hamstrings of the Roman infantry so that, incapacitated, they could be slaughtered later, once the battle was won. An estimated seventy thousand Roman soldiers were killed and another ten thousand captured in what was one of the bloodiest encounters the world has ever seen. By some cruel irony, Varro, largely responsible for the defeat, survived while the reluctant Paullus, who didn't even want to be there in the first place, perished.

According to Livy, Maharbal, the leader of the Numidian cavalry, urged Hannibal to strike while the iron was hot and march on Rome. But Hannibal hesitated, allowing the Romans to regroup. 'You know how to win victory, Hannibal, but you do not know how to use it,' Maharbal rued, albeit apocryphally in all likelihood.

For Rome was 400 kilometres away from Cannae and defended by at least two legions. Hannibal knew that his army was exhausted and that they lacked the requisite siege engines to breach the 7-kilometre-long city walls. Instead, his plan was to continue marginalizing Rome from its allies in southern Italy and bring about the eventual surrender. Attempting to reverse the conclusion of the First Punic War that so enraged his father Hamilcar, Hannibal sought to make a peace with Rome in which Carthage could dictate crippling terms.

So Hannibal resisted the temptation of displaying the same

impetuousness that proved the downfall for many of his enemy leaders, and continued his quest to extend Carthaginian influence – which included overseeing the arrival of forty new war elephants smuggled past the Roman naval blockade that had been in place since his influence in the south had grown. Capua, then Italy's second largest city, soon defected to Carthage. But the Romans had learnt from their mistakes, finally coming round to the attritional tactics of Fabius the Delayer, who was re-elected as consul on three occasions. Enforcing a policy of strategic stalemate at home, Rome took the fight abroad, attacking the Carthaginians in Spain, Sicily and Sardinia. Once Sicily fell, Hannibal's Italian campaign started to flounder. Sensing a change in the wind, Rome then besieged Capua in 211.

In a likely bid to divert Roman attention from Capua, Hannibal finally marched on Rome – seven years after he had shaken the city's foundations by crossing the Alps. Leaving a trail of devastation in his wake, Hannibal's march seemed designed to cause as much panic as possible. But what then happened proved about as anticlimatic as Wiggo's attempt to become the first Briton to win the Giro d'Italia. Incensed by news that the Romans took his advance so lightly that they were diverting troops to face his brother, Hasdrubal, in Spain, Hannibal even heard rumours that Roman businessmen were successfully selling off plots outside Rome – including the very land where his army was camped.

Incandescent with rage, Hannibal rode up to the gates of Rome and threw his spear over the Servian walls – much like a disgruntled Wiggins tossing his Pinarello into a roadside cliff. Still the Romans refused to come out and fight. To make matters worse, the demoralized Senate at surrounded Capua surrendered to the Roman army and the tables were turned. A disgruntled Hannibal took his army back south and holed up in the Calabrian town of Bruttium in the toe of Italy. Like those belonging to René Vietto and poor Apo Lazaridès, the toe was soon severed from its rightful owner.

After shadowing the bulk of Hannibal's famous march on Rome by cycling 2,800 kilometres over the course of twenty-six successive days (400-odd kilometres more than anyone else who completed the whole tour, I hasten to add), there existed a fear that my own arrival in the Italian capital would also be something of an anticlimax. After all, it was not in the saddle of my trusty Felt road machine that I passed through the Porta San Pancrazio, but fast asleep in the van alongside Terry and Sam, both in a similar state of unconsciousness, as Bob took a series of largely unflattering photos of us drooling.

Any dismay at not riding those final kilometres evaporated once we reached the last in a long line of luxurious temporary residences – a former seventeenth-century convent on the edge of the vibrant Trastevere area of Rome. My mind fluttered back to eating tapas in Barcelona and Paolo's suggestion that the Trastevere was where I'd find the best food in Rome. Well, he wasn't wrong – for that evening, despite following our not inconsiderable late lunch with zero pedalling, we moseyed into the Trastevere for a triumphal Roman banquet.

Our last supper together took place at a wonderfully hectic family-run trattoria called Da Fabrizio, where plates of deep-fried zucchini flowers, artichoke hearts, lumps of tangy pecorino and a wooden tray of cured meats and salamis arrived before we'd even had the chance to sit down. A terracotta bowl of rigatoni all carcerata – rich black truffle and stringy cheese 'prison pasta', a Fabrizio special – would have crowned the meal perfectly. But the coronation was still to come: chef Fabrizio's wife – a real bruiser of a woman who would have given Surus the elephant a run for his money – emerged from the kitchen brandishing a medley of mains for us to share, including meatballs in tomato and pea sauce, veal stew and stuffed beef involtini.

'*Buon appetito*,' she said in a gravelly smoker's voice that befitted someone I had already witnessed sparking up surreptitiously on two occasions behind the curtain that led into the kitchen. Both guilt and shame accompanied half an hour later the clearing of the hearty spread into which we had accumulatively failed to make many meaningful inroads. But judging by the matronal corpulence of the resident dominatrix, the leftovers would not remain left over for long.

After polishing off a light lemon sorbet we then raised a glass of rather sharp local Lazio plonk to toast the completion of our monumental cycling challenge. Perhaps only I saw the irony in acknowledging the culmination of a remarkable journey all-but-finished by Hannibal by drinking the kind of sour wine that would have lifted the spirits of his men in times of need.

'Lovely stuff, this, Dylan,' said Terry before emptying his glass. 'Any chance of another bottle?'

The next morning I confused everyone by turning up at breakfast with my cycling kit on.

'I thought I was having a nightmare,' said Terry when he emerged downstairs after his morning ablutions. 'I saw him getting ready and for a minute I forgot we were in Rome. I cursed my alarm for not going off and was just getting used to the idea of riding that damned bike again when I realized that we were in Rome – and that I had probably drunk too much last night.'

'Please don't tell me you're riding back to Barcelona without me,' enquired Bob, all packed up and ready to fly home to Seattle via London.

'I wish! No, I'm going to check out some cycle shops around town and see if they can pack up my bike for the trip home. I thought I'd also do some sightseeing from the saddle. When in Rome, and all that . . .'

I said my goodbyes and assured Bob that I wasn't going to try and notch 100 kilometres around the hectic streets of Rome. Terry and Steve also had morning flights to catch to the UK. 'It's time to face the music,' sighed Terry, although I could tell that he was actually looking forward to seeing his wife after almost a month away. With his own better half about to give birth to their second child, Dylan's afternoon flight to Sydney couldn't come soon enough. Meanwhile, Sam's brother Ben had arrived in town and the pair were about to embark on a five-day road-trip back to Barcelona to return the hired van and bikes. Finally, the remaining Antipodean element of the trip – troopers John, Kay, Sharon and Bernadette – were, like me, spending a few days acclimatizing in Rome before their respective journeys home.

Taking on the pulsating chaos of Rome by bike seemed about as safe as wandering around Cannae dressed as a Roman soldier with one's thighs exposed to the elements. Not only were most of the wide, unmarked and heavily distressed streets cobbled and dissected by the deep grooves of tram lines, but the confusion of traffic lights on display seemed to be just that – mere decorations offering, if anything, a suggestion as to what drivers could do, should they feel like it.

The past month had seen me emerge relatively unscathed from a gauntlet of underhand obstacles and nefarious challenges – including flash floods and lightning in Tuscany, flying ants in Umbria, militant mosquitoes in Piedmont, boiling wax in Barcelona, blocked bowels in Catalonia and rabid, humping dogs in the Pyrenean foothills. I'd survived being run off the road in Céret and nudged into a ditch near Lucca, possibly by a driver fleeing the advances of two petrol station prostitutes. I'd locked my rear wheel on a tight, slippery bend off the back of Mont Ventoux – and lived to tell the tale. I'd braved the elements to ride the twenty-one hairpins of Alpe d'Huez twice in one afternoon – before descending in the dark past potholes and fallen rocks. I'd tackled some of the most ferocious climbs Europe has to offer, much of the time on a cocktail of painkillers after ravaging my knees on a sodden solo ascent before we'd even left Spain. I'd dodged cows, sheep, goats, marmots and enough roadkill to fill a zoo, even managing to clock up a maximum speed of 93.2 kmph despite a frayed front tyre, worn-out brake pads and my trademark tachophobic tendencies. I'd ridden gung-ho on the wrong side of the road on a blind bend just to beat a Velosophy sparring partner at his own game in the agricultural north of Italy. I'd eaten more duck, cheese and truffles than should be medically advised. I'd even managed to extricate myself from a rum encounter with a crackpot Frenchman calling himself the 'Baron', caught red-handed while taking a leak beside a deserted Roman aqueduct he claims to have inspired the *Mona Lisa*.

None of the above, however, was anywhere near as dangerous or life-threatening as taking on the rush-hour traffic in Rome with said front tyre just one sharp-edged cobble away from exploding.

But I was on a mission. A bike ride to Rome would be incomplete without the money shot: a symbolic photo of one triumphant Lycra-clad amateur cyclist in front of the Colosseum with his bike, punching the air with a huge grin.

Wearing my dayglo green shorts to warn off erring drivers, I powered down the Via di San Gregorio hoping to avoid the fate that befell Denis Menchov on this very road in 2009, when the Russian lost control of his bike on the rain-soaked cobbles during the deciding time trial on the final day of the hundredth Giro, skidding along the surface for 20 metres and tearing into his pink skin-suit, before remounting and doing enough to secure the overall victory in the shadow of the Colosseum. (He needn't have been too concerned – his main rival that year, Danilo Di Luca, was later fingered for taking the same kind of drugs that Michael Rasmussen claims were habitually administered to his former Rabobank team-mates, including, er, Menchov. For his part, the 'Silent Assassin' has always denied any wrongdoing – but after Rasmussen's allegations came to light, Menchov retired and fled the sport quicker than a speeding Ferrari.)

Just as the Eiffel Tower, Buckingham Palace and Opera House

are synonymous with Paris, London and Sydney, so too can the aura of Rome be captured in the crumbling Colosseum. A photo here was essential, as was riding on down the Via del Corso to toss some coins into the Trevi Fountain before sitting for a post-gelato caricature in the Piazza Navona (why the old artist insisted on depicting me with bulging muscles is beyond my comprehension – particularly since I'd lost 7kg since leaving Spain and was almost as spindly as an overweight pro during the off-season).

While posing for the sketch people gathered behind the artist, their early laughs and thumbs-up being gradually replaced by querulous looks of bemusement and so-so signals of appreciation. My mind wandered, as it would every day while on the bike. None of this – the ornate fountains, the nearby Pantheon with its oculus and dome, the Colosseum itself – would be here today had Hannibal managed to bring his bold plan to total fruition.

The Second Punic War was the closest Rome came to destruction – before Rome had even become everything that it became for us today. A victorious Hannibal would have shifted the focus of ancient history across the Mediterranean and towards Carthage. There would have been no Caesars, no Roman Empire, no school Latin lessons learning the mantra of *Caecilius est in horto*. Grumio might well still be slaving away in the kitchen, but he wouldn't be preparing stuffed dormice for Quintus to eat after a long day in the Forum – no, he'd be filling pig stomachs with sausages and pouring glasses of vintage balsamic for Hanno, his wife Metella and their son Mago before they went to watch the weekly crucifixion and child sacrifice on the spot of land where the Colosseum, in a ghastly alternative universe, might have stood.

Victory, however, eluded Hannibal. No man would ever defy Rome for so long or hold out against such unfavourable odds. But his influence in the toe of Italy slowly dwindled until he was forced to send for his brother Hasdrubal to bring reinforcements from Spain. Hasdrubal led yet another army of elephants across the Pyrenees and Alps before being killed and decapitated in the Apennines by the Romans in 207 BC, his head carried across Italy and tossed into Hannibal's camp.

'At last I see the destiny of Carthage!' Hannibal cried on seeing the (presumably heavily decomposed) face of his dead brother. He wasn't far off the mark: after nearly fifteen years of fighting in Italy, Hannibal was recalled to his native country to face his nemesis Scipio Africanus, who had come on a long way since rescuing his injured father in the battle of Ticinus. Hannibal entered the resulting showdown – the Battle of Zama in 202 BC – with a larger infantry and the presence of eighty war elephants. But the Romans had a cunning plan: they played their trumpets so loudly that the elephants were provoked into stampeding their own lines. Rome's superior cavalry then carried out a two-pronged attack which forced the Carthaginians into surrender after losing twenty thousand troops.

Once again, Carthage was obliged to sue for peace on humiliating terms. Among the conditions was a measure of disarmament whereby no elephants might be kept. Lance Armstrong thought he was hard done by when he copped a lifetime cycling ban – but this penalty was just too much for Hannibal. For seven years he tried his hand at being a de-elefanted statesman, but finally the daily sight of the city's three hundred empty pachyderm stables gathering dust pushed him over the edge.

Outraged, Hannibal went into voluntary exile in Syria, home of his beloved Surus. From here he tried to revive his warmongering credentials until he was betrayed by the king of Asia Minor. With the Romans closing in, Hannibal, aged 65, took a swig of lethal poison. According to Plutarch, Hannibal's last words were: 'Let us now put an end to the life that caused the Romans so much anxiety.' Thirty-five years later, after the Third Punic War, Carthage was obliterated by the Romans: its people killed and its city walls and port destroyed, Rome's great rival city-state ceased to exist.

Over the course of my bike ride in the footsteps of this charismatic general I strove to emulate the movements of the man who brought the young Roman Republic to its knees. I did so by taking up the sport I'd previously (and so feverishly) followed only from afar, and joining a wonderfully diverse group of people to tackle terrain so beautifully woven into the fabric of cycling folklore. Poisoning myself was admittedly one aspect of the Hannibal legend I wasn't prepared to recreate – but neither, too, did I succumb to the temptation of sourcing EPO from a Barcelona pharmacy (as had been suggested by one friend), providing what would have been a welcome stimulant for what seemed like a relentless succession of punishing climbs, brutal gradients and deadly descents.

There is a school of thought that suggests Hannibal's failure to conquer Rome lay with the notion of his mercenary army going soft during its fifteen-year stay in Italy, perhaps enjoying the fresh produce of the countryside so much that they forgot about the conflict that had brought them over three mountain ranges in the first place. I could certainly empathize. Having crossed the biggest natural barrier in Europe, my own fifteen days in Italy seemed to have followed a very similar pattern. Following the victorious photo at the Colosseum I'd put the bike aside and, with it, banished all past conflicts with aching joints, ageing Americans, snoring Scousers and plucky young Australians with a penchant for quoting *South Park*.

For three days I wandered the streets of Rome, initially feeling about as lost as a fully dressed Numidian without his horse. But soon I settled into a routine, maintaining the kind of calorie consumption that I could get away with while cycling 100 kilometres per day for a month. Local specialities of spaghetti cacio e pepe (a simple dish with pecorino Romano and pepper) and cicoria (wild chicory leaves, shredded like spinach and cooked with garlic and chilli) became my staples. I once even had a second lunch to avoid a sudden downpour as bad as the cursed day of the World Championships.

With my legs now less lazy-lady and more pubescent-teenager, I climbed the Spanish steps, descended into the catacombs, danced on the pedlars around the Campidoglio, counter-attacked the crowds crossing the Tiber en route to the Vatican, and, late for my return flight, raced against the clock all the way up the Via Cavour to the railway station at Termini, to view the piece of the Servian Wall allegedly hit by Hannibal's spear – now located, astonishingly, in the downstairs dining area of the local McDonald's. For three days my extra loops usually involved a slight detour to the Gelateria del Teatro, whose flavour combinations would have got a ringing endorsement from the sorely missed Terry: chocolate orange with candied peel, lavender and white peach, dark chocolate and wine sorbet, white chocolate and basil, garden sage with raspberry . . .

Both my body and mind were in denial: if one believed it was still pushing pedals all day, the other, quite simply, wished it still was.

Reality hit home when I arrived at the airport laden with luggage, including a humongous cardboard box containing my dependable Felt, now dismantled, padded up and feeling generally neglected. Telling the amused and confused people in the check-in queue that I had just ridden my bike – *this* bike – from Barcelona to Rome stirred feelings of pride inside, but also served as a bleak reminder that the epic odyssey was now over.

The excitable old dear sitting next to me on the plane home was returning from a package tour organized by a Catholic charity. 'It was marvellous,' she beamed. 'We got to look around the Basilica and we attended a service in St Peter's Square. I stood just metres away from Pope Francis – it was so very inspiring.'

Her unconditional, unwavering support for one man made me think of those crazed cycling fans for whom Lance Armstrong can do no wrong. (Not that the Pope has yet perfected the most sophisticated, professionalized and successful programme of Sacramental wine abuse the Catholic Church has ever seen). Oddly enough, I found her devotion comforting. After all, the new-found verve that I held for the cult of cycling was arguably just as alarming for any outsider. After years of preaching about the sport without ever getting on a bike, I had finally taken the plunge and graduated as a cycling disciple.

As the plane took off I flicked through a colourful history of Hannibal by the eccentric English zoologist Sir Gavin de Beer, chuckling at a typically coltish analogy. 'Let us suppose,' the honey-tongued academic wrote in a bid to put an Anglo-centric spin on Hannibal's achievements, 'that during the battle of Britain in 1940, Rommel landed in Scotland with 20,000 men and thirty-seven tanks, that he destroyed half a dozen British armies in as many battles, and roamed about the country from Edinburgh to Plymouth, ravaging and living on the land for fifteen years until, in 1955, having failed to detach the Scots and the Welsh from the English or to capture London, he re-embarked and sailed home to defend the Fatherland, which Britain had at last succeeded in invading.'

If a better sentence has been written about Hannibal then I've yet to read it. Likewise, as we flew back over the same Alpine ridges that Hannibal and now I had traversed, I felt with utmost conviction that there could be no better cycling journey than the one I had just completed. Pedal power had been the perfect vehicle for tracing the military mastodon behind one of the most gripping episodes in ancient history, and for stepping in the seasoned cycling shoes of those spindly sportsmen whose antics have curiously become my bread and butter. I was returning to the UK a changed man: no longer a saddle-shy outlier in a world of wheels, I had been well and truly initiated into the ever-expanding Lycra army, my subsequent coverage and enjoyment of the sport enriched and permanently changed for the better.

Under bright sunshine the following spring, the peloton will gather beneath the towers in the main square of San Gimignano – perhaps after an early visit to sample some of Dondoli's finest – ahead of the 2014 Strade Bianche race over the Tuscan dirt roads. I'll watch on as the riders skirt the familiar towns of Pienza and Asciano, passing the cypress-lined driveway where I stopped to chomp a banana during that world champion downpour. I might even catch a glimpse of a solitary black horse experiencing one of his better days, keeping an eye on proceedings from his field beside the chalk road as Peter Sagan launches a pulverizing attack, taking only the eventual race winner – Polish youngster Michal Kwiatkowski – with him. The next day, in the Roma Maxima semi-classic, Alejandro Valverde will make his own decisive assault on the Campi di Annibale ramp south of Rome before defying the peloton by one slender second to take victory in front of a Colosseum clad in scaffolding.

Days later the 2014 Tirreno-Adriatico route will spirit the peloton past San Miniato and Cortona, along the west bank of Lake Trasimeno and through once-pigeon-infested Bevagna, while the Giro d'Italia's main time trial in May will tackle the same undulating roads around Alba and Barolo as we did – though the pros won't have the welcome distractions of wine tasting and truffle guzzling to alleviate their suffering. Later in the summer, Yves and Nanine may dress up their donkeys Félix and Margot in cycling regalia as a stage of the Critérium du Dauphiné passes a cheesy gratin's whiff away from their home in the Alpine foothills. Weeks later, the obligatory photo of the *maillot jaune* reading a copy of *L'Équipe* during the second rest day of the Tour de France will no doubt be shot in the shadow of the lofty ramparts at Carcassonne, behind which tourists will feast on viscid cassoulet and steaks bathed in warm Roquefort.

This is what the future holds for me. While I'll never be a *campionissimo* in anything but amateurishness, now that I've tested my mettle on the mythical roads of Europe my own comparatively minuscule cycling achievements will be indelibly linked to those of the pros. Experiences will mount up, for this is merely the beginning: an amuse-bouche; a foie gras macaron, if you will. The race is only just edging out of the neutral zone. Yes, I may be ten years older than Warren Barguil, the debutant stage winner back in Castelldefels, but like the scrawny Frenchman, my cycling career is very much in its infancy. This may be a sport whose reporters have a tendency to call anyone over thirty a 'veteran' but I have a whole decade on a recent Grand Tour champion and almost four on our very own Bob Berg, who last year clocked up a staggering 10,000 miles. My life on a bike has only just started, the knee pains will certainly return, but both the tastiest delicacies and hardest climbs are still on the horizon. The road ahead is long and, like Hannibal, I don't intend on taking the easy route.

# ACKNOWLEDGEMENTS

This book would not exist had Dylan Reynolds not read my maiden column in *Cyclist* magazine and sent a speculative email my way about the Hannibal Expedition. In this respect I must thank Pete Muir at *Cyclist* for recruiting a gangly, non-cycling cycling reporter to recount, month-by-month, blow-by-blow, his often catastrophic attempts to join the ever-swelling two-wheeled fraternity. Without Pete's belief in my writing and riding abilities, *Climbs and Punishment* would have merely been the headline of one of my weekly pun-fuelled *Blazin' Saddles* blogs.

With that in mind, I am clearly indebted to Alex Chick and everyone at Eurosport for publishing my pieces and letting me cover all the big races. A huge thank you must also go to former *Eurosport.com grand fromage* Lee Walker for giving me the *Blazin' Saddles* gig in the first place – and, of course, an even bigger *merci* to François Picard, *le plus grand des fromages*, for making a gaffe-prone rookie the winter sports and cycling co-editor of the website back in those halcyon days in Paris.

The transition from jeans and loafers to spandex and cleats would have been even trickier without the help and support of many people. I'd like to thank James in Sydney for lending me his Trek (shame you didn't also have size-twelve feet) and Al and Chris for chaperoning me on those initial tentative rides. Back in Blighty, I was lucky to be able to borrow my brother Alex's Bianchi and my brother-in-law Gavin's Ribble. Then James Booth at Specialized stepped in to lend me the exquisite Roubaix Comp which, for the criminally short time during which it was in my possession, rode like a dream.

I owe a huge debt of gratitude to Richard Mardle at the Bristol-based bike store Saddleback, who, in my time of need, allowed me to keep hold of the top-of-the-range road bike that I was testing for the 2013 Time Megève Sportive, which I rode for a feature in *Cyclist*. The trusty Felt Z4 carried me through my training rides and performed beyond expectation throughout the 2,796 kilometres of my ride to Rome. Training for such a daunting challenge became a brilliant hors d'oeuvre to the Hannibalic main course, thanks to the help of a number of people and organizations: Raymond Leddy at Cycle Gran Canaria for having the courage to welcome me back for a stab at the VOTT; the Haute Route for inviting me on their Alpine event for two brutal stages in the high mountains; and HotChillee for allowing me to gatecrash the opening stage of their annual London to Paris ride. Thanks, too, to everyone who joined me on training rides in and outside the M25: Alex, Gavin, Reece, George, Tom, Rowan, Mike and many others.

Writing the Last Gasp column at *Cyclist* had its perks and helped lay down some strong foundations ahead of the tour. In no particular order, a hearty thanks to: Sigma Sports and the Specialized Concept Store in Kingston for the bike fitting and for hosting my car-crash interview with Bjarne Riis; Richard Simmonds for the coaching tips; Sportstest's Dr Garry Palmer and Bespoke Cycling in Farringdon for the VO2 Max test; Jonathan Sangan at Fisher Outdoor for the Santini and Union 34 kit; George Garnier at Ragpicker UK; Maxifuel for the energy gels and nutritional advice that I failed to adhere to; John MacLeary at *telegraph. co.uk* for publishing a series of my Hannibal blogs; Greg LeMond for the

# Acknowledgements

advice and unofficial mentorship; sports photographer James Carnegie for taking some great shots of me in action, and Cinzano for the year's supply of vermouth (if only my grandmother were still alive).

Twitter and other social media have completely revolutionized the world of cycling for riders, reporters and fans alike. Through these avenues my blogs and columns reached a larger audience and numerous friendships and collaborations became possible. Aaron, aka UCI Overlord: you may have gone completely awol but before the craziness there were some good times – and you did introduce me to the awesome Justin Pickens and Dave Smith of *Road Reel*, plus the fabulous Lesli Cohen at the sadly now-defunct *Cyclismas*, who so kindly helped me set up my personal Hannibal blog while I was in transit to Barcelona. A sturdy pat on the back to Scott at Velocast for kindly designing my official Hannibal kit and for Ken at Bioracer for bringing it alive – next time I'll order the slim-fit version in red! As for my close friends who supported me in this quest – thanks for your encouragement, interest and feedback (especially Mike, Becks, Sinje, the Clodes, and my fellow British Library regulars).

Now for the big guns . . . A mammoth thank you to Dylan Reynolds and Sam Woods at Ride & Seek for putting on what was perhaps the best experience of my life so far. Riding through three countries and over three mountain ranges – while eating like a king and staying in the most extraordinary locations – was a joy and a privilege from start to finish (and beyond, for the memories linger on). Thank you for accommodating my eagerness to disappear off the beaten track and for energetically sharing the historical framework which made the Hannibal tour stand out above all others and provided the inspiration for this book. I can't wait to work and ride together on the next adventure in 2015.

Such a tour is nothing without its participants and I was blessed with a revolving door of incredible people during the epic journey.

Above all I must thank my inimitable room-mate Terry for his patience and decency while being lumbered with me for a month – as well as for his steady stream of hilarious anecdotes and witty remarks, which kept morale sky-high. I'd like to thank Bob too, whose fitness, passion and tenacity I found inspiring, as well as guides James and Steve for their input on the second and third legs. I'm extremely lucky to have met and spent time with the four other Hannibal stalwarts – Bernadette, Sharon, John and Kay – as well as the Velosophy Six, who certainly ramped up the competitive edge. To them and everyone else who joined the ride: I hope this book serves as a little memory of a huge adventure in which you all played a significant role. And please forgive me for any playful embellishments or risqué caricatures.

Of course, riding to Rome was only half the challenge; once back I had to write a book about it. This would have been impossible without my agent Charlie Brotherstone at A.M. Heath, who approached me off his own bat, had the confidence in supporting my idea from the outset and helped me get the best publisher on board. Thank you to Henry Vines, my editor at Transworld, for his patience, support and enthusiasm, without which this book would be completely awash (as opposed to merely partially) with pachyderms and poo. Both Henry and my copy-editor, Mari Roberts, deserve recognition for their professionalism, diligence and honesty. I also owe a huge thank you to Micaela Alcaino for producing the quite wonderful cover design in the face of my spurious demands and indecisiveness.

Most notably, I'd like to thank my parents for their unwavering love, support and generosity, as well as the uplifting presence of, and help and advice from, my four incredibly talented siblings and their other halves – with a special mention to my sister, the brilliant artist Francesca Lowe, for the magnificent map and chapter illustrations. *Climbs and Punishment* would never have happened without my family and its pages brim between the lines with everything that you have given me over the years and will give me in the future. This book is me trying to even things out a little and give something back.

Finally, I'd like to doff my cap to the hallowed ghost of Hannibal – the greatest military strategist of all time – and, last but not least, salute the professional peloton past and present for the on-going intrigue and drama, without which my day job would be far less entertaining. *'Chapeau!'* to you all.